Supervision and Management

LIBRARY SUPPORT STAFF HANDBOOKS

The Library Support Staff Handbook series is designed to meet the learning needs of both students in library support staff programs and library support staff working in libraries who want to increase their knowledge and skills.

The series was designed and is edited by Hali Keeler and Marie Shaw, both of whom teach in support staff programs and have managed libraries.

The content of each volume aligns to the competencies of the required and elective courses of the American Library Association-Allied Professional Association (ALA-APA) Library Support Staff Certification (LSSC) program. These books are both textbooks for library instructional programs and current resources for working library staff. Each book is available in both print and e-book versions.

Published books in the series include:

1. *Foundations of Library Services: An Introduction for Support Staff*
2. *Library Technology and Digital Resources: An Introduction for Support Staff*
3. *Cataloging Library Resources: An Introduction*
4. *Working with Library Collections: An Introduction for Support Staff*
5. *Communication and Teamwork: An Introduction for Support Staff*
6. *Supervision and Management: An Introduction for Support Staff*

Supervision and Management

An Introduction for Support Staff

Marie Keen Shaw
Hali R. Keeler

Library Support Staff Handbooks, No. 6

ROWMAN & LITTLEFIELD
Lanham • Boulder • New York • London

Published by Rowman & Littlefield
An imprint of The Rowman & Littlefield Publishing Group, Inc.
4501 Forbes Boulevard, Suite 200, Lanham, Maryland 20706
www.rowman.com

Unit A, Whitacre Mews, 26-34 Stannary Street, London SE11 4AB

British Library Cataloguing in Publication Information Available

Library of Congress Cataloging-in-Publication Data

Names: Shaw, Marie Keen, author. | Keeler, Hali R., 1952– author.
Title: Supervision and management : an introduction for support staff / Marie Keen Shaw and Hali R. Keeler.
Description: Lanham : Rowman and Littlefield, [2019] | Series: Library support staff handbooks ; no. 6 | Includes bibliographical references and index.
Identifiers: LCCN 2018020511 (print) | LCCN 2018043090 (ebook) | ISBN 9781538107676 (electronic) | ISBN 9781538107652 (cloth : alk. paper) | ISBN 9781538107669 (paperback : alk. paper)
Subjects: LCSH: Library administration—United States—Handbooks, manuals, etc. | Library personnel management—United States—Handbooks, manuals, etc.
Classification: LCC Z678 (ebook) | LCC Z678 .S52 2018 (print) | DDC 023/.9—dc23
LC record available at https://lccn.loc.gov/2018020511

Printed in the United States of America

To the communities of library users around the world
and the dedicated library staff who serve them

Contents

Figures

Tables and Textboxes

TABLES

TEXTBOXES

Preface

Aligned with the revised national American Library Association–Library Support Staff Certification (ALA-LSSC) competency standards, *Supervision and Management: An Introduction for Support Staff* provides clear explanations on key principles and concepts of library administration and how library support staff (LSS) can support or perform its functions. In today's libraries, LSS often serve in supervisory roles, particularly in schools and small or rural public libraries. Such LSS need to know the basic concepts of supervision and management to effectively oversee a library department or, in some cases, an entire library building and its staff, services, and programs.

This book is essential for those who work in libraries who need to know and apply the fundamental policies and practices that guide library services and programs. It is also essential for those LSS who have been or will be undertaking administrative roles in areas of leadership, professional learning, fundraising, budgeting, hiring staff, customer service, planning, and many other aspects of library management. Embedded throughout the book are textboxes that provide examples or give easy-to-understand information about a concept or topic. At the end of each chapter is an extensive list of online references and suggested readings for further exploration of library management. This important handbook is geared to improve the reader's knowledge and skills of library supervision and management. Each chapter is broken down into short subheadings to make complex topics easy to find, read, and understand. Tables and illustrations are abundantly used throughout the text to present key ideas simply and clearly.

The text is written for three intended audiences: working library staff, college instructors, and students in college library certificate or degree programs. No matter the type of library, there is even greater need today for LSS to understand how library management supports the work of staff, the needs of customers and library functions, services, and programs.

There is a shortage of practical texts written for library staff on supervision and management. Other books on this topic of supervision and management are written at a level that is aimed for professional librarians and not support staff. However, while the majority of LSS do not hold professional degrees in library and information science, many will become department managers or library directors. By writing in clear language, we hope to help LSS understand the context behind the principles of library management with many examples and practical suggestions.

Students who are training to work in libraries and those who currently are employed as LSS will want this book because it provides understandable explanations about today's challenges and accepted practices of library administration. At the end of each chapter, there are discussion questions and guided practice exercises for situational practice and problem solving of some of the issues library supervisors may encounter.

Professors in library technology certificate or associate degree programs will want this book as a primary instructional resource. With extensive chapter bibliographies, this book supports the curriculum and instruction in supervision and management in library support staff academic programs.

Students will find this a useful text for the way the information is presented in clear, nontechnical language. An abundance of tables and figures makes concepts easier to understand. Suggested websites and readings at the end of each chapter can further students' knowledge of topics that are introduced in the book. Many references are from academic journals that are cited for further reading.

The scope of the book addresses many different aspects of supervision and management staff should know about and be able to perform in their working with others and with patrons. Sequenced in thirteen chapters, this book contains:

- *Basic Regulations and Laws*—Libraries employ personnel; purchase materials, electronic equipment, and furniture; and provide a service to their constituency. In this respect, they are also considered businesses. As such they must comply with federal employment laws. This ensures fairness in the hiring and dismissal process as well as in the workplace overall.
- *Principles of Management and Supervision*—The purpose of management is to support work. These supports may be concrete resources such as providing time, staff, materials, or funding. Supports may also be nontangible qualities of encouragement, mentoring, or sharing ideas to solve issues.
- *Staff Hiring, Evaluation, and Promotion*—Libraries are as good as the people who work there. Caring, dedicated, and knowledgeable staff members contribute to excellent library services. It is through the recruitment and hiring process that libraries, or their human resources departments, attract and hire these candidates. It is also through staff training, evaluation, and promotion that they retain them. In this chapter, we will look at these processes.
- *Performance Expectations*—In the library, as in virtually every workplace, there comes a time when employees are evaluated on their work performance. From a manager's point of view, the employee is an investment: he or she was chosen to perform a job and is being paid to do so. It is to no one's advantage if he is not doing the job well.
- *Principles of Leadership and Professional Learning*—Ideally, managers are strong leaders, but they often require two different sets of skills. While the focus of library management is primarily on planning, staffing, organization, budget, and problem solving, leadership is about developing common vision, strategic planning, aligning people, communication, motivation, and inspirations.

Good leaders also recognize and support the need for ongoing staff development and professional learning of their workers.

- *Policies and Procedures*—According to the American Library association, when developing policies, each library needs to consider the community that it serves. Policies define the values of the organization, and they also help managers and staff translate those values into service priorities. Policies establish a standard for services that can be understood by users and providers. Policies ensure equitable treatment for all and provide a framework for delivery of services. Libraries' governing boards formally adopt policies that are consistent with local, state, and federal laws.

- *Budgeting and Fiscal Management*—A library budget is an annual process that involves the planning for acquiring the income and matching it to the anticipated expenditures needed to run the library for the coming year. There are many steps in budgeting, such as securing quotes and estimating costs for future purchases of materials and databases and allocating sufficient funds for staff salaries, benefits, and other compensation; capital expenses for the building and equipment, maintenance, and replacement of technology; and many other predictable—and unpredictable—costs for maintaining library staff and services.

- *Fundraising and Grant Writing*—Funding is how many libraries pay the bills. Local taxes financially support public schools and most public libraries through their local town or county municipalities. What they receive impacts what services they can offer and can affect the quality of their services. The funding they receive may come from their state library through various programs, but these are in turn dependent on how well the state is funded by its governing body. There are various methods of fundraising that libraries can use to augment their financial situation, including grant writing, so they can continue to provide the services that their patrons rely on.

- *Community Demographics and Customer Service*—For a library to service its community, it must know who, and what, a community is. A community is usually considered to be all the people who live in a particular area or place. While the members of a community could share characteristics, it is made up of a variety of people of different races, ages, incomes, and tastes. Learning who is in the library's community is important so the library can understand and best serve their needs. Library staff also need to serve this population with the best customer service they can provide.

- *The Value of Partnerships*—Before meaningful partnerships can take place, work must be done to ensure the commitment will be sustained. Library partnerships or cooperatives go beyond agreements between staff members. It is most beneficial when the expectations as well as the obligations of each library are clearly stated and agreed to as part of the commitment.

- *Library Marketing*—Marketing is part of any library's public service. Besides wanting to bring attention to programs or services, libraries are in competition with so many other options including bookstores and the Internet. There are those, of course, who predict the end of libraries, but we are finding that they are still relevant both as a place to find materials and services and as the "third place"—the social area separate from home and work. People are living increasingly more isolated lives, as evidenced by the upswing in social networking. Libraries are often the social center of a community. LSS who work in supervisory positions must recognize this and work with other library staff to effectively communicate it.

- *Planning, Goal Management, Objectives, and Assessment*—Successful administrators and leaders plan their work around the current and future goals and needs of the library that have been identified by representatives of the library community. There are many models for planning in business, education, libraries, and other nonprofits. Each model develops steps and actions to best achieve target goals. This chapter explains how the need for a new plan is determined, the elements of planning, and how LSS can align their work to help meet the library mission.

- *Conducting Meetings and Effective Decision Making*—All libraries are governed by boards who represent the community they serve. Common to all of these governing boards are the regular meetings where important group decision making and actions take place about mission, goals, facilities policies, personnel, and fiscal oversight. There are many other types of meetings that involve library staff and the community to discuss ideas and take action. These could be meetings for staff or departments, project management teams, special events, new programming, or friends groups. LSS make important contributions when they understand the basics of meetings and how to participate in and conduct meetings effectively and efficiently. This chapter also introduces strategies LSS can use to help make appropriate decisions both as individuals and with others in meetings.

The structure of each chapter begins with the specific ALA-LSSC supervision and management competency standard it will address. Following subchapter headings are definitions of key terms that explain how the term applies in library administration. The key terms are defined in the context of their importance to administration but also how that effective library supervision and management relates to library customer services and enhanced library functions. Each chapter has an introduction where the upcoming topics and content are foreshadowed. Background knowledge, practical examples, and many step-by-step instructions abound in every chapter. The aim of this book is to describe library supervision and management in clear and direct ways so that the reader has both a basic understanding and the immediate knowledge of how to apply principles and processes to their work. This book has broad appeal because of its topic coverage and practical suggestions. The reader can immediately put into practice many of the ideas and skills gleaned from each chapter.

Supervision and Management: An Introduction for Support Staff covers new ground with its content aligned with the supervision and management competencies established by the American Library Association–Library Support Staff Certification Program (ALA-LSSC). Each chapter addresses one or more of the competencies in ways such that the reader can understand each requirement in real and practical applications and examples. In this book, the supervision and management competencies are turned into examples of library practice that LSS can absorb and practice daily at work.

This text provides a different perspective than most books or materials written for library professionals. Simply put, the majority of library literature is aimed at professional librarians. Works are often highly theoretical and not practical. Other books on this topic of supervision and management are written at a level that is aimed for professional librarians and not support staff. However, 85 percent of library support staff does not hold professional degrees yet will assume many of the functions and responsibilities of library supervision and management.

The many examples within this book can help the reader become more proficient and confident supporting library administration and performing some of its tasks. At the end of each chapter are discussion questions that are written to refocus the reader onto the more important or salient parts of the chapter. There is a learning activity at the end of each chapter that either an instructor can use with a class or the reader can work through independently or with other staff to gain experience or additional practice with ideas or process described in the text. Using this handbook as a guide, LSS will be able to apply the ALA-LSSC standards of supervision and management and demonstrate their understanding of these important competencies in their daily practice and work performance.

Acknowledgments

We acknowledge all of the librarians, library support staff, library boards, users, and community members who guided and supported our own practice in library administration. We are appreciative of those who afforded us leadership and decision-making opportunities and encouraged us to become library supervisors, managers, and teachers.

With special appreciation, we acknowledge our editorial advisory board, who provided us important feedback during the stages of writing this book.

As coauthors, Marie Shaw and Hali Keeler are grateful for this time to collaborate with each other to create together this new addition, Book 6, to the series *Library Support Staff Handbooks*. We thank our executive editor, Charles Harmon, for his confidence in us as authors and for his supportive advice throughout our writing process.

Editorial Advisory Board

CHAPTER 1

Basic Regulations and Laws

Library Support Staff (LSS) know basic regulations and laws that govern employment, library policies, and procedures; and how policies are influenced by local, state, and federal laws and regulations. (ALA-LSSC Supervision and Management Competency #1)

Topics Covered in This Chapter:

- Fundamental Employment and Labor Laws
  - The Equal Employment Opportunity Commission (EEOC)
  - The Family Medical Leave Act (FMLA)
  - Occupational Safety and Health Administration (OSHA)
  - The Americans with Disabilities Act (ADA)
- Employment Policies
  - Personnel Policies
- Legal Employment-Related Issues
  - Background Checks
  - Labor Unions
  - Worker's Compensation
  - Wrongful Discharge and Termination of Employment

Key Terms:

501(c)(3): Section 501(c)(3) is the portion of the U.S. Internal Revenue Code that allows for federal tax exemption of nonprofit organizations, specifically those that are considered public charities, private foundations, or private operating foundations. It is a public benefit category under which libraries fall.[1]

The Americans with Disabilities Act (ADA): The Americans with Disabilities Act, or the ADA, was passed in 1991 as an act of Congress and bans discrimination against the approximately fifty-seven million Americans—19 percent of the population—who are hearing impaired, legally blind, epileptic, paralyzed, developmentally disabled, speech impaired, mentally impaired, and HIV positive. It applies to anyone with a condition that substantially limits one's life actions. It is of interest to libraries in regard to patrons and staff alike.

At will employment: At will employment means that library employees can be fired anytime and for any reason other than those that are illegal (discrimination for age, disability, gender, genetic information, national origin, race, religion, or sex).

Employment laws: Employment laws and regulations seek to protect employees from discrimination and harassment. Employment legislation is important because it provides protection and job security for employees against malpractices in all workplaces, including libraries.

The Equal Employment Opportunity Commission (EEOC): The U.S. Equal Employment Opportunity Commission (EEOC) is responsible for enforcing federal laws that make it illegal to discriminate against a job applicant or an employee because of a person's race, color, religion, sex (including pregnancy, gender identity, and sexual orientation), national origin, age (forty or older), disability, or genetic information. These rules must be part of library employment practices.

Fairness: Fairness includes the concept of equal employment opportunity for all regardless of race, religion, origin, gender, or sexual orientation. Fairness is a key component of the hiring process in libraries.

The Family and Medical Leave Act (FMLA): The Family and Medical Leave Act (FMLA) is a federal labor law that allows an eligible employee to take an extended leave of absence from work due to illness or to care for a sick family member and is guaranteed for libraries, and all employers, with fifty or more employees.

Labor laws: The Department of Labor (DOL) administers and enforces more than 180 federal laws. These mandates and the regulations that implement them cover many workplace activities, including all types of libraries, for about 10 million employers and 125 million workers.[2]

Occupational Safety and Health Administration (OSHA): OSHA's mission is to ensure that every working man and woman in the nation is employed under safe and healthful working conditions.[3] Nearly every employee in the United States comes under OSHA's authority. The only exceptions are those who are self-employed, workers in mining and transportation industries (who are covered by other agencies), and most public employees.

Personnel policies: Personnel policies define the rights, obligations, treatment, and relations of people in a workplace. Personnel policies can vary from library to library but generally cover the hours worked, schedules, vacation and sick time, and rules for dealing with issues and obstacles.

Libraries, whether public, school, or academic, are nonprofit organizations. This means that they have **501(c)(3)** exemption status from the IRS and are recognized by tax officials as a governmental unit under that provision of the IRS, which exempts them from federal taxes. Libraries also employ personnel; purchase materials, electronic equipment, and furniture; and provide a service to their constituency. In this respect, they are also considered businesses. As such they must comply with federal employment laws. This ensures fairness in the hiring and dismissal process as well as in the workplace overall.

FUNDAMENTAL EMPLOYMENT AND LABOR LAWS

Compliance with federal employment law was not always the case. In colonial and revolutionary times, labor disputes often consisted of illegal strikes—there was no other recourse to what workers deemed unfair. The shift from rural to urban worker migration, because of the Industrial Revolution in the eighteenth century, brought with it reliance on machines, from the coal engine to steam engines; from cotton fields to textile factories. "At one time, humans, fueled by the animals and plants they ate and the wood they burned, or aided by their domesticated animals, provided most of the energy in use. . . . Everything changed during the Industrial Revolution, which began around 1750. People found an extra source of energy with an incredible capacity for work. That source was fossil fuels."[4]

With this new revolution came new opportunities, and with them, worker dissatisfaction in the conditions under which they worked. Some formed illegal unions to improve wages and hours, and over time several cases and laws resulted from these actions. It wasn't until 1938 that Congress passed the Fair Labor Standards Act. Although lengthy, in summary it "establishes minimum wage, overtime pay, recordkeeping, and youth employment standards affecting full-time and part-time workers in the private sector and in Federal, State, and local governments."[5] It addressed a minimum wage, the forty-hour workweek, overtime pay, the abolishment of child labor (creating the new minimum worker age of sixteen), and sweatshop conditions. All employees have basic rights in the workplace—including the right to privacy, fair compensation, and freedom from discrimination. A job applicant also has these rights even prior to being hired as an employee.

Employment laws are numerous and complex because there are a variety of federal laws, state laws, and executive orders. The Department of Labor (DOL) administers and enforces more than 180 federal **labor laws**. These mandates and the regulations that implement them cover many workplace activities, including all types of libraries, for about 10 million employers and 125 million workers. Local laws and regulations also impact the selection and treatment of employees. Many employment laws and regulations seek to protect employees from discrimination and harassment. Employment legislation is important because it provides protection and job security for employees against malpractices in the workplace.[6]

As a manager, you may be responsible for hiring, firing, payroll, and dealing with disputes among staff and with the public. There are federal and local laws that govern how this is done, but there are also practices with which a manager needs to become familiar. You need to be aware of everything that is happening in

Figure 1.1. Employment rights graphic. *istock/Rawpixel*

the workplace. If there are problems that come to your attention, then it is likely that others are aware of them as well. If you choose to ignore a problem, it won't go away; rather it is likely to become larger. As manager, you are responsible for following the library's policies, particularly those based on employment laws. Ignorance of the issue, or of the applicable rules or laws, won't make the problem go away, and you can be held liable. Neglecting to act can set you up on the losing end of a suit against you or the library. Ignorance of the law is no excuse.[7] In fact, failure to act can result in an employee winning a complaint or a suit against your organization because you neglected to act. Protect yourself by creating a collaborative workplace instead of a litigious environment.

The manager can begin by employing the concept of **fairness**: determine what defines fair treatment in your department or the library. Fair is not treating everyone the same but means everyone can compete for advancement within their own realm. For example, say you as manager decide to reward LSS for their performance based on their individual jobs. The person who oversees the interlibrary loans will not be evaluated the same as a person who does the technical processing of materials. Yet they can both receive recognition for their excellence based on what the expectations are for their own work. They are not competing for recognition because their jobs are different; rather they are each recognized for excellence for the work they do. This helps to create a good working environment where staff are productive and feel respected. For a manager to practice fairness, he must do so consistently, reasonably, and in an unbiased manner. He can't have any underlying motives.

Many policies that relate to fairness began with the Civil Rights Act of 1964—which includes the concept of Equal Employment Opportunity (EEO) for all regardless of race, religion, origin, gender, or sexual orientation. Even in 2017, the time of this writing, these issues are as critical as they were when created.

> The U.S. **Equal Employment Opportunity Commission (EEOC)** is responsible for enforcing federal laws that make it illegal to discriminate against a job applicant or an employee because of the person's race, color, religion, sex (including pregnancy, gender identity, and sexual orientation), national origin, age (40 or older), disability or genetic information. It is also illegal to discriminate against a person because the person complained about discrimination, filed a charge of discrimination, or participated in an employment discrimination investigation or lawsuit.
>
> Most employers with at least 15 employees are covered by EEOC laws (20 employees in age discrimination cases). Most labor unions and employment agencies are also covered.
>
> The laws apply to all types of work situations, including hiring, firing, promotions, harassment, training, wages, and benefits.[8]

Significant employment laws in the United States besides the Fair Labor Standards Act include the Family Medical Leave Act (FMLA), the Occupational Safety and Health Act (OSHA), the Americans with Disabilities Act (ADA), the Immigration and Nationality Act (INA), and the Civil Rights Act. Still others address harassment, labor unions, workers' compensation, wrongful termination, and myriad others. Here are examples of a few of them:

The Family and Medical Leave Act (FMLA)[9] is a federal labor law that allows an eligible employee to take an extended leave of absence from work due to illness or to care for a sick family member. The leave, guaranteed by FMLA, is unpaid and is available to those working for employers with fifty or more employees.

Figure 1.2. FMLA graphic. *istock/designer491*

The Family and Medical Leave Act (FMLA) entitles eligible employees of covered employers to take unpaid, job-protected leave for specified family and medical reasons, with continuation of group health insurance coverage under the same terms and conditions as if the employee had not taken leave. Eligible employees are entitled to take up to twelve workweeks of FMLA leave in a twelve-month period for the birth of a child (including adoption or foster care); a serious health condition that prevents a person from performing their job; to care for a spouse, son, daughter, or parent who has a serious health condition; any qualifying exigency arising out of the fact that the employee's spouse, son, daughter, or parent is a military member on covered active duty; to care for a covered service member with a serious injury or illness if they are the next of kin. It is illegal for an employer to deny this leave or to terminate that employee.

Congress created the **Occupational Safety and Health Administration (OSHA)**[10] to assure safe and healthful working conditions for working men and women by setting and enforcing standards and by providing training, outreach, education, and assistance. OSHA was established by the Williams-Steiger Occupational Safety and Health Act (OSH Act) of 1970, which took effect in 1971. OSHA's mission is to ensure that every working man and woman in the nation is employed under safe and healthful working conditions. Nearly every employee in the United States comes under OSHA's jurisdiction. The only exceptions are people who are self-employed, workers in mining and transportation industries (who are covered by other agencies), and most public employees. All employers in the United States need to be aware of OSHA rules and regulations.

The Americans with Disabilities Act,[11] or the ADA, was passed in 1991 as an act of Congress and bans discrimination against the approximately fifty-seven million Americans—19 percent of the population—who are hearing impaired, legally blind, epileptic, paralyzed, developmentally disabled, speech impaired, mentally impaired, and HIV positive. It applies to anyone with a condition that substantially limits one's life actions.

Most of these provisions went into effect in 1992, which meant that businesses were required to remove physical barriers and assist communication and new buildings had to be physically accessible. It was amended in 2008 to shift the focus from whether an employee had a disability to whether the employer had made reasonable accommodations. Exceptions are made for existing businesses with fewer than fifteen employees. An employer is required to make a "reasonable accommodation to the known disability of a qualified applicant or employee if it would not impose an undue hardship on the operation of the employer's business. Reasonable accommodations are adjustments or modifications provided by an employer to enable people with disabilities to enjoy equal employment opportunities. Accommodations vary depending upon the needs of the individual applicant or employee. Not all people with disabilities (or even all people with the same disability) will require the same accommodation."[12] Examples of this would include a deaf applicant requiring an interpreter for an interview, a diabetic employee needing breaks to monitor blood sugar, or an employee with cancer needing time off for treatments. However, as mentioned above, an employer does not have to provide reasonable accommodations if it imposes undue hardship relative to the size of the business or the number of employees.

There are no specific remedies, penalties, or guidelines in the law itself. Complaints may be made to the Equal Employment Opportunity Commission, or the employee may file a lawsuit against the offending business. Businesses are then required to make reasonable efforts, but changes requiring "undue hardship" such as significant difficulty or expense may not be required. If, however, the law finds in favor of the employee, they may then be entitled to reinstatement, back pay, attorney's fee, and other costs. Intentional violation of the law may incur financial penalties or other punitive damages to the offending business.[13]

These policies apply to all library employers and employees. This protection has been hard won and cannot be ignored. (It should be noted that employers with fewer than fifteen workers are not required to comply with all of them.)

EMPLOYMENT POLICIES

Written policies are necessary for any organization to spell out what is expected. A policy is a set of rules and principles that aims to guide managers and workers in how to behave in the workplace, and they should be in place for numerous issues. However, they only work if they are used and enforced.

Having well-developed policies and procedures in place can provide the following benefits to your workplace:

1. They help employees know what is expected of them with respect to standards of behavior and performance.
2. They set rules and guidelines for decision-making in routine situations so that employees and managers do not need to continually ask senior managers what to do.
3. They help you to adopt a consistent and clear response across the company to continually refer to in situations involving employee interaction.
4. They allow you to demonstrate good faith that employees will be treated fairly and equally.
5. They allow you to have an accepted method of dealing with complaints and misunderstandings in place to help avoid favoritism.
6. They set a framework for delegation of decision-making.
7. They give you a means of communicating information to new employees.
8. They offer you protection from breaches of employment legislation, such as equal opportunity laws.[14]

Personnel Policies

Employment policies are those that relate directly to the employee. The most obvious one is the **personnel policy**, which defines the rights, obligations, treatment, and relations of people in a workplace. Personnel policies can vary from library to library but generally cover the hours worked, schedules, vacation and sick time, and rules for dealing with issues and obstacles. They should address:

- equal employment opportunity
- anti-harassment

- alcohol or drugs in the workplace
- the use of computers and other electronic equipment
- contracts and agreements
- confidentiality
- safety
- smoking
- grievances

A sample personnel policy outline may follow this format:

TEXTBOX 1.1: SAMPLE PERSONNEL POLICY OUTLINE

1. Policy Statement regarding Equal Employment Opportunity/Affirmative Action
2. Employment Procedure
3. Probationary Period
4. Evaluations/Terminations/Resignations
5. Absenteeism and Tardiness
   a. Work Hours/Payroll
6. Benefits
   a. Holidays
   b. Vacation
   c. Paid Sick Leave
   d. Leaves of Absence without Pay
   e. Weather-Related Closings
7. Other
   a. Jury Duty
   b. Staff Development/Education/Training/Conferences
8. Harassment
   a. Statement of Policy
   b. The Rule
   c. Violation of Policy
   d. Procedures for Complaints

Policies are also a guide to making personnel decisions. If questioned about a personnel decision, a manager should use a clear and predetermined set of criteria. Always review any notes about how decisions were made, and focus on the staff member who questioned the decision. Be direct and factual—this is no time to let personal feelings get in the way. Focus on that person's strengths and make suggestions on how they can improve their work; be aware that they may not agree with the outcome. Above all, maintain confidential information. What goes on between manager and employee is no one else's business.

Policies and procedures will be explored in more detail in chapter 6.

LEGAL EMPLOYMENT-RELATED ISSUES

Whenever someone is hired, the possibility arises that at some point employment-related issues might occur. It is important to be aware of relevant employment
laws. The ADA, mentioned previously, is one that addresses remediation of discrimination in the workplace for those with a disability. The Occupational Health and
Safety Act ensures safe and healthful working conditions. Here are several other legal
employment-related issues that can impact the workplace.

Background Checks

Hiring a new employee can be risky. You, as manager, may receive dozens of applications, and at first glance they all look like great candidates with excellent qualifications. It may be difficult to determine who stands out. Looking at a candidate's
background may help determine, at the very least, if the information they provide
is accurate. It can also serve to protect your library and ensure the safety of other
employees. The information gathered must be relevant to the position; medical and
credit history requires consent of the candidate and would generally not be applicable for a position in the library. "Background checks may be somewhat different
for applicants and should be planned on a case by case basis, however they must
be *consistent* for all candidates. If an applicant feels they were discriminated against
for not being selected for a job, they can file a lawsuit against the hiring authority. If
subject to review, any background investigation needs to reflect being strictly part of
the hiring process based on ability and not personal private information."[15]

Performing a background check on a potential employee can be a requirement of
the library and is routinely done by local, state, federal, or private employers. Employers do this for a variety of reasons—to see past employment history and length
of employment, abilities and employment performance, and academic and professional qualifications. As a search can reveal criminal or arrest records, some may see
it as a violation of their civil rights—even if it has no bearing on their hiring. (In
some cases, it may be a factor as a drug conviction would disqualify someone applying for a position in a hospital or medical office.) However, "the general exclusion of
applicants based on arrest or conviction records violates Title VII of the Civil Rights
Act (although employers are required to consider the seriousness of the offense, how
it relates to the nature of the job and the time elapsed since the offense)."[16]

Labor Unions

A labor union is a group of workers who form to protect their interests and rights.
Originally created during the Industrial Revolution in support of better wages, reasonable hours, and safer working conditions, today unions bargain on behalf of
employees in negotiation with their employers, usually over pay and benefits, complaint procedures, hiring and firing guidelines, and unfair labor practices. Today,
LSS from many town, school, and academic libraries are members of a labor union.
(Typically, management and supervisors are exempt.)

Unions can give workers the ability to earn higher and more equitable salaries and receive COLAs from year to year. In addition, organizing a library's staff into a union may help to improve the working conditions in the library. As well, unionizing can give librarians and library paraprofessionals benefits such as health and dental insurance, things that may not be offered normally to the paraprofessionals of the library, particularly if they are part-time employees. In addition to the tangible benefits, the library staff will gain a voice to make grievances against what they see as unfair treatment and allow them to become a more important player in the decision-making process.[17]

Libraries in Providence, Rhode Island; King County, Washington; and Indianapolis, Indiana, all voted to form unions from 2003 to 2006. LSS from all types of libraries—public, private, federal, and state—enjoy this privilege.

There is a long tradition of library unionization and library strikes, lockouts, and closings in protest over labor disputes. In 2013, labor unions in New York City's library system advocated against budget cuts.[18] A search of the literature will reveal numerous instances of library union actions and strikes over the past three decades.

The American Federation of State, County, and Municipal Employees (AFSCME) represents public workers; when a library decides to organize, they can be represented by the Service Employees International Union (SEIU), which also represents public library workers, and the American Federation of Teachers (AFT), which represents teachers and librarians/media specialists.

Worker's Compensation

Worker's compensation is insurance to provide medical expenses and lost wages to employees who are injured while working. Employers, including libraries, may be required to carry it although laws vary from state to state (and may not be applicable to those employing under a minimum number of employees). Working in a library can be very physical: lifting, bending, stooping, and repetitive hand motions at the circulation desk can cause serious injuries. Carpal tunnel syndrome and neck and back injuries are common.[19] Library staff are subject to a variety of ergonomic hazards from using computers, and from reaching and stretching to take books from a shelf. Other hazards can range from tripping over cables or loose carpeting to being exposed to dust and airborne pollutants from a poor ventilation system. "Library employees are among the 1.8 million workers the U.S. Bureau of Labor Statistics says typically can suffer 'musculoskeletal disorders' (MSD), i.e., usually repetitive stress injuries. That was 26.2 percent of all workplace injuries in 2000. The **worker's compensation** system, which is meant to pay workers for the cost of injuries and wages lost, is an increasingly serious financial burden on library budgets across the country."[20]

Worker's compensation ensures that injured workers receive fixed payments for injuries suffered on the job and provides benefits to the families of those who die from a workplace injury. As a manager, it is important to understand the law on worker's compensation in your state and be prepared to address workplace injuries, subsequent claims, and their resolution.

Wrongful Discharge and Termination of Employment

As you hire, so must you occasionally fire—and deal with the blowback if an employee believes she was unfairly terminated. Unless a written contract or verbal agreement is made, most employees in the United States are at will employees. **At will employment** means that an employee can be fired anytime and for any reason other than those that are illegal (discrimination for age, disability, gender, genetic information, national origin, race, religion, or sex). Although an employer may require a new hire to sign an at will agreement (and can refuse to hire an applicant who does not), it is not in a manager's best interest to arbitrarily fire someone; rather they are encouraged to work through whatever the workplace issues are before taking such measures.

For example, an LSS consistently makes poor use of his time with the result that assignments are late or do not get done. The manager meets with the employee to discuss what is happening and why; each incident must be documented. After three such meetings, a warning is given, with the understanding that if the problem continues and additional warnings are given, the LSS may face termination. This allows the LSS to improve and face the consequences if he does not.

But what if this employee was encouraged to sign an at will agreement that gave him a full year to learn the job and was fired after only a few months? The at will agreement allows for the employee to be let go, even as the employer promised a one-year training period. If the employee did not get that promise in writing, there may be no recourse. This would constitute wrongful termination, and it is at this point that legal recourse may be sought.

If the LSS can answer yes to any of the following questions, they may have a valid case for wrongful discharge based on discrimination:

- Is there direct evidence that you were terminated because of discriminatory reasons? (This may include direct statements verbally or in writing.)
- Is there circumstantial evidence of discrimination (e.g., only women were fired in a recent layoff)?
- Are similar employees treated differently based on age, gender, race, or another protected category (such as tardiness by younger employees is tolerated while that of older ones is not)?
- Did an employer or supervisor make comments or take action that indicates they have a bias against certain groups? Was this done in front of others?
- Did an employer or supervisor make comments indicating preference over one group, such as college graduates?

The same goes for harassment if:

- an employer or supervisor made offensive or insulting comments about a person's age, race, gender, etc.;
- an employer or supervisor made unwelcome sexual advances or requested sexual favors; or
- an employer and employee were in a romantic relationship that ended, and the employee was treated poorly or terminated.[21]

Retaliation, such as firing an employee because of his or her involvement in reporting illegal behavior or unsafe workplace practices, is also considered wrongful termination.

While these are important examples of legal employment-related issues, it is only a sample of the labor laws that affect the employee. For a more complete list of labor laws, please refer to the references at the end of this chapter, or visit www.usa.gov/labor-laws.

CHAPTER SUMMARY

We learned in this chapter that basic regulations and laws govern employment, library policies, and procedures. We also looked at how local, state, and federal laws influence these policies. We examined such fundamental employment and labor laws as the Family and Medical Leave Act and the Americans with Disabilities Act, among others. Employment policies and related issues including worker's compensation were also covered, giving LSS an understanding of how basic laws and regulations affect the library.

DISCUSSION QUESTIONS

1. Libraries of all types are considered nonprofits. In what ways are they also considered businesses?
2. What effect, if any, did the Industrial Revolution have on today's libraries and the modern workplace?
3. What are some significant employment laws in the United States and how do they impact the library?
4. Explain why written policies are necessary for any organization.
5. Choose one legal employment-related issue that could occur in the library and explain how and why it could be a problem.

ACTIVITIES

1. As the new manager of a library department, you and the other department heads are tasked with creating a new personnel policy. Choosing a public, school, or academic library setting, write a policy using at least five of the elements in the chapter. Explain why you chose them and whom they would benefit.
2. After work on a wintry night, several staff members are leaving the library when one falls on the ice and hurts herself. She is seeking redress. In your opinion is the library liable? Why or why not? Which employment law(s) introduced in this chapter would be helpful to know, and why?

NOTES

1. IRS.gov, "Exemption Requirements—501(c)(3) Organizations," accessed June 7, 2017, www.irs.gov/charities-non-profits/charitable-organizations/exemption-requirements-section-501-c-3-organizations.

2. U.S. Department of Labor, "Summary of the Major Laws of the Department of Labor," accessed May 18, 2017, www.dol.gov/general/aboutdol/majorlaws.

3. Inc., "Occupational Safety and Health Administration (OSHA)," Inc.Brand/View, accessed May 22, 2017, www.inc.com/encyclopedia/occupational-safety-and-health-admin istration-osha.html.

4. Khan Academy, "The Industrial Revolution," last modified 2017, accessed May 22, 2017, www.khanacademy.org/partner-content/big-history-project/acceleration/bhp-acceleration/a/ the-industrial-revolution.

5. Society for Human Resource Management, "Fair Labor Standards Act (FLSA) of 1938," last modified October 7, 2008, accessed May 22, 2017, www.shrm.org/resourcesandtools/ legal-and-compliance/employment-law/pages/fairlaborstandardsactof1938.aspx.

6. Joan Giesecke and Beth McNeil, *Fundamentals of Library Supervision*, 2nd ed., ALA Fundamentals (Chicago, IL: ALA, 2010), 73.

7. U.S. Legal, "Ignorance of Law Law and Legal Definition," accessed May 23, 2017, definitions.uslegal.com/i/ignorance-of-law/.

8. U.S. Equal Employment Opportunity Commission, "Overview," accessed May 22, 2017, www.eeoc.gov/eeoc/.

9. U.S. Department of Labor, "Fact Sheet #28F: Qualifying Reasons for Leave under the Family and Medical Leave Act," accessed May 22, 2017, www.dol.gov/whd/regs/compliance/ whdfs28f.pdf.

10. Inc., "Occupational Safety."

11. U.S. Equal Employment Opportunity Commission, "'Facts About the Americans with Disabilities Act,' accessed May 22, 2017, www.eeoc.gov/eeoc/publications/fs-ada.cfm.

12. U.S. Equal Employment Opportunity Commission, "Facts About the Americans with Disabilities Act."

13. Hali Keeler, *Foundations of Library Services* (Lanham, MD: Rowman & Littlefield, 2016), 124.

14. Charles Power, "8 Advantages of Having Workplace Policies," *Employment Law Practical Handbook*, last modified June 13, 2012, accessed May 23, 2017, www.employmentlawhand book.com.au/8-advantages-of-having-workplace-policies/.

15. The Advance Group, "Why It's Important To Conduct Background Checks and How To Do It Legally," last modified September 23, 2011, accessed May 24, 2017, theadvancegroup jobs.com/2011/09/23/why-its-important-to-conduct-background-checks-and-how-to-do-it -legally/.

16. Cynthia Gordy, "When Background Checks Violate Civil Rights," *The Root*, last modified April 25, 2012, accessed May 24, 2017, www.theroot.com/when-background-checks-vio late-civil-rights-1790884189.

17. A. C. Hawley, "A Few Easy Steps to Unionizing Libraries," *Library Worklife*, last modified December 2006, accessed May 24, 2017, ala-apa.org/newsletter/2006/12/17/a-few-easy-steps -to-unionizing-libraries/.

18. Stephon Johnson, "Workers Tell City to 'Save Our Libraries,'" *New York Amsterdam News*, March 14, 2013, 10.

19. Robert E. Kaehr, "What Do Meatpackers and Librarians Have in Common? Library Related Injuries and Possible Solutions," *Teacher Librarian* 36, no. 2 (December 2008): 39–42.

20. Anne B. Turner, "It Hurts to Ignore Work Injury Roots," *Library Journal* 129, no. 1 (January 5, 2004): 64.

21. Lisa Guerin, "Employment at Will: What Does It Mean?" Nolo, last modified 2017, accessed May 25, 2017, www.nolo.com/legal-encyclopedia/employment-at-will-defini tion-30022.html.

REFERENCES, SUGGESTED READINGS, AND WEBSITES

The Advance Group. "Why It's Important to Conduct Background Checks and How to Do It Legally." Last modified September 23, 2011. Accessed May 24, 2017. theadvancegroup jobs.com/2011/09/23/why-its-important-to-conduct-background-checks-and-how-to-do -it-legally/.

Giesecke, Joan, and Beth McNeil. *Fundamentals of Library Supervision*. 2nd ed. ALA Fundamentals. Chicago, IL: ALA, 2010.

Gordy, Cynthia. "When Background Checks Violate Civil Rights." *The Root*. Last modified April 25, 2012. Accessed May 24, 2017. www.theroot.com/when-background-checks-vio late-civil-rights-1790884189.

Green, Alison. "5 Workplace Laws Your Employer Might Be Violating." *U.S. News & World Report*. Last modified February 1, 2016. Accessed May 18, 2017. money.usnews.com/money/ blogs/outside-voices-careers/articles/2016-02-01/5-workplace-laws-your-employer-might -be-violating.

Grossman, Jonathan. "Fair Labor Standards Act of 1938: Maximum Struggle for a Minimum Wage." United States Department of Labor. Accessed May 22, 2017. www.dol.gov/oasam/ programs/history/flsa1938.htm.

Guerin, Lisa. "Employment at Will: What Does It Mean?" Nolo. Last modified 2017. Accessed May 25, 2017. www.nolo.com/legal-encyclopedia/employment-at-will-definition-30022 .html.

Hawley, A. C. "A Few Easy Steps to Unionizing Libraries." *Library Worklife*. Last modified December 2006. Accessed May 24, 2017. ala-apa.org/newsletter/2006/12/17/a-few-easy -steps-to-unionizing-libraries/.

Hearst Newspapers, LLC. "Examples of Employee Policies." Chron. Accessed May 23, 2017. smallbusiness.chron.com/examples-employee-policies-11564.html.

HSA. "Library." Health and Safety Authority. Accessed May 29, 2017. www.hsa.ie/eng/ Your_Industry/Healthcare_Sector/Occupational_Hazards_in_Hospital_Departments/De partment_Hazards/Library/.

Inc. "Occupational Safety and Health Administration (OSHA)." Inc.Brand/View. Accessed May 22, 2017. www.inc.com/encyclopedia/occupational-safety-and-health-administration -osha.html.

IRS.gov. "Exemption Requirements—501(c)(3) Organizations." Accessed June 7, 2017. www.irs.gov/charities-non-profits/charitable-organizations/exemption-requirements-sec tion-501-c-3-organizations.

Johnson, Stephon. "Workers Tell City to 'Save Our Libraries.'" *New York Amsterdam News*, March 14, 2013, 10.

Kaehr, Robert E. "What Do Meatpackers and Librarians Have in Common? Library Related Injuries and Possible Solutions." *Teacher Librarian* 36, no. 2 (December 2008): 39–42.

Keeler, Hali. *Foundations of Library Services*. Lanham, MD: Rowman & Littlefield, 2016.

Khan Academy. "The Industrial Revolution." Last modified 2017. Accessed May 22, 2017. www.khanacademy.org/partner-content/big-history-project/acceleration/bhp-accelera tion/a/the-industrial-revolution.

Kramer, Rob, and Phil Rabinowitz. "Section 5. Developing Personnel Policies." Community Tool Box. Last modified 2016. Accessed May 23, 2017. ctb.ku.edu/en/table-of-contents/ structure/hiring-and-training/personnel-policies/main.

Power, Charles. "8 Advantages of Having Workplace Policies." *Employment Law Practical Handbook*. Last modified June 13, 2012. Accessed May 23, 2017. www.employmentlawhand book.com.au/8-advantages-of-having-workplace-policies/.

Society for Human Resource Management. "Fair Labor Standards Act (FLSA) of 1938." Last modified October 7, 2008. Accessed May 22, 2017. www.shrm.org/resourcesandtools/legal-and-compliance/employment-law/pages/fairlaborstandardsactof1938.aspx.

Tess-Mattner, Marna S. "Employer-Employee Issues: Eight Danger Areas." *GPSolo Magazine.* Last modified April/May 2004. Accessed May 18, 2017. www.americanbar.org/newsletter/publications/gp_solo_magazine_home/gp_solo_magazine_index/employeremployeeissues.html.

Turner, Anne B. "It Hurts to Ignore Work Injury Roots." *Library Journal* 129, no. 1 (January 5, 2004): 64.

USA.gov. "Labor Laws and Issues." Accessed May 18, 2017. www.usa.gov/labor-laws.U.S. Department of Labor. "About OSHA." Accessed May 22, 2017. www.osha.gov/about.html.

———. "Employment Law Guide: Laws, Regulations, and Technical Assistance Services." Accessed May 18, 2017. www.dol.gov/compliance/guide/.

———. "Fact Sheet #28F: Qualifying Reasons for Leave under the Family and Medical Leave Act." Accessed May 22, 2017. www.dol.gov/whd/regs/compliance/whdfs28f.pdf.

———. "Summary of the Major Laws of the Department of Labor." Accessed May 18, 2017. www.dol.gov/general/aboutdol/majorlaws.

U.S. Equal Employment Opportunity Commission. "Facts About the Americans with Disabilities Act." Accessed May 22, 2017. www.eeoc.gov/eeoc/publications/fs-ada.cfm.

———. "Overview." Accessed May 22, 2017. www.eeoc.gov/eeoc/.

U.S. Legal. "Ignorance of Law and Legal Definition." Accessed May 23, 2017. definitions.uslegal.com/i/ignorance-of-law/.

CHAPTER 2

Principles of Management and Supervision

LSS know basic principles of staff management, supervision, and discipline. (ALA-LSSC Supervision and Management Competency #2)

Topics Covered in This Chapter:

- Hierarchy of Library Management
- Management Principles
  - o Nonprofit Organizations
- Successful Principles and Strategies
- Principles of Supervision
  - o Supervisor Principles
- Supervision Methods
  - o Formative Performance Appraisal Methods
  - o Summative Performance Appraisal Methods
- Disciplinary Principles
  - o Harassment and Discrimination
  - o Violence and Bullying
  - o Social Media
  - o Substance Abuse
  - o Other Disciplinary Actions

Key Terms:

Active listening: This is a communication technique that requires the listener to fully concentrate, understand, and respond to the speaker. Managers who perfect this skill enhance their ability to discuss and communicate issues with their staff.

Advocacy: This is the process of demonstrating support, usually to government officials, library administration, or the public, for a policy, decision, or the people with whom you work.

Code of conduct: These are the written expectations of behavior that govern how employees act on the job or in the community.

Consensus: This is the process of a group reaching a common decision or action. When the decision has been agreed upon, the group can typically go forward or advance with their work or planning.

Formative: The term means beginning form or shape and idea or development of a skill or process. In a staff supervision context, the term refers to informal steps or the initial processes of evaluation.

Hierarchy: Used in the context of the library, it is the system of management organization in which people or groups are ranked one above the other according to authority.

Library board of trustees: Typically a volunteer group of people who represent the community and serve the library and its director in an advisory capacity. Some boards also have management oversight of the library director and/or fiscal responsibility for the library budget.

Mission: This is a guiding statement of the purpose of the library and its work. All employees should know the library mission and align their work with it.

Nonprofit: Libraries and other institutions that either are publicly funded or have endowments and other means of raising revenue that cover the annual operating expenses. They are not "in business" to have a profit. Nonprofits typically do not pay state or federal taxes.

Summative: This term as it relates to evaluation means a cumulative or summary assessment of what a person can do or perform. For library staff, the summary evaluation could be an annual performance appraisal or review.

Supervision: The act or process of monitoring work performance of others that includes administering and delegating library activities and responsibilities.

Termination: Simply stated, this is when an employee is severed from their employment and let go due to just cause.

The purpose of management is to support work. In this chapter, we will explore many ways management supports the work of library services. These supports may be concrete resources such as providing time, staff, materials, or funding. Supports may also be nontangible qualities of encouragement, mentoring, or sharing ideas to solve issues.

HIERARCHY OF LIBRARY MANAGEMENT

There are an abundance of management theories and practices. Typically, the larger the library, the more structured the management. The smaller the library, the more informal the management process.

In each type of library, be it school, academic, public, or special, there is a management **hierarchy**. While every library has its own unique hierarchy, figure 2.1 shows management examples for each type of library.

K-12 School	Academic	Public	Special (Corporate)
Board of Education	Board of Regents	Board of Trustees	Stockholders
Superintendent	College President	Library Director	CEO
Principal	Academic Dean	Assistant Director	Vice-President
Assistant Principal	Library Director	Department Librarian	Library Director
Library Media Specialist	Department Librarian	LSS	Librarian
Library Support Staff (LSS)	Librarian		LSS
	LSS		

Figure 2.1. Management hierarchy for four types of libraries. *Courtesy of the author*

MANAGEMENT PRINCIPLES

Management is the process of controlling things, projects, and people. Management is an accepted practice in businesses, schools, nonprofits, and organizations to maximize the productivity and services of the workforce. There are basic principles of management depending upon whether the organization is for-profit or **nonprofit**.

Nonprofit Organizations

Managers of for-profit organizations measure success by how much revenue they generate for their goods or services. For-profit organizations strive to be better than the competition and to make the most money for its owners. Management strategies and incentives of for-profit organizations are extrinsically linked to the balance sheet.

Libraries, however, are not owned by individuals or stockholders, nor do they generate revenue. As a nonprofit, a library requires a different set of management principles and incentives than a business. The mission of a nonprofit is to create a community or public benefit, securing enough funding to sustain the organization.[1] The book *Managing the Nonprofit Organization* by Peter Drucker identifies seven "best practices" for managing nonprofit organizations that can also be applied to managing libraries. According to Drucker, nonprofit management should focus on (1) identifying, communicating, and understanding the **mission**; (2) embracing change and innovation; (3) adopting the team concept; (4) being accountable; (5) welcoming dissent but targeting consensus; (6) benefiting from lessons learned; and (7) celebrating accomplishments and contributions.[2]

As libraries are nonprofits, they can also benefit from Drucker's best practices in management.

**TEXTBOX 2.1: SEVEN BEST PRACTICES
IN NONPROFIT MANAGEMENT**

1. Identify, communicate, and understand the mission.
2. Embrace change and innovation.
3. Adopt the team concept.
4. Be accountable.
5. Target consensus.
6. Benefit from lessons learned.
7. Celebrate accomplishments.

In addition to adopting Drucker's seven best practices for nonprofit management, there are seven additional basic principles of library management that should be considered by LSS staff **supervision**:

**TEXTBOX 2.2: SEVEN BASIC PRINCIPLES
OF LIBRARY MANAGEMENT**

1. Maintain a welcoming, respectful, and safe library environment.
2. Advocate for the staff and yourself.
3. Understand the community and align the work of the library closely to it.
4. Build and support an inclusive and diverse workforce.
5. Be knowledgeable of and support library policy as well as all local, state, and federal laws that pertain to the library, its staff, and its patrons.
6. Learn and use practices of fiscal management.
7. Manage facilities and resources to support users' needs.

LSS are in many supervisory and managerial positions. We manage the work of volunteers and students. We are supervisors of departments such as circulation, technical services, and children's or teen services. We often have designated responsibility for the staff and the building during extended hours the library is open during evenings or weekends.

Successful managers know how to do the work of those whom they supervise. Combining both the best practices and basic library management, how do we implement these practices and principles at work?

SUCCESSFUL PRINCIPLES AND STRATEGIES

In this subchapter, each of the fourteen principles is explained from a library management perspective. Following are three practical strategies a new library manager can use to improve their own or their staff's performance.

1. Identify, communicate, and understand the mission. Libraries are mission driven. The mission states the purpose of the library. Succinctly written, the mission is a statement of the main goals of the library. Library management is responsible to ensure all services, programs, and work by the staff align with the mission.

   Strategy 1: Read and initiate discussion with supervisor and staff about the library mission for your better understanding.

   Strategy 2: Focus on one aspect of the mission and embed it into your daily work.

   Strategy 3: Volunteer to serve on a strategic planning or other committees that may be developing or revising the library mission statement.

2. Embrace change and innovation. The purpose of having libraries is continually challenged with funding and technology. Managers should seek to adopt change and innovation when libraries are successful to continually improve upon the services and programs offered, thus positioning libraries as a critical community resource if times get bad.[3]

   Strategy 1: See change as an opportunity and not a threat. Encourage staff to embrace change as an opportunity for them to grow where maintaining the status quo does not.

   Strategy 2: Reach out to vendors to be a beta or pilot site to test new databases, technology, or programs. This is often a low-cost way to bring innovation into the library.

   Strategy 3: Seek partnerships with local colleges or other nonprofit institutions for shared programs or services. Not only will resources expand, but also sharing learning and expertise with others enhances growth and innovation for the staff.

3. Adopt the team concept. Libraries are most successful when staff are a functional team. As a team, they work to implement the library mission and goals. The library management fosters trust and collegiality among staff. Staff are encouraged to discuss their opinions and ideas for the betterment of library services.

Figure 2.2. Library team meeting. *istock/UberImages*

Strategy 1: Continually work to build upon and improve the team concept. Communicate each day with staff to develop their trust and their perception of the manager's honesty.

Strategy 2: Encourage staff to participate in group decisions. Understand and work with different personality and communication styles of staff.

Strategy 3: Have frequent meetings for staff (one-on-one, department, inter-department, etc.) to discuss and prioritize their work. These are also opportunities for staff to learn about what other departments are doing. Work with other managers for sharing projects so that all staff feel they are an important member of the whole library staff.

4. Be accountable. Everyone needs to know what they are accountable for in the library. Make sure the people whom you manage and on whom you depend understand what you intend to concentrate on and should be held accountable for.[4]

Strategy 1: Set expectations for reasonable time periods for when work is to be completed. Communicate these expectations clearly with staff.

Strategy 2: Work closely with staff so that they understand the parameters and expectations of the work product or project. Check in regularly to monitor progress and to offer support as needed.

Strategy 3: In addition to goals and deadlines, help the staff develop a reasonable work plan. Create steps or phases of a project that are accomplishable early on by reason of priority or because they are "easy to do." In the work plan, provide for training of staff if this is new learning. Training could be setting up mentor partnerships, internal or external workshops, and so on.

5. Target consensus. Managers who develop and support the synergy and energy of the team encourage members to voice opinions so that ideas for change and innovation in the library will be heard. Best results are **consensus** decisions whereby staff agree upon what the team must do to move forward on a plan or project.[5]

Strategy 1: Library staff form opinions about their work processes and experiences servicing patrons. Encourage staff to express their point of view. Ask for disagreement openly to give opportunity for everyone to express their opinion. Do not be quick to discredit divergent ideas.

Strategy 2: Use **active listening** skills during meetings. Repeat important points that are made for clarity and understanding.

Strategy 3: Reach agreement in steps. Use a technique several times during the discussion whereby you ask for a show of hands or a nod of heads to express agreement or dissension about a part of an idea to help move agreement on a larger concept forward.

6. Benefit from lessons learned. Library resources in funding and staff are limited and cannot continue with a project that does not achieve results. Managers need to evaluate how resources are being used for the betterment of library services.

Strategy 1: Gather data to assess the success of library services, projects, and programs. Keep statistics. In regular meetings with staff, share and compare statistics and other data on patrons served that help give the picture of how successful a program or service is.

Strategy 2: Learn by doing. As we grow as managers, we get further away from hands-on serving the patrons. Successful managers know and can perform the work they expect of their staff. Be familiar with the tasks they do. Step in and do the work of your staff to experience what they are telling you.

Strategy 3: Use the long-term collective memory of staff to help make decisions (The library friends failed ten years ago because . . . We tried this before and this is what happened . . .). Learn from mistakes of the past.

7. Celebrate accomplishments. Successful managers support the development of their staff, emphasizing people's strengths and not their weaknesses. Delegate without micromanaging, giving employees opportunities to try new ideas and expand their knowledge and skills on the job. Most library staff are intrinsically motivated and receive satisfaction from the work they do.[6]

Strategy 1: Library staff are typically underpaid and obtain satisfaction from the services they perform and their work achievements. Successful managers provide regular praise and recognition for successful work.

Strategy 2: Create an event to celebrate a successful project where patrons and staff are invited. Give credit where it is due.

Strategy 3: Use social media and traditional reporting sources, such as local newspapers, to announce new projects, ongoing progress, and completion. Provide recognition to all team members who contributed to the success of the project.

8. Maintain a welcoming, respectful, and safe library environment. Patrons and staff expect and deserve to find the library to be a place that is comfortable to them, where all people are treated equally without discrimination or prejudice.[7] The library is safe from any kind of outside threat or environmental insult. Work closely with library director, board, and other administration to continually improve the environment.

Strategy 1: Provide training to staff on customer service, including how to deal with difficult patrons. Observe how staff treat patrons, and provide constructive feedback and support.

Strategy 2: Review library polices to ensure there are regulations about the desired library environment and procedures in place for staff to follow if it is disrupted. Provide information and training about these policies, practicing drills for staff in case of a safety evacuation or threat by intruders.

Strategy 3: Managers should be visible and model welcoming and respectful behavior for both staff and patrons. When disruption occurs, handle the situation in a calm and respectful manner. In case of emergencies, act immediately to call police, fire, or other support.

9. Advocate for the staff and yourself. As a professional, you must learn to speak up for your own abilities, taking on projects others may not want to do as you work up the management ladder.[8]

Strategy 1: Volunteer for additional work and show those in library administration you can manage a project. Use the project to develop professional skills in communication, planning, personnel, and project management.

Strategy 2: Promote the good work of your department. Be sure staff has a clear sense of why a project is important and the impact their contribution will have on it.

Strategy 3: Learn the skills of **advocacy** and participate on all levels within the library community with administration and board, at the local governmental level, and, if possible, at the state level.[9] Challenge yourself to become involved by writing letters and speaking before governmental groups and other constituencies for the library and its work.

10. Understand the local community and align the work of the library closely to it. Library managers are most successful when they understand the culture and background of a community, know its key leaders, and work to unite dissenting and dissociated groups through library services and programs.

Strategy 1: Attend library board and important governmental meetings that have a library or community focus. Make a point of introducing yourself.

Strategy 2: Analyze library programs and services and identify "gaps" where members of the community may be overlooked. For example, meet with LGBT leaders to discuss informational programs or other services the library may offer.

Figure 2.3.   Library outreach. *istock/KatarzynaBialasiewicz*

Strategy 3: Provide outreach services for the community members who may not be able to visit the library. These could be in nursing homes, assisted living, and senior centers as well as schools, town recreation programs, shelters, or other places where people live or gather. Adapt resources and services to outreach populations.

11. Build and support an inclusive and diverse workforce. Libraries serve communities made up of all kinds of people differing in race, gender, age, religion, political and sexual orientation, abilities, socioeconomic status, and so forth.[10] Managers should strive to hire a diverse workforce who will relate to and best serve the community.

    Strategy 1: If the library staff is diverse, they will better be able to meet patrons' customer needs.

    Strategy 2: Managers free of direct or indirect bias have a wider pool of talented applicants to select from.

    Strategy 3: Having a wider pool of talent to select from may result in developing a more skillful workforce.

12. Be knowledgeable of and support library policy as well as all local, state, and federal laws that pertain to the library, its staff, and its patrons. Managers should become knowledgeable of and be able to apply library policy and uphold the law to protect interests of staff and patrons.

    Strategy 1: Seek discussion with administration about policies and laws in handbooks and obtain their advice on how to uphold and apply them in the library as a manager.

    Strategy 2: Research and keep current with professional organizations for how they advise interpretation and meaning of policies as they apply to libraries, staff, patrons, and services.

    Strategy 3: Research and keep current with new state and federal laws, following pending legislation. Contact legislators or their offices for updated information.

13. Learn and use practices of fiscal management. Managers plan budgets, advocate for funding, authorize expenditures, and are accountable for the financial status of their department.

    Strategy 1: It is strongly recommended managers take an introductory accounting course to become familiar with terminology and acceptable practices of budgeting.

    Strategy 2: Volunteer to serve as treasurer of a nonprofit organization as you will become familiar with reading and interpreting balance sheets.

    Strategy 3: As a first step, ask to help other library administrators construct their budgets to learn how budgets are developed. Work with a library accountant to learn the budget structure. Follow the budget process along, attending meetings of finance committees or other groups who make decisions about funding. Understand the fiscal constraints of the community.

Attend meetings where budget presentations are made and action is taken on the final budget.

14. Manage facilities and resources to support users' needs. Patrons visit the library for its resources and space. Managers work with maintenance and other staff to ensure the building is attractive, clean, and in good working order. Managers also make critical decisions about acquisition of resources.

Strategy 1: Learn the local building and safety codes of the town and state that govern use of the library. Discuss these codes with town experts (fire, health, etc.) to understand and assess how they are being applied in the library. Inform staff of the codes and why they are necessary to be followed.

Strategy 2: Ask the head of maintenance to give you a thorough building tour, from top to bottom. Learn about the infrastructure of the building. Be aware of its valuable assets as well as areas in need of maintenance or replacement. Work with others to develop a maintenance plan.

Strategy 3: Keep current with trends and demands of library resources. Attend workshops on what successful materials and equipment libraries are acquiring as well as collection types that are losing popularity. For example, does it make sense to continue funding the acquisition of DVDs if more people each year are streaming video?

These basic principles apply to managers of any library department in all types of libraries. Most people who become library managers did not begin their careers on this track. Most people who become managers took on leadership roles unexpectedly. Key to becoming a successful manager are the ability to think on your feet, a willingness to take on tasks that others may not want, excellent communication skills, the ability to negotiate and bring others to consensus, an adherence to standards and rules, and the motivation and caring to work with others to bring out the best in them.

PRINCIPLES OF SUPERVISION

Libraries by type have different types of supervision models at the higher administration (see figure 2.1). The library director or chief executive often reports to a board of trustees, superintendent, academic dean or president, or a city or town manager. All other library staff report to their direct supervisor who works in the library. LSS in all types of libraries often advance to manager positions in a group or department.

Library managers apply supervisory techniques, principles, and procedures to assign work, schedule, train, and evaluate the work of assigned staff. They have experience and skill in personnel recruitment, selection, and the use of personnel information systems.[11] Supervision is a process of monitoring work performance of others that includes administering and delegating activities and responsibilities. There is no one comprehensive or accepted list of supervision principles. Desired behaviors vary from person to person and institution to institution. Below is a summary of supervisory principles from the human resources department of the state of Maine. A few are cloaked in "Downeast" humor, and all are very practical principles that can apply to most any library supervisor:[12]

Supervisor Principles

1. Build positive experiences into the workplace as 50 percent of what we successfully do comes from our experience.
2. Most people use a few basic techniques to handle most situations.
3. When planning work go beyond the "must do." Add some "should do" and "nice to do" items.
4. Determine if a person can do the task requested and provide support if needed.
5. Have success and failure standards for projects to avoid a "risk-adverse" climate.
6. Send the indispensable person away at times to give others the opportunity to get proficient with critical tasks.
7. Delegate with clear expectations.
8. Avoid people who won't do what you ask of them and those who only do exactly what you ask them to do.
9. Your best and worst people are rule breakers. Be aware of why staff break rules.
10. Give authority along with responsibility.
11. Motivation has, at its root, dissatisfaction.
12. People think they are better than their boss thinks they are.
13. 80/20 rule: 80 percent of the power is in 20 percent of the staff. Eighty percent of the problems come from 20 percent of the staff. Eighty percent of the work is done by 20 percent of the staff.
14. There are two "tyrannies"—change and another's opinion. A tyranny is something you do not have any control over.

As you read the principles, think about both supervisors and colleagues you have worked with. You may find that if supervisors applied these principles to their management, improved work performance would result from a more supportive relationship between staff and supervisor.

SUPERVISION METHODS

Supervision is both formative and summative. An example of formative supervision is informal day-to-day observations while summative supervision may be an annual review linked to promotion or compensation.

If an employee does not meet performance standards, disciplinary action may occur. LSS should know the basics of management, supervision, and discipline to understand the structure of the library workplace and so they can use this knowledge to improve their own work performance.

There are many ways managers supervise their staff. These range from no supervision to very formal and scripted methods. Depending on whether the library is
school, public, academic, or special, and other measures such as private or municipal, large or small, city or rural, and so forth, supervision methods will vary. Let us
examine two broad categories of supervision methods: formative and summative.

Formative Performance Appraisal Methods

Formative appraisal methods are those that provide an informal feedback exchange between the supervisor and staff. In classrooms, teachers check student
learning progress with formative assessments, such as the teacher calling on students,
walking around the room to observe, or assigning homework and daily practice.

Formative performance appraisal methods of staff performance are also ongoing
and informal. The supervisor is forming her opinion of what the employee can
do and how she performs her work. This can be done by daily observations, walk-
throughs, informal meetings, periodic checking of work, or patron or staff input.

One formative performance appraisal method is the check-in. Managers and
employees meet intermittently throughout the year for unstructured chats about
achievements, expectations, goals, and concerns.[13] The talks allow employees to give
and receive feedback and allow managers to guide their career development. There's
no schedule to adhere to and no paperwork to be filed.

Another informal method of supervision some experience, and which is popular
in many businesses, is called a walk-through. The supervisor, unannounced, walks
into the employee's workspace and, without interruption or conversation, observes
the employee at work for about ten minutes. The employee has been told there will
be walk-throughs and to keep working as if the supervisor was not there. After each
walk-through, the supervisor provides the employee written notes of what she observed and any other feedback is discussed.

A third formative appraisal method is the checklist. With a list of expected positive behaviors and skills, the supervisor and employee mutually evaluate the consistency with which the employee applies them in his work.

In the busy library environment, and with some staff being part-time, many supervisors use formative methods in their supervision of employees.

Summative Performance Appraisal Methods

Summative performance appraisal methods are formal processes used by supervisors to improve staff performance, adjust compensation, provide feedback to workers,
create documentation for future decisions, set goals for future work and evaluation,
make promotion decisions, and identify training and staff planning. Goals are mutually established and staff is supported to expand their knowledge and experience as
they grow in their work. Most often the appraisal is done by an employee's manager,
and the process may be reviewed by a manager one level higher. While most summative methods involve the employee and manager, some seek opinions from peers or
team members or, as in the 360-degree appraisal interview, feedback from those with
whom the employee interacts, such as customers, students, or patrons.

Library managers need to prepare for an employee's review. Ways they can do this are to:

1. Become knowledgeable of any library or umbrella institutional policies that govern how to conduct performance reviews.
2. Develop and use a system for documentation, such as notes, papers, and other materials related to the performance of the employee. Review any documentation collected since the last evaluation.
3. Be prepared to give an above- or below-average performance rating of the employee.
4. Determine beforehand what changes may need to be made. Present them in the review as clearly written, measurable objectives.
5. Determine appropriate recognition where warranted, approved by upper management.
6. Anticipate the important goals for the library you would like to guide the employee to set for the next year.

A prepared and organized manager leads a productive and efficient summative appraisal. There are many kinds of summative methods, but common in most library organizations are two key systems.[14] First, they involve a continuous process of ongoing feedback and coaching to provide advice to improve employee's performance. Managers, supervisors, and employees frequently analyze their colleagues' performances and other behaviors to boost motivation and job effectiveness. Second, they set objectives, which are clearly defined tasks to achieve. Objectives align the employee's work to the library mission and goals. In other words, the tasks staff perform should support the library mission. Often managers and employees, working as a pair or in larger groups, develop important objectives that they are mutually excited about and motivated to achieve.

DISCIPLINARY PRINCIPLES

However necessary, discipline of an employee is unfortunate and often very difficult for the manager. Other than ethical or legal abridgements, discipline should occur after an appropriate number of attempts of coaching and other supports have failed. Employee disciplinary action could be as severe as being arrested for breaking the law or being fired on one extreme to a mild reprimand or referral on the other. Most disciplinary actions are around correctable job performance issues. Documentation is made, often in the form of a letter or an employee review sheet. In some libraries, there is a process for employee rebuttal. In larger institutions where there is a human resources (HR) department, HR is involved and lends support to both the manager and employee in the process.

All libraries should have a staff handbook that outlines labor practices aligned with civil, state, and federal law. Staff handbooks should also have an employee **code of conduct** with explicit statements of expected behavior. For example, many libraries require library staff to be held to the same standards of Internet use as the public. Outlined in a staff handbook are the process and steps for disciplinary action as well as a statement of the employees' rights.

Library managers should be prepared to take or be involved in disciplinary actions. It comes with the territory of being a manager. Principles to consider:

1. Treat all employees fairly and equally.
2. Be as neutral and without bias as possible. This particularly is true for being anti-discriminatory in all aspects with staff.
3. Meet with the employee and suggest corrective actions. Provide supports such as training if needed.
4. Unless the infraction is a critical emergency or legal violation, take time to gather data, obtain the "big picture," and explore options. Speak with immediate supervisor and/or HR for guidance.
5. Observe the employee at work. Intervene and suggest corrections. It is important the manager provides appropriate support to staff.
6. Document the situation over time. Have detailed notes with statements, dates, actions, and other information that may be needed to support disciplinary action or termination.
7. Understand state and federal law as well as library board and other policies that govern workplace conduct, legal and ethical behavior, disciplinary action, and termination. Seek support from supervisor and HR to ensure disciplinary actions and/or notice of termination is written with cause and consistent with library policy.

The following are areas of employee conduct that may require disciplinary action and some steps library mangers may consider.

Harassment and Discrimination

Libraries are public spaces, and as such they do not tolerate any form of harassment between or among patrons and staff. Discrimination and harassment include bias against those of a certain race, culture, gender, sexual orientation, religion, disability, medical condition, mental disability, or any other distinguishable attribute. Staff and patrons expect a library climate that is safe and respectful. Any staff member who does not adhere to discrimination or harassment law and policies should receive immediate disciplinary action and, if warranted, **termination**.

Violence and Bullying

Workplace violence and any threat to others cannot be tolerated and requires immediate action and possible termination. Violence or its threat is cause for arrest and civil prosecution. Library management supports outside investigations by police or other qualified personnel. If the violence is related to a health issue, the manager should see that the employee or family is knowledgeable of all medical supports the library extends to its employees. Bullying in any form—verbal and nonverbal—is a type of harassment and is not to be tolerated. It may even be illegal. All employees deserve a workplace environment free of bullying.

Social Media

Many library staff are public employees, meaning they work for a municipal or public library, public school, or public academic institution. Regardless of the First Amendment, as public employees, if they post inflammatory or other such statements on social media, there can be disciplinary ramifications. Public employees have been suspended for all manner of speech—supporting the shooting of police officers, lauding officers for shooting citizens, criticizing their students or coworkers, mocking minorities or religions, and a litany of other messages on social media.[15] When a public employee's social media posts create a fear of backlash from the community, the courts often defer to the opinion of the employer. In other words, if a public library employee posts a comment deemed inappropriate to the community on social media, the library administration most likely will be upheld in court if they decide to discipline the employee.

Figure 2.4. LSS use social media. *istock/dima_sidelnikov*

Substance Abuse

Library boards and administration should have a strategy that includes raising awareness about the consequences of staff drug and alcohol misuse and a policy on how the employer will respond to employee substance abuse. As part of the strategy, employers should provide line managers with specialist training to handle conversations about substance misuse.[16] The staff policy manual should have clear language about the disciplinary actions that will follow if an employee abuses substances on the job. Managers who suspect an employee has a problem with substances can encourage the person to seek treatment and support the employee by adjusting hours, offering sick leave, or referring the employee to counseling.

Other Disciplinary Actions

Insubordination to a supervisor may be a disciplinary offense. Many K–12 schools have insubordination clauses with disciplinary consequences stated in staff handbooks.

Library administration expects honesty of its employees. Lying, stealing, or other ethical breaches cannot be tolerated. When managers suspect such behavior, they need to follow disciplinary principles. Depending on the degree of the offense, such as stealing a large amount of funds, the matter could be referred to the police.

Library staff are seen by the public as professionals. As such they should conduct themselves in a professional manner in the community.

CHAPTER SUMMARY

LSS know basic principles of staff management, supervision, and discipline. Most LSS who move into managerial positions have a great potential to succeed because they are familiar with the work they are asking others to perform from their own firsthand experience. Because of this, they have the expertise to be mentors and coaches in their management and supervisory roles.

Library staff mostly work with the public, and as such they are expected to adhere to a standard of conduct. Disciplinary actions, when necessary, should align with library board and staff policies as well as civil, state, and federal law. Library managers seek guidance and support from their supervisors and HR when there is a need to discipline or terminate an employee.

DISCUSSION QUESTIONS

1. What are some of differences in management principles between for-profit and nonprofit organizations?
2. Why are team building and being able to reach consensus important to successful library management?
3. Why are LSS most often good managers? What reason does the author give?
4. What is the purpose of library staff supervision? How do formative performance appraisal methods differ from summative appraisal methods?
5. What are the two main processes or techniques successfully used in most summative performance appraisal methods?
6. How should supervisors prepare themselves for taking necessary staff disciplinary action?

ACTIVITY

Read the situation below. As the library manager for these workers, what supervisory steps would you take? Would you take disciplinary action? If so, in what form?

Write a report, no more than two pages, summarizing the situation. Describe the action you will take, using the management principles you learned in this chapter. What supervisory and, if necessary, disciplinary actions will you use to resolve the problem?

You are the supervisor of the circulation department of a large public library. Over the past few months, you notice that two of your employees, Alice and Pat, have not been getting along. They have not been cooperating with each other on the desk, and they have been a source of disruption in the department as people are uncomfortable with their name calling and other signs of disrespect. You are told today by another staff that patrons are beginning to complain about them as they are more preoccupied with their disagreements than with customer service. Work performance for the whole department is being negatively affected.

You have ignored this up until now thinking it was temporary and would soon blow over. But their situation has escalated now and you are afraid customer service is being affected as well as the morale of the department. Coworkers are starting to complain that they can't concentrate and do their own work with the disruptions. When you try to sit them down and talk to them, they are belligerent and tell you to stay out of the situation. They tell you this has nothing to do with work and they will handle it on their own. They get up and leave your office.

NOTES

1. Samuel A. Thumma and Meredith Marshburn, "Applying Successful Nonprofit Management Principles in the Courts," *Judges' Journal* 55, no. 2 (Spring 2016): 1, search.ebsco host.com/login.aspx?direct=true&db=aph&AN=117595984&authtype=cookie,cpid&custid= csl&site=ehost-live&scope=site.

2. Peter F. Drucker, *Managing the Nonprofit Organization* (New York: HarperBusiness, 2006).

3. Thumma and Marshburn, "Applying Successful Nonprofit Management Principles."

4. Ibid.

5. Janie Pickett, "First Steps with a Library Advisory Committee," *Knowledge Quest* 42, no. 1 (September/October 2013): 14–17, search.ebscohost.com/login.aspx?direct=true&db= aph&AN=90230621&authtype=cookie,cpid&custid=csl&site=ehost-live&scope=site.

6. Michelle Renard, "How Can Work Be Designed to Be Intrinsically Rewarding? Qualitative Insights From South African Non-Profit Employees," *South African Journal of Industrial Psychology* 42, no. 1 (2016), search.ebscohost.com.trcc.idm.oclc.org/login.aspx?direct= true&db=buh&AN=118204858&site=ehost-live&scope=site.

7. Vanderbilt University, "A Welcoming Library Environment," Jean and Alexander Heard Library, accessed May 12, 2017, www.library.vanderbilt.edu/policies/welcoming.php.

8. Jennifer A. Dixon, "The Next Step: Manager," *Library Journal* 142, no. 5 (March 15, 2017), search.ebscohost.com/login.aspx?direct=true&db=aph&AN=121964277&authtype= cookie,cpid&custid=csl&site=ehost-live&scope=site.

9. Jonathan A. Segal, "10 Keys to Grassroots Advocacy," *HR Magazine* 62, no. 3 (April 2017), search.ebscohost.com/login.aspx?direct=true&AuthType=cookie,ip,cpid&custid=csl &db=f5h&AN=122259404&site=eds-live.

10. Rachel O'Neill, "The Importance of a Diverse and Culturally Competent Workforce," *BusiDate* 24, no. 3 (July 2016), search.ebscohost.com/login.aspx?direct=true&db=aph &AN=117152574&authtype=cookie,cpid&custid=csl&site=ehost-live&scope=site.

11. City of Newport News, Virginia, "Job Description: Supervising Librarian, Libraries & Information Services," Human Resources Department, last modified August 1, 2015, accessed May 29, 2017, www.nnva.gov/DocumentCenter/Home/View/2827.

12. State of Maine, Human Resources, *Supervisor Skills Reference Guide*, 2015, 11–12, accessed May 29, 2017, www.maine.gov/bhr/employee_center/Supervisor%20Skills%20Refer ence%20Guide.pdf.

13. Catherine McIntyre, "Manage Performance Intelligently," *Canadian Business* 89, no. 14 (December 2016), search.ebscohost.com/login.aspx?direct=true&db=aph&AN=119324740& authtype=cookie,cpid&custid=csl&site=ehost-live&scope=site.

14. Michell Zeng, "What Alternative Performance Appraisal Methods Have Companies Used to Replace Forced Rankings?" Cornell University ILR School, last modified 2016, accessed May 29, 2017, digitalcommons.ilr.cornell.edu/cgi/viewcontent.cgi?article=1101&con text=student.

15. David L. Hudson, "Public Employees, Private Speech: 1st Amendment Doesn't Always Protect Government Workers," *ABA Journal*, May 2017, 1, search.ebscohost.com/login.aspx ?direct=true&db=aph&AN=122789040&authtype=cookie,cpid&custid=csl&site=ehost-live& scope=site.

16. Qian Mou, "Employee Substance Misuse: 5 Workplace Tips," *Occupational Health* 68, no. 10 (October 2016): 23, search.ebscohost.com/login.aspx?direct=true&db=aph&AN= 118726564&authtype=cookie,cpid&custid=csl&site=ehost-live&scope=site.

REFERENCES, SUGGESTED READINGS, AND WEBSITES

City of Newport News, Virginia. "Job Description: Supervising Librarian, Libraries & Information Services." Human Resources Department. Last modified August 1, 2015. Accessed May 29, 2017. www.nnva.gov/DocumentCenter/Home/View/2827.

Collett, Stacy. "How Do You Get a Fair Assessment?" *Computerworld Digital Magazine*, January 2016, 19–26. search.ebscohost.com/login.aspx?direct=true&db=aph&AN=112012702&auth type=cookie,cpid&custid=csl&site=ehost-live&scope=site.

Dixon, Jennifer A. "The Next Step: Manager." *Library Journal* 142, no. 5 (March 15, 2017): 68–69. search.ebscohost.com/login.aspx?direct=true&db=aph&AN=121964277&authtype= cookie,cpid&custid=csl&site=ehost-live&scope=site.

Drucker, Peter F. *Managing the Nonprofit Organization*. New York: HarperBusiness, 2006.

Hudson, David L. "Public Employees, Private Speech: 1st Amendment Doesn't Always Protect Government Workers." *ABA Journal*, May 2017, 1. search.ebscohost.com/login.aspx?di rect=true&db=aph&AN=122789040&authtype=cookie,cpid&custid=csl&site=ehost-live& scope=site.

LA Law Library. "Employee Handbook LA Law Library." Employee Handbook and Personnel Policies. Last modified 2013. Accessed May 30, 2017. www.lalawlibrary.org/pdfs/ Agenda_20130214a.attachment.pdf.

McIntyre, Catherine. "Manage Performance Intelligently." *Canadian Business* 89, no. 14 (December 2016): 37. search.ebscohost.com/login.aspx?direct=true&db=aph&AN=119324740& authtype=cookie,cpid&custid=csl&site=ehost-live&scope=site.

Mou, Qian. "Employee Substance Misuse: 5 Workplace Tips." *Occupational Health* 68, no. 10 (October 2016): 23. search.ebscohost.com/login.aspx?direct=true&db=aph&AN=118726564& authtype=cookie,cpid&custid=csl&site=ehost-live&scope=site.

O'Neill, Rachel. "The Importance of a Diverse and Culturally Competent Workforce." *BusiDate* 24, no. 3 (July 2016): 9–13. search.ebscohost.com/login.aspx?direct=true&db= aph&AN=117152574&authtype=cookie,cpid&custid=csl&site=ehost-live&scope=site.

Pickett, Janie. "First Steps with a Library Advisory Committee." *Knowledge Quest* 42, no. 1 (September/October 2013): 14–17. search.ebscohost.com/login.aspx?direct=true&db=aph&AN=90230621&authtype=cookie,cpid&custid=csl&site=ehost-live&scope=site.

Renard, Michelle. "How Can Work Be Designed to Be Intrinsically Rewarding? Qualitative Insights from South African Non-Profit Employees." *South African Journal of Industrial Psychology* 42, no. 1 (2016): 1–12. search.ebscohost.com.trcc.idm.oclc.org/login.aspx?direct=true&db=buh&AN=118204858&site=ehost-live&scope=site.

Segal, Jonathan A. "10 Keys to Grassroots Advocacy." *HR Magazine* 62, no. 3 (April 2017). search.ebscohost.com/login.aspx?direct=true&AuthType=cookie,ip,cpid&custid=csl&db=f5h&AN=122259404&site=eds-live.

State of Main, Human Resources. *Supervisor Skills Reference Guide.* 2015. Accessed May 29, 2017. www.maine.gov/bhr/employee_center/Supervisor%20Skills%20Reference%20Guide.pdf.

Thumma, Samuel A., and Meredith Marshburn. "Applying Successful Nonprofit Management Principles in the Courts." *Judges' Journal* 55, no. 2 (Spring 2016). search.ebscohost.com/login.aspx?direct=true&db=aph&AN=117595984&authtype=cookie,cpid&custid=csl&site=ehost-live&scope=site.

Vanderbilt University. "A Welcoming Library Environment." Jean and Alexander Heard Library. Accessed May 12, 2017. www.library.vanderbilt.edu/policies/welcoming.php.

Zeng, Michell. "What Alternative Performance Appraisal Methods Have Companies Used to Replace Forced Rankings?" Cornell University ILR School. Last modified 2016. Accessed May 29, 2017. digitalcommons.ilr.cornell.edu/cgi/viewcontent.cgi?article=1101&context=student.

CHAPTER 3

Staff Hiring, Evaluation, and Promotion

LSS participate in recruiting, hiring, training, evaluating, and promoting library staff. (ALA-LSSC Supervision and Management Competency #3)

Topics Covered in This Chapter:

- Hiring
  - o Policies
  - o Benefits
  - o Recruitment
- Interviewing
- Training
- Evaluating Staff
- Staff Promotion

Key Terms:

Anniversary date: An employee's anniversary date corresponds to the date on which they were hired. It is significant in the library in that this date may be the beginning of the employee's fiscal year, used for annual evaluations, salary increases, vacations, or promotions.

Benefits: In the library and other workplaces, benefits refer to compensation other than wages, such as holidays, sick time, medical insurance, and pensions.

Diversity: Diversity refers to hiring and maintaining a staff that represents a variety of backgrounds and abilities. Having diversity in the staff is important for serving a multicultural and multiethnic demographic.

Evaluation: An evaluation is an assessment of the work that a library staff member is doing. Also referred to as a performance review, it is a measurement of an employee's success in meeting goals and objectives for his or her position. Usually performed annually, it may be more frequent for the new employee during his probationary period.

Hiring: Hiring, for most organizations including libraries, is a complex process involving several steps: applications from interested candidates, selecting those who qualify for an interview, checking their references, and so on to determine who is offered the job.

Inclusion: Inclusion is a concept similar to diversity in that it recognizes people of all abilities but goes on to assure their participation in library employment and activities.

Interview: An interview is a meeting between a prospective employee and employer to determine the subject's qualifications and suitability for a position in a library or other workplace.

Policies: Policies are a set of rules and guidelines that help employees know what is expected of them with respect to standards of behavior and performance. In the library, they are usually set and adopted by a board of trustees.

Probationary period: The probationary period, often the first sixty or ninety days of a new job in a library, determines if the new employee is suited for the job and serves as a time for training and evaluation. Benefits may begin to accrue at the end of the probationary period.

Procedures: Library procedures are the steps taken to carry out a policy. They may be a set of instructions, a chart, or a list.

Recruitment: Recruitment, in a library, is the process of finding appropriate candidates for an open position. Usually carried out by human resources, it may also be done by others in library management.

Shadowing: Shadowing is a strategy where a new staff member follows another staff member during their daily routine. They can observe how a task is done by watching someone doing it. This is useful for new LSS to learn hands-on how to do their job.

Libraries are as good as the people who work there. Caring, dedicated, and knowledgeable staff members contribute to excellent library service. It is not by luck that these people find their way to a library near you. It is through the recruitment and hiring process that libraries, or their human resources departments, attract and hire these candidates. It is also through staff training, evaluation, and promotion that they retain them. In this chapter, we will look at these processes.

HIRING

Hiring, for most organizations including libraries, is a complex process involving several steps: soliciting and reviewing applications from candidates, selecting those who qualify for an interview, checking their references, and so on to determine who is offered the job. Some libraries incorporate these steps in a hiring policy; for others, it may be part of the personnel policy.

Policies

If the library is part of a town, college, or multibranch system, the hiring process may be part of the human resources department, or HR. (In schools, the librarians, or media specialists, are often hired by the school principal and are employed by the local board of education. They are considered faculty, and while they can have input, they would not hire.)

A sample hiring **policy** may follow this model:

The Objective:
Anywhere Library believes that hiring qualified individuals to fill positions at the Library contributes to the success of the Library. To hire the most qualified candidate this process should be followed.

The Hiring Process:
Open positions must include:

- Job title
- Hours
- Job functions and qualifications
- Any specific instructions

Job posting:

- All openings are posted on the library intranet and bulletin boards.
- Position remains posted until the job is filled.
- Job postings are updated [daily].

Internal transfer:

- Current employees may apply.
- Employees must complete the application and submit to HR.
- All applicants will be considered according to their qualifications and ability to perform the job.

Advertising:

- HR will advertise the position externally by use of print, listservs, and social media.

Interview process:

- HR will screen applications and résumés prior to scheduling interviews.
- HR will conduct initial interviews.
- Results will be forwarded to the library director or department head for individual or team interviews.
- HR will notify those applicants who are not selected.

Reference checks:

- HR will check references for all candidates.
- HR will conduct criminal background checks.

Job offer:

- Upon satisfactory reference and background checks, the candidate will be offered the position.

Start date:

- On the agreed-upon start date, the new hire will complete the proper paperwork including state and federal employment forms.[1]

If a library does not have a human resources department, this policy, or elements of it, may be part of the library's personnel policy or the employee handbook. (The employee handbook can serve as the list of **procedures,** or the steps taken to carry out employment policy.) In this case, hiring would be carried out by the library director or an authorized department head. Among the responsibilities of the HR or library director tasked with carrying out the process of hiring are to:

- negotiate the most cost-effective salary and benefit program,
- ensure equity in pay practices,
- ensure compliance with local and federal regulations,
- identify and use diverse sources of recruitment, and
- efficiently process and maintain employee records.[2]

Once the hiring process is complete, the new employee must be informed of their **probationary period**. A probationary period is a designated number of weeks or months when the employee's status is not yet considered permanent. Say the probationary period is six months. During this time, the new hire may be evaluated at one-month, three-month, and six-month intervals. If there are areas of concern, the employee will be given constructive directions for improvement. If after three evaluations, the employee is not working up to expectations, then their employment may be terminated. If the previous six months have been satisfactory, then at this point their holiday, sick, and vacation benefits can begin to accrue. However, the initial start date is considered the LSS's employment **anniversary date** for subsequent annual reviews and evaluations.

The new hire may be offered an employment contract. In chapter 1, the concepts of at will employment and representation by unions were discussed. If the new employee works for a school district, university, or municipal library, he may have a contract through the union representing the library. Otherwise LSS would likely be at will employees. Employee contracts are not common for LSS who are not part of the above scenarios but work in association or public libraries that are not town or county departments. Even so, LSS are entitled by law to certain benefits.

Benefits

Benefits are nonwage additions to an employee's wages or salary. By law, employers are required to provide certain benefits. They must:

- Give employees time off to vote, serve on a jury, and perform military service.
- Comply with all workers' compensation requirements.
- Withhold FICA taxes from employees' paychecks and pay their own portion of FICA taxes, providing employees with retirement and disability benefits.
- Pay state and federal unemployment taxes, thus providing benefits for unemployed workers.
- Contribute to state short-term disability programs in states where such programs exist.
- Comply with the Federal Family and Medical Leave Act (FMLA).[3]

Additionally, some libraries or systems may include medical and dental insurance; contribution to a defined retirement plan; and paid sick leave, holidays, and vacations. Just because the law does not require it does not mean the library should not offer or provide such benefits. On the contrary, it makes sense to offer at least some of these benefits to foster LSS's feeling of being valued.

Benefits are expensive, but when libraries skimp on them, they are likely to experience lower morale, less productivity, and more turnover—which is also costly. Because they are expensive, it is in the library's best interests to let employees know how much their benefits cost, so they can better appreciate them. According to the most recent report from the Bureau of Labor Statistics, employers spend between 30 and 37 percent for benefits compared to between 63 and 69 percent for wages.[4] (Some libraries may provide a benefit statement along with the offered wages, so the staff member can see how much is really being invested in them.)

In chapter 1, we were introduced to the concept of fairness. Benefits is one area where fairness is important. If one employee gets a paid holiday or sick day, so should all employees, including those who work part-time. It is the nature of libraries—the many days, evenings, and weekends that need coverage by staff—that there are a lot of part-time and flexible work hours. Libraries could not operate without them. Recognizing the value of these employees contributes to the overall well-being and morale—and is well worth the investment.

Additional benefits may be offered in the form of professional development—encouraging and offering opportunities and funding for LSS to improve their education through workshops, mini-courses, or online classes and other learning opportunities. This will be discussed in chapter 5.

Recruitment

It's been determined that there is an opening to fill in the library. You now know about the hiring process, but how do you find the right candidate? If the library has a human resources department, it would come under their purview, but the process is the same regardless of who at the management level does the search. The library should have a policy or statement regarding **diversity** in hiring, such as that used by the University of Michigan:

> The Library complies with all applicable laws regarding non-discrimination. **Recruiting** procedures disregard the irrelevant factors of race, creed, color, national origin, sexual orientation, religion, ancestry, sex, and age, except when sex and age are bona fide occupational requirements or when affirmative action considerations apply. The Library is committed to the recruitment and retention of a staff that represents diverse backgrounds in order to serve effectively the multicultural academic community.[5]

Diversity, however, is not enough. **Inclusion** must be considered as well. If diversity is the "what"—recognizing that people are different—inclusion is the "how"—doing something about it. "Diversity is being invited to the party; inclusion is being asked to dance."[6] Another way of looking at it is that diversity is quantifiable—having people of differing ethnicities or varying abilities on staff. Inclusion then is about the quality of their experience. It means valuing their contributions as individuals, not as representatives of a group or ability.

According to the Inclusion Network, an affiliation of organizations and individuals that provides access to learning opportunities, dialogues, and experiences that support actions toward equality and justice to strengthen our communities, "diversity includes all human differences. Valuing diverse people strengthens our workplaces, organizations, governments and communities, and enriches our personal lives."[7] They say:

- Inclusion is about ALL of us.
- Inclusion is about living full lives—about learning to live together.
- Inclusion makes the world our classroom for a full life.
- Inclusion treasures diversity and builds community.
- Inclusion is about our "abilities"—our gifts and how to share them.
- Inclusion is NOT just a "disability" issue.[8]

Next, the job description must be written using inclusive affirmative action language. It will consist of such elements as job title, job summary, work activities, performance expectations, and qualifications. It may also contain a statement about working conditions and physical requirements (e.g., must be able to lift twenty-five pounds). The library may require an application as well as a cover letter and résumé. It may also ask for the names of several references. Finally, it may or may not include the salary or hourly rate.

The job description for library support staff for a school, public, or academic library may look like this:

TEXTBOX 3.1: SAMPLE JOB DESCRIPTION

Library Support Staff

Summary: Facilitates the use of library resources by performing varied clerical and customer-service oriented tasks. Charges and discharges materials, registers patrons, records statistics, processes reserves, performs information searches, and instructs patrons. Keeps current with materials added to the library collection and makes recommendations to patrons. Performs all delinquent material functions. Assists throughout library.

Work activities: 25 hours per week, Monday–Friday, including some evenings and Saturdays. Ability to sit or stand for prolonged periods of time and ability to do repetitive movement. Frequently required to stoop, kneel, crouch, or crawl and lift and/or move up to 10 pounds.

Qualifications: Skills and knowledge required would usually be acquired with a high school education and two years' experience in public library work. Library Support Staff Certification preferred. Excellent communication and customer service skills required. Successful candidates will have demonstrated proficiency with computers, office equipment, and an Integrated Library System. Current minimum starting hourly rate of $12.50/hr.

Send résumé, cover letter, and names, addresses, and phone numbers of three references to HR. Applications accepted until filled. The library is an Equal Opportunity Employer.

All successful applicants must pass a drug test and a criminal background check.

The position may first be advertised in-house to qualified library staff. It may be advertised in the library, town, or institution's newsletter, website, Facebook page, other social media, or blog. To attract outside interest, do some research to identify the newspapers in the immediate and surrounding area and their requirements and prices for job postings both in print and online. Also find out what other media sources are available in the area that would accept a job posting. Most state library associations have an online job or career center that will post it. Other sources for job postings include such websites as Monster, Library Spot, and Indeed; LinkedIn (an employment-focused social media site) is another option for greater exposure. For LSS positions, advertising locally but widely is a good strategy. (ALA offers Joblist through their website, as do LibGig and Lyrasis, for example. These are national search sources that chiefly advertise positions that require the MLS and would not be a likely resource for support staff jobs.)

Most library employment ads do not differ significantly from the actual job description, although some may offer a summary with a link to a more detailed description. Textbox 3.2 shows what a sample ad might look like.

TEXTBOX 3.2: SAMPLE JOB AD

Anytown Library has an immediate opening for a part-time library support staff, 12 hours per week, $17.13/hour. Duties include direct customer service at the circulation desk and a variety of clerical duties in the Technical & Circulation Services Department. Schedule includes morning and/or afternoon hours Monday–Wednesday. Additional hours may be available on an as-needed basis. High school diploma or equivalent and proficiency with computers required. Previous library experience and work with an Integrated Library System a plus. To apply, please send a cover letter and résumé to Anytown Library, 123 Main Street, Anytown, Your State. Applications accepted until position filled. EOE.

INTERVIEWING

Congratulations! You have received several good applications that have passed the initial screening; now it's time to schedule **interviews** for the top five candidates. Perhaps your library's practice is to create an interview panel of staff members or librarians from other area libraries. Perhaps, as a manager, you will perform the interview by yourself. Now it's time to create the questions that will be asked of all the candidates. Here is where fairness comes up again: every candidate must be asked the exact same questions. Their answers must be evaluated by the same standards, and using a rating sheet (or evaluation form) assures it. The rating sheet may be incorporated into the interview question form or be provided separately. Examples will be provided later in the chapter.

After reviewing and culling the applications, it's time to set up interviews. What to ask is as important as what *not* to ask. Five common mistakes that interviewers make include:

1. Using subjective criteria: Rather than "screening-out" candidates based on an initial gut feeling, the address on the résumé, or the sound of a name, the interviewer should make sure that the job-evaluation process is as structured, job-specific, and objective as possible.

2. Checking social media: Social media profiles often contain pictures of candidates, as well as a plethora of information that is irrelevant to the job. Research has repeatedly shown that images and other irrelevant information can unconsciously undermine rational decision making.
3. Too much chatting: During the interview, it is common for the interviewer to slip into monologues about the opportunity, the company, the culture, and other job attributes. While this can be an important part of getting acquainted, it's important not to monopolize the conversation and to give the candidate opportunities to talk.
4. Asking ad-lib questions: During the structured section of the interview, people often go off-script and wander off into something that more closely resembles a friendly discussion. One should only ask the questions that are prepared as well as scripted follow-up questions.
5. Personal preferences: As humans, we tend to like people who share our personal preferences and interests . . . and other behaviors that aren't relevant to the job. While interviewing, keep in mind that liking the same TV shows is not related to on-the-job performance. Interviewers should not let "being like me" unconsciously sway their judgment.[9]

Other questions that cannot be asked include any personal questions designed to elicit information that is irrelevant or illegal based on anti-discrimination laws mentioned previously. There are many different state and federal anti-discrimination laws in place that work to curb discriminatory hiring practices. While some questions on their face are not explicitly illegal, the motive behind them may be and can be used as evidence of discrimination.

Here are some questions that should never be asked:

1. What is your race?
2. What is your national origin?
3. What is your religious affiliation?
4. How old are you?
5. Are you married? What is your maiden name? Do you have children or plan to? Are you pregnant?
6. Do you have any disabilities?
7. Have you ever been arrested?
8. What type of military discharge did you receive?
9. Have you ever filed for bankruptcy? Are you in debt?
10. Do you belong to any organizations?
11. Do you drink socially or smoke?[10]

There are, however, many acceptable questions that are quite typical when inter-viewing for library positions. Examples of these include:

- Why do you want to work here?
- How would your coworkers describe you?
- What are your strengths? Weaknesses?
- Describe what qualities and skills you have that would contribute to your work.
- Have you visited the library? What do you think of it?
- How would you handle an irate patron?
- Describe your experience using technology.
- Tell us what being a good team member means to you.
- Describe a conflict you had at a previous job, and tell us how it was resolved.
- Many say that libraries are dead. What is your response?

Figure 3.1.   Job interview. *istock/Squaredpixels*

There are many more possible questions that can be used, those that are general and those that are specific to the job. As long as they stay within the boundaries of what is legal, interviewing can be both challenging and enlightening.

TEXTBOX 3.3: SAMPLE JOB INTERVIEW SCORE SHEET

Candidate _____

Date _____

Interviewer _____

Table 3.1. Sample Job Interview Score Sheet

Circle a score for each question	Excellent	Good	Fair	Poor
Answer to Question #1	4	3	2	1
Answer to Question #2	4	3	2	1
Answer to Question #3	4	3	2	1
Answer to Question #4	4	3	2	1
Answer to Question #5	4	3	2	1
Answer to Question #6	4	3	2	1
Totals				

TRAINING

From the initial training of a new hire to seasoned staff, all LSS should have access to some forms of training or continuing education. These options may be outlined in an employee manual; they may be part of regular library operations; or they may be offered by management when outside training opportunities become available. All personnel—full- and part-time—should be included. In fact, it may be even more important to part-time staff as they don't have the benefit of being there to observe and learn from full-time or senior staff members.

Beginning with new employees, the first thing to do is to give them a tour. Show them where everything is—the restrooms, the breakroom (let them know when their breaks are and where they can eat lunch), office supplies, technical services, and the offices of key personnel. Let them know if there is a coffee pool to which they contribute or if they make their own—or where the closest coffee shop is. Then introduce them around, to those with whom they will be directly working as well as to those in other departments. Give them a list of key personnel and their contact information. If you think someone on staff shares their interests, make that connection. It helps a new employee to feel welcome and more comfortable.

Provide resources for them—an employee handbook if you have one, as well as relevant materials that will help acclimate them, such as an annual report or other library-produced materials that will help them understand the culture and environment. Make yourself available by checking in on them periodically throughout the first few days, and encourage them to ask questions. "Take the time to help your new employee feel welcome and comfortable and support her as she learns the ropes of her new gig. Remember: the more time you're able to invest in the beginning, the faster you'll have a dynamite team member—and the better off you'll start your relationship with her."[11]

Another good option for training is **shadowing**. Shadowing is a simple strategy whereby a new staff member follows another staff member during their daily routine. They can observe how a task is done by watching someone doing it. This is useful for new employees to learn hands-on how to do their job. During this process, encourage them to take notes that can reinforce that learning and provide the new hire with a "cheat sheet" for future reference.

It is also useful for seasoned LSS who can become familiar with how different departments work. When someone from cataloging, for instance, shadows someone in reference, they are cross training, which allows them to learn additional skills; it is especially valuable in small libraries that don't have enough staff to specialize in only one department.

Webinars are another tool that can be offered for training. A webinar is an informational seminar, meeting, or conference that is offered over the Internet, to be viewed at a prearranged time or archived to be viewed at the convenience of the LSS. Webinars are an excellent and cost-effective way to provide training to new and longtime employees alike. Typically sponsored by a library journal, library organization, or other educational facility, webinars are often presented as a PowerPoint program. If offered live, there are opportunities to ask questions or offer other feedback via computer or voice. Webinars run the gamut from specific subjects (such as reference skills, cataloging basics, or new software products) to training sessions for customer service or placing reserves.

They are often available for free, though some may be accessed for a fee, but registration is required. In spring of 2017, *Library Journal* offered webcasts on graphic novels, new apps for audio and e-books, open access (free, online use of research), and collection development, to name only a few. ALA offers webinars on advocacy

Figure 3.2. Webinar. *istock/anyaberkut*

and marketing, literacy, and youth services. TechSoup for Libraries presents software-related programs. At OCLC's WebJunction, one can find webinars on staff motivation, how best to use Wikipedia, and managing technology. These are only several examples of hundreds of topics. Other sites include LibraryConnect, Infopeople, and state library organizations, among others that will be discussed in a later chapter. Searching any of these sites will show the range of topics available for library staff training; as a manager, it is in your best interests to make them known and encourage staff to participate.

EVALUATING STAFF

As mentioned previously, new staff members are often subject to a probationary period during which their performance is **evaluated**. Once the probationary period is past, they, and all personnel, should be evaluated for their performance on an annual basis. This may be on their anniversary date or coinciding with a new **fiscal year** when budgets, and raises, are calculated.

To evaluate someone, she needs to know what is expected of her. Having standards and goals will help. Performance standards describe what you want workers in a job to accomplish and how you want the job done. Goals are tailored to each employee and will depend on her own strengths and weaknesses. When this has been done, be sure the employee gets a copy so she can know exactly what the expectations are. Then track her performance throughout the year. If she does something very well, or if she makes mistakes, give her immediate feedback. This can be done orally or in writing. Let her know when she has done something good or if you are concerned about her performance.[12] Whichever way you choose, document it in writing in their (electronic) file. This is how you as manager can keep track of the performances of all employees. This cannot be overstated, particularly if a dispute arises over elements of a job performance.

What some managers like to do in addition is to give the employee the means to create a self-appraisal. It is helpful for the manager to see how the employee feels he or she is performing relative to goals and standards. This gives employees the opportunity to address their strengths and weakness and to explain how or why an aspect of their job isn't working for them. This tool, along with the formal evaluation, can create a better picture of an employee's success. Some sample questions that can be included in a self-evaluation include:

- Identify any components of the job description that you no longer do or that now take additional time.
- Determine the components of your job that you would like to change or eliminate. Why?
- What accomplishment and achievements are you the proudest of since your last performance evaluation?
- What job-related goals would you like to accomplish during this evaluation period?
- List your areas of strengths and areas needing improvement.

- What skills or new knowledge would you like to develop to improve your performance?
- List your most significant accomplishments or contributions since last year. How do these achievements align with the goals/objectives outlined in your last review?[13]

This input from your employees can be a valuable tool when it comes to giving them their performance appraisal, which can be a difficult task.

Figure 3.3. Performance appraisal graphic. *istock/vinnstock*

However, some employees get very defensive in this situation. For example, one LSS was extremely defensive, and not only refused to accept her evaluation, she wrote a letter reviewing the evaluation to show why it was wrong—and then quit two days later. On the other hand, sometimes there are employees who accept their evaluation, improve for a short while, then backslide. After receiving several such warnings, which again were acknowledged, one LSS continued to make the same mistakes. When she was then let go, as warned—she was caught completely by surprise! Clearly, she did not take the warnings seriously. In a similar instance, when after numerous warnings another LSS was let go, she cried and asked for yet one more chance. By this time, her performance so affected the morale of the entire staff that there was no choice but to terminate her employment. Fortunately, good evaluations outnumber the difficult ones. It is critical to remember that when performing evaluations, you are working with real people and their reactions cannot always be predicted.

Nolo, a respected publisher of legal books and software, gives advice for performing an evaluation:

- Be specific. When you set goals and standards for your workers, spell out exactly what they will have to do to achieve them.
- Give deadlines. If you want to see improvement, give the worker a timeline to turn things around. If you expect something to be done by a certain date, say so.
- Be realistic. If you set unrealistic or impossible goals and standards, everyone will be disheartened—and will have little incentive to do their best if they know they will still fall short. Don't make your standards too easy to achieve, but do take into account the realities of your workplace.
- Be honest. If you avoid telling a worker about performance problems, the worker won't know that he or she needs to improve. Be sure to give the bad news, even if it is uncomfortable.
- Be complete. Write your evaluation so that an outsider reading it would be able to understand exactly what happened and why.
- Evaluate performance, not personality. Focus on how well (or poorly) the worker does the job—not on the worker's personal characteristics or traits.
- Listen to your employees. The evaluation process will seem fairer to your workers if they have an opportunity to express their concerns, too. Ask employees what they enjoy about their jobs and about working at the company. Also ask about any concerns or problems they might have.[14]

There are several ways to document a performance appraisal, and using a standard evaluation form, like using standard interview questions, both simplifies and equalizes the process. An evaluation may be done using a format such as the one provided.

TEXTBOX 3.4: PERFORMANCE APPRAISAL FORM

Name:

Position:

Date of Evaluation:

Date of Hire:

Evaluator:

Please use the following guideline when evaluating the employee's performance.

Above Standard: Employee performance is consistently above the standards for the position. Specific examples of above standard performance must be documented.

Meets Standard: Employee performance consistently meets standards for the position.

Below Standard: Employee performance is consistently below acceptable standards for the position. Specific areas requiring improvement must be documented.

QUALITY OF WORK

☐ Knowledge and ability to perform duties

Above ☐   Meets ☐   Below ☐

Comments:

WORK HABITS

☐ Punctuality, attendance, effective use of time, communication, follow-through

Above ☐   Meets ☐   Below ☐

Comments:

WORK INITIATIVE

☐ Resourcefulness, ability to carry out new assignments, adaptability.

Above ☐   Meets ☐   Below ☐

Comments:

INTER-PERSONNEL AND CUSTOMER RELATIONS

☐ Ability to get along with coworkers, acceptance of supervision, tact and courtesy
in dealing with the public.

Above ☐   Meets ☐   Below ☐

Comments:

LIBRARY STANDARDS/OBJECTIVES

☐ Adheres to policies/procedures

Above ☐   Meets ☐   Below ☐

Comments:

OVERALL PERFORMANCE

Above ☐   Meets ☐   Below ☐

Comments:

SIGNATURES:

Employee: _____   Date: _____

Evaluator: _____   Date: _____

Figure 3.4.   Performance appraisal form. *Courtesy of the author*

STAFF PROMOTION

The American Library Association Office for Library Personnel Resources Standing Committee on Library Education issued a paper in 1991 that stated, "Paraprofessional library positions offer limited advancement opportunities."[15] While at one time this may have been true, the graying of the library profession has created new opportunities. Support staff are now filling positions formerly only held by MLS librarians; increasing technology has also created a niche for talented LSS. Today, LSS hold positions of responsibility as department heads and even as directors of small public libraries. Fortunately, the educational opportunities for LSS are preparing them for a bright future.

As with most aspects of working in a library, there needs to be a policy in place that concerns the promotion of all library staff, including LSS. "Unclear promotion policies can create conflicts and high turnover rates among employees who don't understand why co-workers received a promotion instead of them. Problems may not end there if vague promotion procedures also appear discriminatory. Employers can avoid such difficulties by creating a transparent promotion policy and consistently applying that policy's standards to each employee seeking advancement."[16]

Advancement for LSS, as with any profession, depends on openings in the field; any qualified employees are eligible to apply. Promotion to these jobs depends on skills and past performance. A promotion policy may contain the following considerations:

Function: An effective promotion policy focuses on advancing employees based on their skills and performance, not favoritism. Companies risk putting people in jobs they can't handle when promotions aren't based on workers' abilities.
Setting criteria: It's important to determine the minimum criteria for advancement and make employees aware of the standards they need to meet to earn promotions. For example, employees may need to work with a company for at least two years before they're eligible for any type of promotion or meet certain quotas to advance within a company.
Posting jobs: Make posting all job openings in the workplace part of your promotion policy so advancement opportunities are open to all qualified candidates.
Assessing candidates: Assess all qualified employees for a promotion in the same manner to avoid the appearance of favoritism or discrimination. For example, ensure a hiring manager examines performance appraisals and uses them to select the top candidates for a promotion. Keep the application review process consistent by determining the importance of various qualifications and judging all candidates on those factors.[17]

The promotion process won't differ significantly from the hiring process; indeed, many of the elements are the same. A new opening, for which existing personnel might be qualified, still must be posted, even if the policy is to first consider internal candidates. Promoting from within is a viable option, particularly if someone has already been doing similar work or assisting on the available job.

Another way to "promote" staff, besides moving into a new position, is to offer incentives for the job they already do. This kind of promotion recognizes their work and encourages the employee to strive. Many employers encourage staff members to volunteer at an outside organization and offer recognition of that effort. Leaving early one day a month to work at a community center, youth organization, or a blood drive are examples of community involvement that can inspire employees. They feel valued, and they value the library for supporting investment in the community. This also raises the profile and visibility of the library; if the library thrives, it trickles down.

Simply thanking staff boosts morale, as does offering physical incentives. These typically consist of small rewards for a job well done, such as coupons for coffee at the local café, points toward earning flex time or an early dismissal, or a certificate of achievement. Sharing notice of excellent employee performance with the library board, with the local paper, or on social media is an immediate bolster. Have a prize for brainstorming—the best idea for rearranging a workspace wins $20—and so on. Giving LSS a chance to feel vested in the outcome of library decisions is a positive improvement.

Research shows that feeling appreciated is a driver of employee engagement. *Forbes*, the business magazine, offers twenty-five great ideas that libraries can adopt for promotion. While some are more practical than others, who wouldn't appreciate any of these?

1. A sincere word of thanks . . . is very effective.
2. Post a thank you note on their door in their honor.
3. Throw a pizza party or cake party in their honor.
4. Create a simple "ABCD" card that is given when someone goes "Above the Call of Duty."
5. Write about them in a [library]-wide e-mail.
6. Give a long lunch, extra break, or comp time.
7. Honor them at the start of the next staff meeting.
8. Post a "thank you" sign in the lobby with their name on it.
9. Gift them flowers, a book, or other small gift.
10. Invite them to a one-on-one lunch.
11. Give them a card with lottery tickets inside.
12. Give them a card with movie tickets inside.
13. Give them a card with a Starbucks gift certificate.
14. Have the entire team sign a framed photo or certificate of appreciation.
15. Arrange for a boss several levels up to stop by to say thanks.
16. Send a thank you note or gift basket to their spouse.
17. Arrange to have their car washed.
18. Arrange to have their home cleaned.
19. Let them bring their pet to work.
20. Buy a dozen donuts and announce to the department that they are in the honoree's office; they should stop by to say hi and get one.
21. Feature them in the company newsletter.
22. Pick an unusual or funny object and place it on their desk for a week.
23. Let them dress casually for a day.
24. Have entire team honor them with a standing ovation at the start of the next staff meeting.
25. Offer to swap a task with them for a day or week.[18]

Thus, there are many ways to promote LSS—from new positions to a simple note of appreciation. Anything that you, as manager, can do to make library staff happy is a successful promotion.

CHAPTER SUMMARY

In this chapter, we learned about the recruiting, hiring, training, evaluating, and promoting of library staff. As a manager, it is your job to oversee and be a part of this process, even if the library has a human resources department. Fairness is the overriding factor, and sensitivity to personnel is required. The entire process demands a knowledge and understanding of diversity, management, and local and federal regulations. No library can be successful without competent and satisfied staff; it is imperative that all is done to ensure it.

DISCUSSION QUESTIONS

1. Name several steps involved in the hiring of a new staff member at the library.
2. What are some of the elements that should go into a job description?
3. Many library positions come with benefits. Discuss what they are; should they be offered to all staff members, and why?
4. How do you conduct a successful interview?
5. Once you have hired a new staff member, what will you do to train him; what will you do to ensure he stays?

ACTIVITIES

1. Search local and national media for library job descriptions. Using them as a model, write a new job description for an opening in your (school, public, or academic) library. Make a list of media outlets to which they could be sent to recruit candidates.
2. Create an interview and rating sheet for a new position. Consider what questions need to be asked, taking into consideration those that cannot. Working with two other students or colleagues, interview the candidates, and rate the answers. Which one would you hire, and why?

NOTES

1. Society for Human Resource Management, "Hiring Policy: Process and Procedures May 30, 2016," last modified May 30, 2016, accessed June 14, 2017, www.shrm.org/resourcesand tools/tools-and-samples/policies/pages/cms_001677.aspx.

2. American Library Association, "Human Resources," accessed June 13, 2017, www.ala .org/offices/hr.

3. Entrepreneur Media, "The Basics of Employee Benefits," last modified 2017, accessed June 16, 2017, www.entrepreneur.com/article/80158.

4. U.S. Bureau of Labor Statistics, "Employer Costs for Employee Compensation News Release," last modified March 17, 2017, accessed June 16, 2017, www.bls.gov/news.release/archives/ecec_03172017.htm.

5. University of Michigan Library, "Staff Manual: Recruiting for Library Staff Positions," last modified December 2015, accessed June 19, 2017, www.lib.umich.edu/library-human-re sources/staff-manual-recruiting-library-staff-positions.

6. Verna Myers, "Diversity Is Being Invited to the Party; Inclusion Is Being Asked to Dance," *GPSolo eReport*, last modified June 2012, accessed July 6, 2017, www.americanbar.org/publi cations/gpsolo_ereport/2012/june_2012/diversity_invited_party_inclusion_asked_dance.html.

7. Inclusion Network, "We Value Diversity," accessed July 8, 2017, www.inclusionnetwork .org/.

8. Shafik Assante, "What is Inclusion?" Inclusion Network, accessed July 6, 2017, www .inclusion.com/inclusion.html.

9. Chad Brooks, "5 Common Mistakes Job Interviewers Make," *Business News Daily*, last modified October 10, 2013, accessed June 21, 2017, www.businessnewsdaily.com/5261-com mon-job-interview-mistakes.htm.

10. Emily Casey, Esq., interview by the author, Groton, CT, April 25, 2017.

11. Jessica Taylor, "5 Tips for Training New Hires," The Muse, last modified 2017, accessed June 27, 2017, www.themuse.com/advice/5-tips-for-training-new-hires.

12. Amy DelPo, "How to Conduct Employee Evaluations," Nolo, last modified 2017, ac cessed June 27, 2017, www.nolo.com/legal-encyclopedia/employee-evaluations-how-to-con duct-29547.html.

13. Susan M. Heathfield, "Sample Questions for an Employee Self-evaluation," The Balance, last modified April 3, 2016, accessed June 27, 2017, www.thebalance.com/sample -questions-for-an-employee-self-evaluation-1918891; Boise State University, "Self-Evaluation Questions," accessed June 27, 2017, vpfa.boisestate.edu/process/uformsdocs/pfm/SelfEvalu ationQuestions.pdf.

14. DelPo, "How to Conduct."

15. American Library Association, "Advancement for Support Staff," last modified Septem ber 17, 1991, accessed June 27, 2017, www.ala.org/educationcareers/education/3rdcongress onpro/advancementsupport.

16. Frances Burks, "Employee Promotion Policy Guide," Chron, last modified 2017, accessed June 27, 2017, smallbusiness.chron.com/employee-promotion-policy-guide-40500.html.

17. Ibid.

18. Kevin Kruse, "25 Low-Cost Ways to Reward Employees," *Forbes*, last modified March 1, 2013, accessed June 27, 2017, www.forbes.com/sites/kevinkruse/2013/03/01/25-low-cost -ways-to-reward-employees/#76bb0a03246b.

REFERENCES, SUGGESTED READINGS, AND WEBSITES

ALA-APA.org. "7 Common Employee Gripes (and How to Silence Them)." *Library Worklife*. Last modified June 2017. Accessed June 13, 2017. ala-apa.org/newsletter/2017/06/13/ 7-common-employee-gripes-and-how-to-silence-them/.

Allard, Suzie. "Bouncing Back: Placements and Salaries 2016." *Library Journal* 141, no. 17 (October 15, 2016): 30–36.

American Library Association. "Advancement for Support Staff." Last modified September 17, 1991. Accessed June 27, 2017. www.ala.org/educationcareers/education/3rdcongress onpro/advancementsupport.

———. "Human Resources." Accessed June 13, 2017. www.ala.org/offices/hr.

————. "Overview of Library Support Staff." Last modified 2017. Accessed June 13, 2017. www.ala.org/offices/hrdr/librarysupportstaff/overview_of_library_support_staff.

Assante, Shafik. "What is Inclusion?" Inclusion Network. Accessed July 6, 2017. www.inclusion.com/inclusion.html.

Boise State University. "Self-Evaluation Questions." Accessed June 27, 2017. vpfa.boisestate.edu/process/uformsdocs/pfm/SelfEvaluationQuestions.pdf.

Brooks, Chad. "5 Common Mistakes Job Interviewers Make." *Business News Daily.* Last modified October 10, 2013. Accessed June 21, 2017. www.businessnewsdaily.com/5261-common-job-interview-mistakes.html.

Burks, Frances. "Employee Promotion Policy Guide." Chron. Last modified 2017. Accessed June 27, 2017. smallbusiness.chron.com/employee-promotion-policy-guide-40500.html.

Carter, Jami, Steve Peay, and Rachel Gull. "Self-Directed Achievement: If You Give Library Staff An Hour." WebJunction. Last modified February 3, 2013. Accessed June 13, 2017. www.webjunction.org/content/dam/WebJunction/Documents/webJunction/slides_Self_Directed_Achievement_webinar.pdf.

Casey, Emily, Esq. Interview by the author. Groton, CT. April 25, 2017.

DelPo, Amy. "How to Conduct Employee Evaluations." Nolo. Last modified 2017. Accessed June 27, 2017. www.nolo.com/legal-encyclopedia/employee-evaluations-how-to-conduct-29547.html.

"Dimensions Autism Friendly Libraries Training Video For Library Staff." Video file, 9:51. YouTube. Posted by Dimension UK, July 1, 2016. Accessed June 13, 2017. www.youtube.com/watch?v=BJLbbJW1BpA.

Entrepreneur Media. "The Basics of Employee Benefits." Last modified 2017. Accessed June 16, 2017. www.entrepreneur.com/article/80158.

Gutsche, Beth, and Elizabeth Iaukea. "12 Anytime + Anywhere = Never: Motivating the Self-Directed Learner." WebJunction. Last modified June 16, 2016. Accessed June 13, 2017. www.webjunction.org/news/webjunction/anytime-anywhere-never-sda.html.

Heathfield, Susan M. "Sample Questions for an Employee Self-evaluation." The Balance. Last modified April 3, 2016. Accessed June 27, 2017. www.thebalance.com/sample-questions-for-an-employee-self-evaluation-1918891.

Inclusion Network. "We Value Diversity." Accessed July 8, 2017. www.inclusionnetwork.org/.

Kruse, Kevin. "25 Low-Cost Ways to Reward Employees." *Forbes.* Last modified March 1, 2013. Accessed June 27, 2017. www.forbes.com/sites/kevinkruse/2013/03/01/25-low-cost-ways-to-reward-employees/#76bb0a03246b.

"Library Assistant Interview Questions." Video file, 1:00. Posted by AlphaCode System, May 12, 2017. www.youtube.com/watch?v=zuiuAdnqgcQ.

Martinez, Edward B. "In the Beginning, There Was Support Staff . . ." American Library Association. Accessed June 13, 2017. www.ala.org/offices/hrdr/librarysupportstaff/history_of_library_support_staff.

Myers, Verna. "Diversity Is Being Invited to the Party; Inclusion Is Being Asked to Dance." *GP-Solo eReport.* Last modified June 2012. Accessed July 6, 2017. www.americanbar.org/publications/gpsolo_ereport/2012/june_2012/diversity_invited_party_inclusion_asked_dance.html.

National Law Forum. "Five Essential Elements of a Good Job Description." *National Law Review.* Last modified October 24, 2012. Accessed June 19, 2017. www.natlawreview.com/article/five-essential-elements-good-job-description.

"Performance Appraisal Training Part 1." Video file. YouTube. Posted by UNI Human Resource Services, March 15, 2016. Accessed July 6, 2017. www.youtube.com/watch?v=hM2H3wo2Qf8.

Schwartz, Meredith. "Reworking the Workforce." *Library Journal* 121, no. 20 (December 15, 2016): 42–45.

Society for Human Resource Management. "Hiring Policy: Process and Procedures May 30, 2016." Last modified May 30, 2016. Accessed June 14, 2017. www.shrm.org/resourcesand tools/tools-and-samples/policies/pages/cms_001677.aspx.

Taylor, Jessica. "5 Tips for Training New Hires." The Muse. Last modified 2017. Accessed June 27, 2017. www.themuse.com/advice/5-tips-for-training-new-hires.

"Top Library Assistant Interview Questions." Video file, 1:32. You Tube. Posted by Mock Questions, March 1, 2016. Accessed June 13, 2017. www.youtube.com/watch?v=TzO 5QEmgN1Q.

University of Michigan Library. "Staff Manual: Recruiting for Library Staff Positions." Last modified December 2015. Accessed June 19, 2017. www.lib.umich.edu/library-human-re sources/staff-manual-recruiting-library-staff-positions.

U.S. Bureau of Labor Statistics. "Employer Costs for Employee Compensation News Release." Last modified March 17, 2017. Accessed June 16, 2017. www.bls.gov/news.release/archives/ ecec_03172017.htm.

Weak, Emily. "The Interview Questions Repository." *Hiring Librarians: An Inside Look at Library Hiring.* Last modified April 19, 2015. Accessed June 13, 2017. docs.google.com/spread sheets/d/1N9segNyNeOssPYqfZ1pacKEHYDPpETKI00lHW_ppJF0/edit#gid=0.

Yale University Library. "Working at the Library: Performance and Promotion Criteria." Last modified April 24, 2017. Accessed June 13, 2017. guides.library.yale.edu/c.php?g=296164 &p=1976544.

CHAPTER 4

Performance Expectations

LSS set clear performance expectations for staff linked to the library's strategies and priorities. (ALA-LSSC Supervision and Management Competency #4)

Topics Covered in This Chapter:

- Performance Expectations
  - o Evaluations
  - o Documentation
- Annual Performance Plans
  - o Strategic Plan
  - o Annual Plan
- Linking Expectations to the Library's Strategic Directions

Key Terms:

Annual performance plan: The annual plan provides the link between long-term strategic goals outlined in the library's strategic plans and what managers and LSS are expected to accomplish in a single fiscal year.

Documentation: Documentation is information that serves as a record of what took place, the record of an employee's performance.

Evaluation: An evaluation is another term for a performance appraisal. In the library, it is a way to judge a staff member's work, usually on an annual basis, and is based on a predetermined set of standards.

Feedback: Feedback is the process whereby the results of something you do are "fed back" or returned to you; between manager and LSS, it is an important part of the performance review process.

Job description: A job description is a statement or document that describes the duties and responsibilities of an employee in the workplace.

> *Performance appraisal:* A performance appraisal, also known as a performance evaluation, is a process by which a manager examines an employee's work by comparing it to a set of previously determined standards.
>
> *Strategic plan:* A strategic plan is the clearly worded description of the library's mission, what it wants to achieve over the next few years, and the strategic priorities to guide the organization toward achievement of the vision.

In the library, as in virtually every workplace, there comes a time when employees are evaluated on their work performance. From a manager's point of view, the employee is an investment: he or she was chosen to perform a job and is being paid to do so. It is to no one's advantage if he is not doing the job well.

A **performance appraisal**, also known as a performance evaluation, is a process by which a manager examines an employee's work by comparing it to a set of previously determined standards. In doing so, she documents the comparison and then uses it to provide feedback to the staff member. The result determines if improvement is needed and why, what further training may be needed, and if the employee is then retained, promoted, or fired.[1]

These appraisals are linked to the library's plan and ultimately to its long-term goals.

PERFORMANCE EXPECTATIONS

As we saw in chapter 3, "libraries are as good as the people who work there." The library has gone through the process of soliciting candidates, reviewing their applications, and interviewing those who appear to be a good fit for the position. Presumably now the library has qualified library staff, and everyone lives happily ever after. If it was only that easy!

To perform well, employees need to know what is expected of them. They need to begin with a current **job description** that lists the essential functions, tasks, and responsibilities of their job. It will also outline the general areas of knowledge and skills required of the employee to be successful in the job.[2]

"Job descriptions clearly define what is expected of an employee. Organizations tend to update a job description when they need to hire, but forget to review these descriptions. As a result, the nature of the person's job has changed, but the description fails to reflect the changes. By updating the job description, you are making sure everyone is on the same page and clearly defining what everyone does in the library."[3]

But that's not all. There are other considerations beyond just the job description. It is helpful if the LSS understands her role in the library—how she fits into the organization; what her relationship is to other employees, such as her peers and supervisors; and how her job contributes to the mission and goals of the library. These expectations serve as a basis for evaluating performance on an ongoing basis.

It should come as no surprise that communication between supervisor and LSS is critical. There can be no misunderstanding of what is expected of the employee, nor can there be any question what the employee needs from her supervisor. While performance evaluations may be performed annually, say on the anniversary of the date of hire, staff members should not be left guessing if they are doing a good job until then. The more communication there is the better the chances that there will be no surprises.

Talking to coworkers and supervisors about what is going on, in casual chat or even if a specific question arises, facilitates an ongoing two-way conversation. This is called **feedback**. As it sounds, feedback is the process whereby the result of something you do is "fed back" or returned to you. For example, your supervisor has asked you to write up a protocol for teaching a student worker the circulation functions in your library. You carefully go through the process, beginning with what items can circulate, how long the loan period is, whether materials can be renewed or reserved, and how to print the date due receipts. You give it to her for review— and she says you have done a good job, but you left out information about late fees; she suggests that once that is done, this revised procedure can be used immediately. Your supervisor has praised you for your work and suggested how to improve it. She has given you feedback.

Keeping the lines of communication open between manager and employee helps the performance expectations serve as a foundation for communicating about performance throughout the year. It also serves as the basis for reviewing employee performance. When the manager and the employee set clear expectations about the results that must be achieved and the methods or approaches needed to achieve them, then a path for success is established.[4] With this knowledge, the LSS can anticipate good results when performance appraisals take place.

However, an employee does not have to be caught off guard; rather he can prepare for performance evaluations. Good communication is the first step; knowing what is expected of you from your job description is the second. Be aware of the essential functions, tasks, and responsibilities of your job, as well as how you relate to your coworkers. Are you always on time for your shift? Do you complete your tasks in a timely manner? It helps to create your own "performance review" file. Keep track of your successes in the various areas of your job, as well as any problems that you may have encountered—and how you resolved them.

Evaluations

In fact, while some libraries may ask an employee to perform a formal self-evaluation, be proactive and create one for yourself based on some of the previous suggestions. In doing so, it will help to determine if you and your manager are on the same page—or if you are not, what you can do to get closer to your goals.[5] Don't be afraid to ask your supervisor for occasional feedback during the year, and ask for specifics. "You're doing fine" doesn't really tell you anything. Expect as well that there may be some areas where you could improve; use this opportunity to add it to your own "performance review" file so that your performance expectations will be in line with your eventual performance review.

TEXTBOX 4.1: SAMPLE STAFF SELF-EVALUATION

Name:

Position:

Date:

This staff self-evaluation form is an opportunity. Your answers can help refine the job you do, making the _____ Library a more efficient place in which to work. This helps the overall function of the library, making us a more effective (and cost-effective) institution.

1. Please write a short report on how you feel you've been doing in your position this past year, and try to include the following. Use the back of the page and additional paper if necessary.
    a. Does your job meet your expectations?
    b. What have you done this year of which you are particularly proud?
    c. Is there anything you've done, or any area you perceive, that could have been improved?
2. What goals would you set for next year [and beyond]?
3. Comments. Questions?

Staff Signature: _____ Date: _____

Received by: _____ Date: _____

From the point of view of the manager or supervisor, performance evaluations can be just as intimidating as they are for the employee. According to an article in *Library Journal* by Steven Bell, associate university librarian at Temple University in Philadelphia, "Despite efforts to make the process meaningful for both worker and supervisor, we still tend to regard performance evaluations as a necessary evil. . . . I think workers value performance reviews and the opportunity to provide an accounting of their contributions and receive feedback from a supervisor."[6] Depending on the library, evaluations may be prerequisites to annual compensation increases, and all staff members—from supervisors to LSS—must endure them.

While it may be unavoidable, the performance evaluation does not have to be a burden. If you as the manager are giving staff members clear goals, their job descriptions are up to date, and communication is open, it should be a fairly simple process. It is important to determine what kind of rating sheet you will be using and then use it for each staff member being evaluated. The rating sheet needs to have objective criteria so all those being evaluated are judged equally. There are numerous evaluation methods and charts that can be used; two samples are presented in table 4.1 and textbox 4.2.

Figure 4.1. Performance evaluation. *istock/fizkes*

Ideally, the evaluation takes place, and everyone is happy—but that isn't always the case. There have been times when, even after multiple interactions throughout the year about an employee's performance, he is still blindsided by his appraisal. For example, say the LSS was cited several times for tardiness. He was warned that it would not be tolerated and given a deadline to improve; the deadline came, and nothing had changed. When he was finally called to task and it affected his evaluation, he was shocked.

It is standard procedure for both the staff member and supervisor to sign the evaluation, accepting the results. In another example, imagine that a staff member did not express any dissatisfaction with her appraisal but came back the next day with a list of rebuttal statements about why her evaluation was not acceptable to her—and she refused to sign it. Some people get very defensive when any part of their performance is called out, even if they have been previously warned, and their reactions can be unexpected. While most evaluations are not this dramatic, be prepared for a variety of reactions, just in case.

Table 4.1.   Sample Evaluation Sheet 1

Employee Info			
Employee Name		Department	
Employee ID		Reviewer Name	
Position Held		Reviewer Title	
Last Review Date		Today's Date	

Characteristics				
Quality	Unsatisfactory	Good	Highly Satisfactory	Excellent
Works to Full Potential				
Quality of Work				
Work Consistency				
Communication				
Independent Work				
Takes Initiative				
Group Work				
Productivity				
Creativity				
Honesty				
Integrity				
Coworker Relations				
Client Relations				
Technical Skills				
Dependability				
Punctuality				
Attendance				

Goals
Achieved Goals Set in Previous Review?

Goals for Next Review Period			
Comments and Approval			
Employee Signature		Reviewer Signature	

TEXTBOX 4.2: SAMPLE EVALUATION SHEET 2

Employee Name:

Supervisor:

Position:

Date of Hire:

Last Evaluation Date:

Position Knowledge
Understands basic principles, techniques, practices, and procedures of position
    Exceeds Requirements   Meets Requirements   Needs Improvement
Understands and supports overall mission of the library
    Exceeds Requirements   Meets Requirements   Needs Improvement
Follows library policies and procedures
    Exceeds Requirements   Meets Requirements   Needs Improvement
Ability to operate library equipment as required
    Exceeds Requirements   Meets Requirements   Needs Improvement
Ability to follow oral and written instructions
    Exceeds Requirements   Meets Requirements   Needs Improvement

Quality of Work
Is diligent about completing tasks with minimum guidance and direction
    Exceeds Requirements   Meets Requirements   Needs Improvement
Accuracy in work
    Exceeds Requirements   Meets Requirements   Needs Improvement
Work consistently meets standards set by supervisor
    Exceeds Requirements   Meets Requirements   Needs Improvement
Completes assignments in a timely fashion
    Exceeds Requirements   Meets Requirements   Needs Improvement

Customer Service
Welcoming and courteous to customers
    Exceeds Requirements   Meets Requirements   Needs Improvement
Offers assistance to customers
    Exceeds Requirements   Meets Requirements   Needs Improvement
Patient and empathetic with customers
    Exceeds Requirements   Meets Requirements   Needs Improvement

Interpersonal Relations
Works effectively and courteously
    Exceeds Requirements   Meets Requirements   Needs Improvement
Offers assistance to others
    Exceeds Requirements   Meets Requirements   Needs Improvement
Demonstrates a willingness to achieve common goals
    Exceeds Requirements   Meets Requirements   Needs Improvement
Accepts constructive suggestions
    Exceeds Requirements   Meets Requirements   Needs Improvement

Attendance
Conforms to a regular work schedule
    Exceeds Requirements   Meets Requirements   Needs Improvement
Reports to work on time
    Exceeds Requirements   Meets Requirements   Needs Improvement

Adaptability
Willingness to learn and perform new duties
    Exceeds Requirements   Meets Requirements   Needs Improvement
Assists with work normally done by others
    Exceeds Requirements   Meets Requirements   Needs Improvement
Is flexible in adapting to daily work situations
    Exceeds Requirements   Meets Requirements   Needs Improvement

Accomplishments
(List a few accomplishments of employee since the last review.)

Goals and Objectives
(What is to be accomplished over the next year and what actions will be taken to achieve the goals?)

Overall Performance
    Exceeds Requirements   Meets Requirements   Needs Improvement

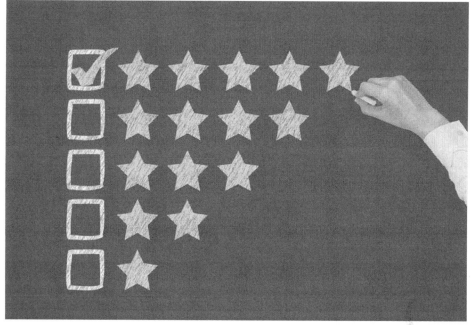

Figure 4.2. Star ratings. *istock/phototechno*

Documentation

That an evaluation is not accepted or understood is not necessarily the fault of the staff member. The manager must be diligent about documenting all behaviors—both good and bad. Just as we talked about a self-evaluation folder, so too must the supervisor keep a folder into which goes **documentation** of any interaction about performance. The manager should discuss each incident with the LSS before filing it. Documentation is essential for managers because you need to make a serious effort to record all the events in their employment history—both positive and negative. You need to document any agreements made during the conversation, any goals set, any improvements required, and the timeline for that improvement—and it needs to be done immediately after the conversation while details are fresh in your mind. Your documentation must be objective, fair, and consistent and should also contain suggestions or offers to assist the employee.

Documentation:

- provides evidence that performance issues were discussed with the employee in a timely and concise fashion.
- offers a history of the employee's improvement or failure to improve performance over time. It is chronological and a precise description of the employee's actions, the manager's actions, and events as they occur.
- provides evidence that supports management decisions to take unfavorable action such as discipline or termination with an employee.
- offers proof that an employee deserves an available promotion or opportunity over other employees who are also eligible.

- provides evidence to justify salary increases, decreases, or why an employee received no raise.
- will protect an employer's interests in the event of a lawsuit; it can support management's actions in terminating an unsuccessful employee.
- can prove that the employee was terminated for reasons that are legal rather than others such as discrimination. (Details of employment and labor laws are found in chapter 1.)[7]

ANNUAL PERFORMANCE PLANS

Annual performance plans provide a link between long-term strategic goals, outlined in a library's strategic plans, and what managers and staff are expected to accomplish in a single fiscal year. To look at an annual performance plan, we first should understand the **strategic plan**.

Strategic Plan

Without putting a name to it, we all have a plan. From "graduate, see the world, get a job" to "plan a party for thirty family members"—we need plans to see it through. This plan takes place over time and has steps toward reaching the goal. For the library, a strategic plan is the clearly worded description of its purpose for being (its mission) and what it wants to achieve over the next few years (its vision). It then decides on a set of three to five strategic priorities to guide the organization toward achievement of the vision.[8] A strategic plan is usually designed to cover a period of three to five years.

This can seem like an enormous task, but it can be manageable. We'll see more about the process in chapter 12; to summarize, according to an article in *Forbes*, it can be done in five steps.[9]

1. *Determine where you are.* This is harder than it looks. Some people see themselves how they want to see themselves, not how they appear to others. Be honest about your organization.
2. *Identify what's important.* Focus on where you want to take your library over time.
3. *Define what you must achieve.* Define the expected objectives that clearly state what your library must achieve to address the priority issues.
4. *Determine who is accountable.* This is how you're going to get to where you want to go. The strategies, action plans, and budgets are all steps in the process that effectively communicate how you will allocate time, staff, and money to address the priority issues and achieve the defined objectives.
5. *Review. Review. Review.* To ensure the plan performs as designed, hold regularly scheduled reviews of the process, and refine as necessary.

Annual Plan

We have established that a strategic plan, for the library, is a document used to communicate the library's goals, the actions needed to achieve those goals, and all the other critical elements developed during the planning exercise. It sets priorities, focuses energy, and strengthens library operations. It also ensures that staff members are working toward the same objectives. The creation of a strategic plan can use different frameworks and methodologies;[10] ultimately it is a process that takes time and effort to create. It covers a defined period of several years.

The annual plan, on the other hand, provides the direct linkage between long-term strategic goals outlined in the library's strategic plans and what managers and employees are expected to accomplish in a single fiscal year.[11] These goals are specific to library staff and their jobs. They may include such examples as improve your customer service skills to patrons and staff; facilitate better access to the library's resources, or (for a manager) maintain diversity in the library's workforce.

Figure 4.3. Calendar years. *istock/Oakozhan*

The annual plan:

- is part of a continuing conversation that should take place between the LSS and manager; it is not a formal part of the review process but may implement suggestions for future directions that were stated in a previous evaluation.
- represents a forward-looking plan of action for an individual staff member for the coming year.
- identifies several areas on which individual staff members will focus during the coming year.
- includes activity planned so the manager and staff member can address the activity in relation to job responsibilities.

- should normally be brief, not a comprehensive work list.
- is normally the product of a collaborative discussion between the LSS and supervisor.
- is a dynamic document that may change during the year based on the needs of the library.

Examples of areas of focus for an annual plan include personal performance goals related to selected primary job responsibilities, activities related to a new project, a temporary assignment, or specific criteria.[12]

One may wonder, how does an annual plan differ from a performance review? The annual plan is a work plan created from the results of the performance appraisal. It takes specific elements and puts them into a plan for the LSS to effect during the coming work year. It is not a pronouncement but a collaboration between staff and manager on the best plan to take going forward. Being dynamic, it may change during the year depending on the needs of the library or the employee.

So, in short, a strategic plan looks out into the future two, three, or even five years to determine what it is you hope to be accomplishing and then prioritizes the essential strategies for achieving those goals. With this strategic framework to guide you, work plans can be developed annually that include specific objectives, outcome measures, and detailed action plans. Your strategic plan and your annual work plan go together. The annual work plan provides the details of how the necessary work will get done, but without the strategic planning framework to guide you, the annual planning process will be anything but strategic.[13]

LINKING EXPECTATIONS TO THE LIBRARY'S STRATEGIC DIRECTIONS

We have been talking about relationships throughout this chapter: the relationship of a performance evaluation to a set of previously determined standards; the relationship of the annual plan to the strategic plan; and the relationship of long-term goals to the library's strategic plan.

Now we will look at how the library links expectations to its strategic directions. Ideally all staff members, on every level, can link their job descriptions, or their roles, to the library's strategic goals. Unfortunately, there is a tendency in libraries for some staff, particularly part-time staff, pages, or clerical workers, to feel marginal. They may only work a few hours a week and may see themselves as peripheral to the operation. When offered opportunities for training or participation in team activities, they may feel they are not important enough to be included. The reaction can be "I'm only part-time. I don't count." They could not be more mistaken. Every employee plays a role, no matter how small, in the operation of the library and, by extension, in the overall strategic goals of the library.

The American National Standards Institute (ANSI), in 2012, established minimum standards for human resources that affect performance evaluation.[14] These include what we have already seen:

- A feedback process so employees know how they are doing and what is expected.
- A dialogue (including performance feedback) measured against specific goals and expectations.
- A process that shows the outcome—documentation.
- A two-way dialogue between employee and manager—at least once annually.[15]

These standards apply to all staff members from pages to managers, as each one contributes to the success of the library. To reach its goals, the library counts on every member to achieve his individual goals. This isn't done in a vacuum—each performance evaluation must be aligned to the library's strategic goals. To do so, each staff member should identify one to three goals from the strategic plan. Then, with his manager, each LSS should write an accompanying objective for each goal. Finally, he must agree on measurable outcomes to ultimately define his success. These can be statistics, patron input, or employee reports, depending on the goal. Incidentally, there should be a standard vehicle for the procedure for this such as a blank objectives, evaluation, and responsibilities form in an employee handbook.

The supervisor and the LSS can work together on this:

- The supervisor will identify the goals from the strategic plan.
- The supervisor and LSS will work together to determine results-oriented objectives.
- Together they will rate the performance (fails goal, meets goal, exceeds goal).
- Together they will
  - o make notes,
  - o sign the form, and
  - o work on the next plan.

In figure 4.4, we can see what this looks like. This chart, from "Linking Performance Evaluation to Strategic Goals" from the Montana State Library,[16] puts the

Performance Evaluation

employee:　　　　　　　　supervisor:　　　　　　　　evaluation date:

Goal (from Strategic Plan)	Results-oriented objective	Performance Result as reported by employee	RATING	Notes
4.4 Expand outreach services to new audiences	Books to 15 day care providers	20 providers now receiving books twice monthly	Exceeds goal	Good implementation; great plan to sustain this new service
6.1 Add stay-&-play activities	Have a Stay&Play activity at every story time	Added a monthly Stay&Play because volunteers were not willing to stay to help with supervising after story time.	Acceptable	This service needs to be sustainable and embraced by volunteers; until there is buy-in from volunteers or more volunteers, once per month is okay.
7.2 Align story time with MT Early Learning Standards	Address MT Early Learning Standards at every story time	Started this, but was unclear how to apply these standards; need more training	Failed goal	Results will be revised to having employee attain the needed training so progress can be made.

Signature of employee: _____　Signature of supervisor: _____

Figure 4.4.　Performance evaluation. *Courtesy of the Montana State Library*

information into five columns. In the first column, we see the goal taken from the library's strategic plan. In the second column are the objectives that the LSS has created. Column three is a description of what happened when the goal was carried out. The rating, given by the supervisor, is in column four; column five includes the notes they worked on together.

We can see that not all the employee's goals and objectives were successful; the supervisor's rating and subsequent notes explain how they can be improved. Thus, the LSS has been evaluated on goals based on previously determined standards (the strategic plan); there is dialogue between supervisor and LSS; and the outcome is mutually agreed upon. Expectations have been linked to the library's strategic direction.

CHAPTER SUMMARY

All library employees, whether staff or management, should expect to have their work performance appraised at least once a year. This evaluation does not occur in a vacuum; rather it is done in the context of the person's job. It begins with a statement or document that describes the duties and responsibilities of an employee in the workplace and evaluates if the person is carrying out them out. There are several methods of evaluations to use, and the one that you, as manager, choose needs to be applied equally to every employee's performance appraisal. All staff members need to understand how they fit into the library's organization; their duties, responsibilities, and goals should be tied to the library's overall strategic plan. In this way, all employees contribute to the success of the library.

DISCUSSION QUESTIONS

1. Please explain what a job description is and why it is necessary for all employees.
2. When management talks about an annual plan, to what are they referring?
3. Why, and how, should a manager document the performance of a library worker?
4. What is feedback, and why is it important for all staff members?
5. How can you, as the LSS, prepare for your performance evaluation—or can you?

ACTIVITIES

1. Create a bibliography of five articles about setting performance expectations. Your bibliography should be both descriptive and evaluative. Using what you learned from these articles and past experience, prepare an annual performance plan for a library employee. Describe how this plan reflects a library's strategies.
2. Using the examples in this chapter, create an evaluation form. Then, with the permission of your supervisor, perform a mock evaluation of two LSS in different positions in your library. Are their duties conforming to their job descriptions? Are they related to the library's strategic plan?

NOTES

1. "Performance Appraisal," Business Dictionary, last modified 2017, accessed August 25, 2017, www.businessdictionary.com/definition/performance-appraisal.html.

2. University of California, Berkeley, "Performance Expectations = Results + Actions & Behaviors," Berkeley Human Resources, last modified 2017, accessed August 25, 2017, hr.berkeley.edu/hr-network/central-guide-managing-hr/managing-hr/managing-successfully/performance-management/planning/expectations.

3. Montana State Library, "Public Library Standards," last modified 2017, accessed August 31, 2017, mslservices.mt.gov/search/default.aspx?q=msl.mt.gov/Library_Development/Standards?Documents/publiclibrarystandards.pdf.

4. UC Berkeley, "Performance Expectations."

5. Joan Lloyd, "It's Wise to Prepare for Your Performance Review," JobDig, www.jobdig.com/articles/888/It's_Wise_To_Prepare_For_Your_Performance_Review.html.

6. Steven Bell, "Rethinking the Much-Dreaded Employee Evaluation | Leading from the Library," *Library Journal*, last modified June 30, 2016, accessed August 24, 2017, lj.libraryjournal.com/2016/06/opinion/leading-from-the-library/rethinking-the-much-dreaded-employee-evaluation-leading-from-the-library/#_.

7. Susan H. Heathfield, "How to Document Employee Performance," The Balance, last modified August 28, 2017, accessed September 2, 2017, www.thebalance.com/how-to-document-employee-performance-1917911.

8. Starboard Leadership Consulting, "The Difference Between Strategic Planning and Annual Planning," accessed August 29, 2017, www.starboardleadership.com/strategic-planning/the-difference-between-strategic-planning-and-annual-planning/.

9. Aileron, "Five Steps to a Strategic Plan," *Forbes*, last modified October 25, 2011, accessed August 29, 2017, www.forbes.com/sites/aileron/2011/10/25/five-steps-to-a-strategic-plan/#42c6ceb35464.

10. Balanced Scorecard Institute, "Strategic Planning Basics," last modified 2017, accessed August 29, 2017, www.balancedscorecard.org/BSC-Basics/Strategic-Planning-Basics.

11. National Archives, "Annual Performance Plans," accessed August 28, 2017, www.archives.gov/about/plans-reports/performance-plan.

12. University of California, Irvine, "Guidelines for Librarians' Annual Plans," last modified August 2015, accessed August 28, 2017, www.lib.uci.edu/sites/all/docs/staff/annual_plans_guidelines.pdf.

13. Starboard Leadership Consulting, "The Difference."

14. Society for Human Resource Management, "ANSI Approves Performance Management Standard," last modified December 18, 2012, accessed September 6, 2017, www.shrm.org/about-shrm/press-room/press-releases/pages/ansiapprovesperformancemanagementstandard.aspx.

15. Joann Flick, Jodie Moore, and Stef Johnson, "Linking Performance Evaluation to Strategic Goals," Montana State Library, last modified April 14, 2015, accessed August 24, 2017, www.slideshare.net/MontanaStateLibrary/linking-performance-evaluation-to-strategic-g.

16. Ibid.

REFERENCES, SUGGESTED READINGS, AND WEBSITES

Aileron. "Five Steps to a Strategic Plan." *Forbes*. Last modified October 25, 2011. Accessed August 29, 2017. www.forbes.com/sites/aileron/2011/10/25/five-steps-to-a-strategic-plan/#42c6ceb35464.

American Library Association. "Outcome Measurement Made Easy with PLA's Project Outcome." Public Library Association. Last modified January 12, 2017. Accessed August 28, 2017. www.ala.org/pla/education/onlinelearning/webinars/archive/projectoutcomeeasy.

Applegate, Mark. "How to Write a Good Performance Evaluation for a Library Staff." Career Trend. Last modified July 5, 2017. Accessed August 24, 2017. careertrend.com/write-good-performance-evaluation-library-staff-39257.html.

"Appraisal Training Video—How to perform a performance appraisal." Video file, 9:03. You Tube. Posted March 20, 2013. Accessed September 8, 2017. www.youtube.com/watch?v=Z3uNkRNhuY4.

Balanced Scorecard Institute. "Strategic Planning Basics." Last modified 2017. Accessed August 29, 2017. www.balancedscorecard.org/BSC-Basics/Strategic-Planning-Basics.

Bell, Steven. "Rethinking the Much-Dreaded Employee Evaluation | Leading from the Library." *Library Journal.* Last modified June 30, 2016. Accessed August 24, 2017. lj.library journal.com/2016/06/opinion/leading-from-the-library/rethinking-the-much-dreaded -employee-evaluation-leading-from-the-library/#_.

Delaney, Meg, and Amy Hartman. "Developing Truly Effective Performance Evaluations Webinar Handouts." American Library Association. Last modified September 7, 2016. Accessed August 24, 2017. www.ala.org/pla/sites/ala.org.pla/files/content/onlinelearning/webinars/2016-09-07_Performance-Evalutions-Handouts_PLA-Webinars.pdf.

"Effective Performance Evaluations." Video file, 26:14. You Tube. Posted April 1, 2016. Accessed September 8, 2017. www.youtube.com/watch?v=HrpfXVVglhU.

"Employee Evaluations for Public Library Staff." Library Research Service. Last modified January 2007. Accessed August 24, 2017. www.lrs.org/documents/field_stats/Employee_Eval uations.pdf.

Flick, Joann, Jodie Moore, and Stef Johnson. "Linking Performance Evaluation to Strategic Goals." Montana State Library. Last modified April 14, 2015. Accessed August 24, 2017. www.slideshare.net/MontanaStateLibrary/linking-performance-evaluation-to-strategic-g.

Heathfield, Susan H. "How to Document Employee Performance." The Balance. Last modified August 28, 2017. Accessed September 2, 2017. www.thebalance.com/how-to-docu ment-employee-performance-1917911.

Leong, Julie. "Purpose-Driven Learning for Library Staff." *Australian Library Journal.* Last modified May 27, 2014. Accessed August 24, 2017. www.tandfonline.com/doi/full/10.1080/00 049670.2014.898236.

Lloyd, Joan. "It's Wise to Prepare for Your Performance Review." JobDig. www.jobdig.com/articles/888/It's_Wise_To_Prepare_For_Your_Performance_Review.html.

Martin, Christine. "Library Worklife: HR E-News for Today's Leaders: How to Prepare for a Performance Evaluation." ALA/APA. Last modified June 2005. Accessed August 24, 2017. ala-apa.org/newsletter/2005/06/17/how-to-prepare-for-a-performance-evaluation/.

Montana State Library. "Public Library Standards." Last modified 2017. Accessed August 31, 2017. mslservices.mt.gov/search/default.aspx?q=msl.mt.gov/Library_Development/Stan dards?Documents/publiclibrarystandards.pdf.

National Archives. "Annual Performance Plans." Accessed August 28, 2017. www.archives .gov/about/plans-reports/performance-plan.

"Performance Appraisal." Business Dictionary. Last modified 2017. Accessed August 25, 2017. www.businessdictionary.com/definition/performance-appraisal.html.

Society for Human Resource Management. "ANSI Approves Performance Management Standard." Last modified December 18, 2012. Accessed September 6, 2017. www.shrm.org/about-shrm/press-room/press-releases/pages/ansiapprovesperformancemanagementstan dard.aspx.

Starboard Leadership Consulting. "The Difference Between Strategic Planning and Annual Planning." Accessed August 29, 2017. www.starboardleadership.com/strategic-planning/the-difference-between-strategic-planning-and-annual-planning/.

University of California, Berkeley. "Performance Expectations = Results + Actions & Behaviors." Berkeley Human Resources. Last modified 2017. Accessed August 25, 2017. hr.berkeley.edu/hr-network/central-guide-managing-hr/managing-hr/managing-successfully/performance-management/planning/expectations.

University of California, Irvine. "Guidelines for Librarians' Annual Plans." Last modified August 2015. Accessed August 28, 2017. www.lib.uci.edu/sites/all/docs/staff/annual_plans_guidelines.pdf.

CHAPTER 5

Principles of Leadership and Professional Learning

LSS know basic principles of leadership. (ALA-LSSC Supervision and Management Competency #5)

LSS plan, implement, and encourage participation in staff development activities. (ALA-LSSC Supervision and Management Competency #6)

Topics Covered in This Chapter:

- Leadership Theories
  - o Situational/Contingency Theory
  - o Transactional Theory
  - o Transformational Theory
- Principles of Library Leadership
- Professional Learning
  - o Adult Learning Theories
- LSS Learning Opportunities
  - o Social Media
  - o Educational Opportunities
  - o ALA-LSSC Certification
  - o Mentors and Internships
  - o Professional Literature

Key Terms:

Active listening: In a library, active listening is the process by which staff repeats what is said so that the speaker knows he has been heard.

Cohort: This is a group of people, for example, LSS students, who are together in a similar situation or academic course that help and support each other through the process.

Convergent thinking: In this type of learning, such as in an LSS course, the instructor expects students to deduce the "right" or correct answer.

Curriculum: This is the specific content or material taught in a course, such as an LSS course in foundations, that can be measured through types of testing or assessments.

Divergent thinking: In this type of learning, there is no one correct or "right" answer. LSS students, for example, may interpret the problem differently and seek multiple creative solutions.

Laissez-faire: A policy or attitude of letting things take their own course, without interfering. A library manager who has this style of leadership will not intervene even if warranted.

Library leadership: These are the supervisors and administrators who manage the library to assure staffing, policies, services, and all operational details are taking place appropriately.

Listserv: This is an application or program that distributes messages to subscribers interested in specific topics, such as on the topic of library children's programming, on an electronic mailing list.

Pedagogy: These are the traditional classroom methods of teaching academic or theoretical subjects that most students, including those who are in library degree programs, are exposed to in school.

Pilot: Before adapting a new policy or procedure in final form, this is a trial run to evaluate and make improvements, such as to a new library policy, before full implementation.

Qualitative data: The opposite of statistics, these are ways to confirm a hypothesis or theory, such as if self-checkout units improve library service, using interviews, observations, and other social or humanistic methods.

Self-regulation: This type of self-management occurs when a person takes charge of his or her own learning or makes other decisions that guide his or her actions, such as when an LSS decides to return to college for an advanced degree.

Situational leadership: This adaptive and flexible leadership style may be temporarily needed when there is a contingency or event, such as an emergency in the library during after hours, that requires someone with confidence and experience to step in to make decisions.

Staff development: Also called professional learning, library staff continue to learn new skills, issues, and theories to improve their work performance by taking courses, attending workshops, reading journals, and learning from others in various other formats.

Transactional leadership: Work performance is primarily influenced by rewards and punishments. These library managers believe library employees are motivated by tangible rewards and use their control to improve employee work performance with money, promotions, or other acknowledgments.

Transformational leadership: A style of leadership whereby library supervisors place a high value on forming a personal relationship with their LSS employees, firmly believing that they have a role to empower others to develop their potential for the long-term good of the institution and its goals.

Peter Drucker's principles of nonprofit management were introduced in chapter 2. Ideally, managers are strong leaders, but they often require two different sets of skills. While the focus of library management is primarily on planning, staffing, organization, budget, and problem solving, leadership is about developing common vision, strategic planning, aligning people, communication, motivation, and inspiration.[1] Good leaders also recognize and support the need for ongoing staff development and professional learning of their workers.

LEADERSHIP THEORIES

Library leadership is about the relationships between the library board, director, department managers, and the staff whom they supervise and support. There are many theories for what makes good leadership. Examined here are five more commonly held theories: Great Man, Traits, Situational-Contingency, Transactional, and Transformational theories.[2]

Great Man theory is grounded in the idea that leadership is inherited at birth and not learned behavior. They will step forward when the need arises. Simplistically stated, great men (and women) are born to leadership and will step forward when there is a need, such as Prime Minister Winston Churchill's presence in World War II or German Chancellor Angela Merkel's influence in sustaining the European Union. While we certainly appreciate great leadership, not too many people really believe this to be the case.

Figure 5.1.   World leaders. *istock/Rawpixel*

Likewise Trait theory proposes that certain people are born with the "right stuff" or traits that leaders must have to be effective. These traits are characteristics such as confidence, intelligence, flexibility, social skills, and so forth. Underlying Trait theory is that a person was either born with these traits or was not. If they are, they can step up to leadership. If not, the traits cannot be acquired through experience or learning.

In reality, most people would agree that leadership can be learned. We know this in ourselves through varied experiences; our confidence grows in how we are able to handle ourselves and influence others. The next three theories suggest leadership is not a trait we are born with but one that can be learned.

TEXTBOX 5.1: KEY IDEAS OF THREE COMMON LEADERSHIP THEORIES

Situational/Contingency Leadership: The ability to lead is contingent on the specific type of event or issue.
Transactional Leadership: People are motivated by rewards and punishment.
Transformational Leadership: Relationships between leader and staff are of critical importance.

Situational/Contingency Theory

Depending upon the circumstances, people rise to the occasion and become ad hoc or temporary leaders to guide others through difficult and unexpected situations. Hershey and Blanchard proposed the idea of situational leadership in 1977 when they observed in certain situations people may "step up" to take on leadership roles in crises that they typically do not assume in normal life.[3] These situational or contingency leaders may make authoritative or decisive decisions for the group to follow. It has been repeatedly shown in unpredictable and dangerous times of natural disasters, school shootings, terrorist attacks, or plane crashes that certain people who have a high level of maturity, adaptability, and confidence will emerge as leaders to help or save others in crisis.[4]

Situational leadership may also be assumed in the normal work environment. It is an adaptive leadership style that encourages managers to demonstrate flexibility depending upon whom they are working with and the changing goals of the organization or team.[5] Leaders modify their management style to best work with others under the circumstances to achieve team success.

Libraries need leaders in both crisis and normal situations. Library staff work with diverse and sometimes unpredictable patrons. Patrons bring into the library both their current positive and negative feelings, and in public libraries no one is barred from entering. In school and academic settings, libraries are large and open gathering spaces. In all libraries, there is the potential for inappropriate patron behavior that could be disruptive or even dangerous. While libraries have policy on how to deal with patrons, in a crisis situation, any library staff may be needed to step up to lead others to safety or make quick decisions about the seriousness of the threat and what actions should take place to minimize it.

Another type of situational leadership requires adaptability and flexibility. In normal situations, libraries are usually governed by community members who serve on library or academic boards or trustees with different backgrounds and work styles. The successful library director adapts his or her style of leadership to successfully work with and execute board policies. Library managers must also be adaptable when working with local and state governing officials who influence or control library funding sources. Similarly, LSS in supervisory roles demonstrate flexibility to support and execute the library mission as well as their manager's goals.

How do LSS step up to become leaders? LSS can develop situational leadership in many ways. They may assume responsibility for building or facility functions, such as learning the procedures for closing down the library in the evening or offering to be cross-trained in other library functions so that they can help out in times of staff shortages. LSS who are motivated to learn new technologies and their uses often step into leadership roles with acquired expertise.

LSS who serve on planning committees or teams may become more flexible and adaptable to change when they believe in and are committed to trying new ways to provide library services to patrons. As they mature in their thinking, LSS may become more willing to pilot changes for the betterment of the patrons. Upon successful engagement on planning teams, the LSS may develop situational leadership roles with other staff.

TEXTBOX 5.2: SOME WAYS LSS ACQUIRE SITUATIONAL LEADERSHIP

1. Become a member of several library committees that work to improve building and patron services. As team members, LSS will learn about how situational leadership is being applied by management.
2. Serve on safety, environmental, and other library committees that have to do with potential crisis. Learn and practice the protocols and procedures for what to do in case of fire, intruders, or other threats to patrons.
3. Become familiar with how the library is funded. Attend public financial meetings where the library budget is determined. By understanding funding, LSS may become more adaptable and supportive when fiscal constraints are applied.
4. Be motivated to learn new technologies and how to apply them in the library setting. LSS can demonstrate situational leadership around technology when they are knowledgeable and confident in its use.

Because there will always be unpredicted contingencies, situational leadership is ongoing. LSS can prepare to be leaders in both crisis and normal times when they are interested and motivated to accept responsibilities outside of their day-to-day work and are actively involved on committees that make important library decisions. The next theory to explore is transactional leadership.

Transactional Theory

Transactional theory suggests work performance is primarily influenced by rewards and punishments. Leaders believe employees are motivated by tangible rewards and use their control to improve employee work performance with money, promotions, or other acknowledgments. Conversely, management may also withhold rewards for unsatisfactory performance in attempts to change employee productivity.[6]

Transactions are often thought of as commercial exchanges between sellers and buyers. An exchange of items takes place when equal value is established. In **transactional leadership**, the manager equates the work of the employee with its value to the institution. Sometimes the transaction is very straightforward. In some libraries, particularly where there are formal municipal or union contracts, LSS may receive a pay increase that is linked to longevity on the job. For example, after three, five, and ten years of service, a percentage pay increase is automatically transacted or given. A transactional leader, however, has more discretion about when and how much pay increase is given. The library supervisor uses an evaluation protocol to assess the employee's work performance. Depending upon the results, the transactional leader or supervisor will equate the success of the employee's performance to a monetary value or raise in pay.

In transactional leadership, clear and mutual goals and expectations are agreed to by both the library supervisor and the LSS employee that relate to the mission of the library. Often the goals or objectives are measurable, such as a goal to increase patron participation in summer programs, develop new outreach opportunities with underserved populations, or improve content and circulation of the materials in certain collections. The success of each of these goals can be measured either statistically or through other means of **qualitative data**. A transactional leadership style would clearly define these organizational goals as well as the expected roles of the employee to achieve success. Three types of transactional leadership that apply to libraries are conditional reward, management by exception, and **laissez-faire**.[7]

With conditional reward, the supervisor determines the tasks and targets for her employees. Employees know they will receive the reward if they meet the target. One simple example of conditional reward could be the goal of having all mediated interlibrary loan (ILL) transactions completed and documented by the LSS prior to shift change at the circulation desk. The supervisor has had too many complaints from both staff and patrons that ILL requests are not being processed in a timely manner. With the target set by the supervisor and agreed upon by staff, the LSS knows that this task is part of his job performance evaluation.

In management by exception, the library supervisor monitors LSS work closely and will intervene when there is a problem in order to keep the goal or task on target. Using the example of ILL, if the supervisor reviews data and sees a discrepancy in the number of transactions a new LSS is creating compared to other staff, he can work with this person to see where the problem is. Thus corrections will be made so that ILL service to patrons will not suffer.

In laissez-faire transactional leadership, the supervisor has a hands-off approach to management. Targets and goals have been mutually agreed upon, but the supervisor does not step in if targets are not being met until annual review. If ILLs are not being processed, so be it. The annual statistics will show there was a problem at the end of the year, and the LSS who did not do her work as expected will receive a poor review. In libraries today, patrons and staff deserve a better approach than a laissez-faire leadership.

Transactional leaders are not particularly interested in developing their staff, but rather they believe staff performance can be improved by exchanging excellent performance for salary increases or promotions. However, when analyzed, salary and titles are only a small part of what motivates workers, and research shows that

TEXTBOX 5.3: THREE TYPES OF TRANSACTIONAL LEADERSHIP STYLES[8]

1. Conditional Reward: The supervisor determines the tasks and sets mutually agreed upon performance targets with rewards for employees who meet or exceed expectations.
2. Management by Exception: The supervisor monitors employees' work and intervenes if there is a problem in order to avoid not meeting target expectations.
3. Laissez-faire: The supervisor leaves their employees on their own and will not intervene. Decisions are not made and responsibilities not fulfilled.

job satisfaction is not highly correlated to transactional leadership.[9] Most employees find support and personal motivation from the third type of leadership, which is transformational.

Transformational Theory

Transformational leaders place a high value on forming a personal relationship with their employees, firmly believing that they have a role to empower others and to develop their potential for the long-term good of the institution and its goals.[10] By transforming employees to accept and create change, they are inspirational leaders who serve as mentors, coaches, and motivators for others. A transformational leader encourages staff to reach beyond their perceived potential, supporting their ideas and suggestions that will better improve work. LSS benefit greatly when they work under supervision of a transformational leader because they will be supported to advance in both the type of work they do and their responsibilities. Ideally, all library supervisors and managers perceive themselves as transformational leaders

Figure 5.2.   Library leadership meeting. *istock/narith_2527*

who place importance on developing and cross-training LSS in ways that enhance their work skills and future employability in libraries.

Transformational leaders promote others to be leaders by preparing staff for leadership roles. These leaders provide opportunities for staff to practice how to best work with others and to broaden LSS's skill sets and education so that they may be considered for future supervisory positions.

LSS who are supervisors in departments or divisions can improve their role by empowering others who will be prepared to help the library achieve both long- and short-term goals. Universal are many attributes that are key to being a transformational leader:

Table 5.1. Attributes of Transformational Leadership

Be flexible and able to deal with unexpected issues.	Make a positive influence and become a role model for others.	Recognize contributions and celebrate successes of others.
Inspire others and earn their trust and confidence.	Be willing to lead others through innovation, change, and reform.	Develop and support teamwork, partnerships, and alliances.
Develop political skills and community awareness.	Solve problems systematically.	Participate in opportunities for continuous learning.

Okcu, Veysel. "Relation between Secondary School Administrators' Transformational and Transactional Leadership Style and Skills to Diversity Management in the School." *Educational Sciences: Theory and Practice* 14, no. 6 (December 2014).

PRINCIPLES OF LIBRARY LEADERSHIP

The nine key leadership attributes listed in table 5.1 are important for LSS to understand and develop in order to become leaders. Each attribute is given a brief explanation below followed by practical strategies LSS can apply to acquire transformational leadership skills that are valued in today's libraries.

1. Be flexible and able to deal with unexpected issues. No two days are alike in libraries, and in dealing with the public, students, vendors, staff, and many external forces, LSS have to be able to adjust on the spot.

   Strategy 1: Learn the library policies for dealing with unexpected situations, such as fire, intruders, or other threats to safety. Talk with others about the procedures and suggest simulated practice sessions.

   Strategy 2: Create a list each day of what must be done. Confirm with supervisor. Set a priority and manage your time around these items. If unexpected issues arise—and they will—these items will not be neglected.

   Strategy 3: Learn to appear gracious, calm, and kind to others, including upset patrons. If appropriate, use humor and always use **active listening** skills to defuse situations that may become charged or volatile. Patrons most likely will follow your example, and now you can be helpful to solving their issue.

2. Make a positive influence and be a role model for others. LSS work in all departments of the library and interact with many staff. Being supportive of the goals and vision library leaders strive to obtain can positively influence other staff.

    Strategy 1: Become involved with staff negotiations or other bargaining units for LSS. In this role, advocate for the important work LSS perform.

    Strategy 2: Rather than complain about administrative decisions, strive to become informed about the fiscal or other reasons that are behind unpopular decisions. Being able to provide unbiased information will earn respect from others.

    Strategy 3: Offer to mentor volunteers, interns, and others who help in the library. By conducting yourself in a professional manner, you will be perceived as a model for others.

3. Recognize contributions and celebrate the successes of others. Library staff who sincerely care about each other have the potential to become a highly functional team. LSS who recognize their peers form positive relationships that may later support them as leaders.

    Strategy 1: Peer recognition is a powerful way for LSS to develop positive relationships. Recognize peers in a simply written card or note to express the appreciation you feel for their help.

    Strategy 2: Throw a lunchtime or after-work reception that honors a peer for significant success, keeping it simple with coffee, cold drinks, and finger appetizers and desserts.

    Strategy 3: Use social media and other forms of communication to recognize others who contribute to the success of the library mission.

4. Inspire others as you earn their trust and confidence. Nothing inspires trust and confidence more than being reliable and accountable.

    Strategy 1: Keep your promises, beginning with being prompt to meetings and on time to work. LSS often job share, and it is critical that schedules are adhered to.

    Strategy 2: Strong leaders are informed. Do your homework! Become competent in all aspects of your work. As people gain confidence in you, they will look to you to help them with more challenging tasks.

    Strategy 3: Exhibit moral and ethical behavior. Keep your word, and be proud of your reputation. We are a summation of our words and deeds. LSS who always act in a professional manner are perceived as trustworthy and situational leaders.

5. Be willing to lead others in times of change, innovation, and reform. While LSS may not supervise change and reform, they have an important role to support and participate in new ways of improving library services.

    Strategy 1: Be curious about new trends and ideas in library service. Research articles in professional journals that relate to change in your library. Armed with information, LSS can be important agents of successful innovation.

Strategy 2: Hold discussions with other LSS about upcoming change, such as a new integrated library system. As you become comfortable with change, support others who may feel threatened or overly challenged.

Strategy 3: Offer to obtain more training. LSS who adapt easily to change do so because they have invested time into learning new systems or processes. The investment not only helps build confidence for the LSS, but also distinguishes them as team leaders for their peers.

6. Develop and support teamwork, partnerships, and alliances. No one person can provide library services without the support and help of others. LSS are integral members of the team in every library and, as such, take on leadership roles.

Strategy 1: Join committees and work teams of interest to you both in the library and in the library community. Team members gain new perspectives on issues and have the opportunity to voice their opinions and volunteer for specific tasks and may receive special training related to new initiatives.

Strategy 2: Look at the work you currently do as an LSS and brainstorm ways to improve or extend the service through programming or outreach to the community. Often when library staff reach out to others to fill a perceived need, they are welcomed wholeheartedly.

Strategy 3: Often LSS are so busy they have no opportunity to partner with peers in other libraries. Join professional organizations and roundtables where LSS who do similar work regularly meet. Forming outside partnerships and alliances contributes to the LSS knowledge base, and partnerships may bring improved programming and services to the larger community.

7. Develop political skill and community awareness. Many public, school, and academic libraries are publicly funded and have government or board oversight. Libraries exist to serve their communities, and LSS can seek opportunities to strengthen external supports.

Strategy 1: Many LSS have direct patron contact. Learn who the patrons are that are involved in political service, community agencies, the library board, and so forth. These decision makers are also library patrons, and how they are greeted and served by LSS can make a positive difference in their advocacy for the library.

Strategy 2: Offer to serve on local governmental, community, or political committees. The library position at budget time will be strengthened by LSS serving on outside committees who become known to others who may be voting on the library budget.

Strategy 3: LSS who are involved in their community may be able to suggest new ideas for library programming that fills a community need. For example, an LSS who volunteers at the local school may be able to suggest joint school/public library programs or services.

8. Solve problems systematically. It is not that leaders have all of the answers, but more likely they take a step-by-step, systematic approach to solving a problem, being sure that as many considerations as possible are examined before a decision is made.

Strategy 1: LSS can learn the steps of project management that include initiation, planning, execution, and closedown. Each of these steps requires thoughtful analysis of the problem solved or the project to be managed.

Strategy 2: Work with others to solve problems. Two heads are often better than one. As LSS work in departments or teams, it is important that the solution to a problem that involves new procedures or ways of doing shared work is vetted with others before implemented.

Strategy 3: LSS can suggest that new solutions are to be piloted. A **pilot** is a trial period when something new is tested, reviewed, and evaluated. During a pilot often new information or ideas are suggested for the final process.

9. Participate in opportunities for continuous learning. Libraries are centers for lifelong learning, and as such LSS must be continuous learners who implement new ways for providing library service, programs, and technology.

Strategy 1: Join professional organizations at the national, state, and local levels that support LSS. These organizations offer professional development workshops as well as numerous opportunities to network with other LSS both in person and via social media.

Strategy 2: Take college courses to advance knowledge and skills. Colleges offer both traditional and online classes in all areas of library technology for LSS. The learning obtained from being in a library technology certificate program or an advanced degree will open employment opportunities for LSS to advance from their current positions.

Strategy 3: Learn from each other. LSS work with both professional librarians and experienced LSS who have much knowledge and skills to share. Likewise, be a mentor to other LSS. It is said that we learn a concept thoroughly when we have to teach it!

This last attribute of successful leaders being continuous learners will segue into the section of this chapter on how LSS plan, implement, and participate in professional learning.

PROFESSIONAL LEARNING

Another name for professional learning is **staff development**. Librarianship is a profession, and similar to health care and education, workers are expected to regularly acquire new learning because there is a need to keep current in how we conduct library service. The American Library Association promotes continuous learning for LSS,[11] providing many ways to advance training.

Adult Learning Theories

Adults learn differently than children, yet often the **pedagogy** or method of instructing adults is presented in the same manner. The pedagogy of traditional teaching has these attributes:

- teacher structured
- minimal control by learner
- focus on training for events to come
- encourages convergent thinking
- focus on memory
- content supplied by teacher/class materials
- based on specific content standards

In traditional teaching, which we are all familiar with, the student has little flexibility as to how and what she learns. Students are rewarded for memorization with an emphasis on **convergent thinking** where there is only one correct answer. Experts in adult learning know that adults do not learn best under these circumstances. With a lifetime of experience, adults learn when they can relate their experience to new ideas that are applicable to their work.

Here are some important theories of adult learning:

- Andragogy (Knowles):[12] Adults are independent and self-directed. We need to know why we should learn. Learning is best when the topic has immediate value to us. Instruction is task-orientated. We approach learning as problem-solving.
- Experiential Learning (Kolb):[13] Successful learning will occur when current tasks are linked to past experiences.
- Self-Directed Learning (Brookfield):[14] Adults learn well when they set their own learning goals, discover resources on their own, chose their own learning methods, and evaluate their own progress. Teacher is facilitator.
- Transformational Learning (Mezirow):[15] Adults learn by examining previously unchallenged assumptions, working through new perspectives, and using critical reflection.

These theorists found in their research that adults learn when the environment has these attributes:

- learner structured
- minimal control by teacher
- focus on assimilation of learning from past experiences
- encourages divergent thinking
- content supplied partially by students
- outcomes evolve as learning progresses

Confirming that adults learn best when they can make connections to their own experiences, they are also successful when they take control of their learning and supply their own content, rather than being presented **curriculum** solely by the instructor. Adults know there may be many answers to a question and seek **divergent thinking**.

A comprehensive adult learning theory is the TRIO Model.[16] This model suggests three interrelated components contribute to professional learning: individual attributes, key experiences, and environmental factors. Individual attributes are such things as personal motivation, mental models, and **self-regulation**. Key experiences

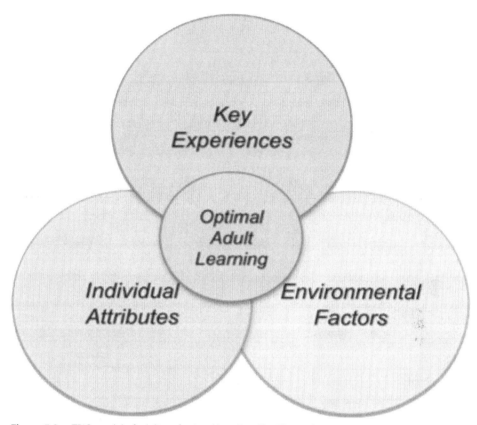

Figure 5.3. TRIO model of adult professional learning. *Sheckley et al. 2008*

are prior experiences that adults use to compare and analyze new learning against as well as deliberate practice and reflection. Environment supports can derive from the supervisor and others, the challenges learners face, or the resources available. All three components must be in place for best learning to occur.

As adults LSS should seek learning opportunities that best match their personal and professional needs. Think about how you learn best today.

LSS LEARNING OPPORTUNITIES

LSS plan, implement, and participate in professional learning. Ideally libraries have sufficient means to offer formal professional learning or staff development for each LSS. But this is most often not the case, and learning is acquired on our own because we are highly motivated to do our work better and to keep abreast of new trends and ideas in libraries. Often LSS plan their own learning by finding workshops, courses, or webinars that they are interested in. Always keep supervisors informed of planning, as they may be able to help financially and certainly will be supportive of the motivation to acquire new knowledge and skills. Sharing learning opportunities with other LSS is important because if a **cohort** can be formed, members will be able to help each other throughout the learning process. If LSS belong to a professional organization or network, it may be possible to have a workshop or speaker present to LSS from several local libraries. Cost sharing of expenses is also beneficial.

Implementing professional development takes on many forms. If you are going it alone, seek guidance from workshop providers or college program coordinators for advisement and questions. Implementation of an in-library session will require support from many. Room and food arrangements will need to be made as well as finding out what technology support the presenter will need. Sometimes the presenter requests reimbursement for travel and lodging. An evaluation process for after the workshop is important to understand what benefit the workshop was to participants and what future learning is desired.

LSS have a variety of learning opportunities they may participate in. Using the American Library Association Library Support Staff Resource[17] web page as a guide, let's explore several of the categories.

Social Media

Social media are valuable resources for students to explore careers, network with professionals, and stay up to date with current trends in the field.[18] LSS use Facebook, Twitter, Instagram, Pinterest, YouTube, and other channels to make connections and keep informed in their work. Today most libraries and librarians use these channels to pose questions, share announcements and ideas, and seek advice from other professionals. **Listservs** and discussion groups are mostly managed through e-mail. There is a hosting institution, often a state library, school of library science, or professional organization. To join a listserv or group, send an e-mail to a specific address. Once a member, you will receive all e-mails automatically. E-mails must be on an appropriate topic or subject around the theme of the listserv. For example, there are library listservs for children's services. All messages are focused on related topics of children and libraries. While there are many options, LSS may consider joining Facebook, Instagram, Twitter, and YouTube. Using just one of many professional organizations, the Public Library Association (PLA),[19] as a model, LSS can enhance their learning by participating in many social media opportunities professional library organizations offer:

Table 5.2.   Professional Organizations Use Social Media

Facebook	www.facebook.com/pla.org
Instagram	instagram.com/ala_pla/
Twitter	twitter.com/ALA_PLA
YouTube	www.youtube.com/channel/UCD9DUiXzel3qpNrj2Rqi1bg
Discussions	www.ala.org/pla/connect

Or join social media channels that are focused on a theme, such as *Every Child Ready to Read*:

Table 5.3.   Social Media Focused on the Theme *Every Child Can Read*

Facebook	www.facebook.com/everychild
Twitter	twitter.com/ALA_ECRR
Ning	everychildreadytoread.ning.com

Educational Opportunities

There are many excellent online resources for professional learning. Some require registration and payment; others are free. Some state libraries offer discounts or support national training sites such as OCLC WebJunction. Check your state library to see if this is the case or if it offers its own staff development opportunities for library staff in the state. Often library supervisors are not aware of current offerings, and if there is nominal or no cost to the library, LSS may ask to take a state-sponsored online workshop that relates to their duties during work hours. Table 5.4 offers some excellent suggestions for continuous learning about library topics, skills, trends, and issues.

Table 5.4. Resources for Professional Learning

ABLE Idaho Commission for Libraries (free)	ABLE provides library basics for library staff and covers a wide range of topics, including collection development, merchandising, cataloging, and reference work. Funded by LSTA and IMLS, it is offered at no cost.
ALA Online Learning (payment required)	Connects school library employees with a wide range of online training. Click on "Online Learning News" to access a list of webinars. See specifics concerning time and fees.
American Libraries Magazine Live (free)	Provides webinars of current trends in libraries.
Infopeople (payment required for some)	Provides webinars and resources for library employees. Some webinars are approved by the ALA's Library Support Staff Certification (LSSC) program.
Library of Congress Professional Development (free)	Targeted for teachers and school librarians, LC provides webinars on copyright, inquiry process, primary sources, etc.
Nebraska Library Commission (free)	Webinars and technology training offered on current topics.
OCLC's WebJunction (payment required unless your state library is subscribed)	Promotes learning for library workers. Each month a state library compiles and shares free training.

In today's competitive job market, formal education is expected because there is little time on the job to learn the knowledge and skills to be successful. Often library managers seek to fill positions with people who can immediately step into the job setting. Being a library user does not prepare one for the responsibilities and skills of working as an LSS.

The American Library Association (ALA) is the key professional organization for librarians in the United States. ALA accredits college and university library science programs that meet its standards for professional librarians at the graduate level for Master of Library Science (MLS) or Master of Information and Library Science (MILS) and the associate degree or certificate programs levels for LSS education.[20]

ALA-LSSC Certification

The Library Support Staff Certification (LSSC) Program is a national certification program that allows library support staff to demonstrate their competencies and become a Certified Library Support Staff (CLSS) either by completing an approved certificate or associate degree program or by petitioning in required and elective competencies by portfolio. The LSSC means that a prospective employee has specific knowledge and skills. Current employees can increase their skills leading to improved performance. At this time there are a limited number of accredited LSSC programs in the United States. Several are offered asynchronously online, meaning that students can take courses remotely and have some flexibility to do their work at times that best meet their weekly schedules.

Of great benefit to LSS who have achieved ALA-LSSC accreditation is that they are highly desirable employees and their degree or certificate is nationally recognized and portable to any library in the country. With the changing and demanding work environment of libraries, it makes great sense for LSS to achieve the ALA-LSSC credential.

Mentors and Internships

LSS both formally and informally learn from each other. New LSS often receive training from other staff who serve as mentors to teach specific applications of technology, work processes, and accepted procedures. Mentors also introduce new staff to others and the library environment. Most often mentor relationships are temporary. However, sometimes LSS are fortunate to be mentored by another who continues to provide professional support and career growth. LSS often serve as mentors to new staff and, with attributes of transformational leadership, can be the provider of professional support to others.

Internships most often take place in another location than the person's workplace. The purpose of an internship is to acquire new learning in authentic settings to gain practice in unfamiliar skills. Sometimes LSS seek internships in different types of libraries than the ones that they work in. LSS in training programs may seek internships to give them first-time experience working in libraries that will be helpful when they apply for positions.

A site supervisor volunteers to guide, teach, and follow the intern, providing ample opportunities to learn and practice the goals of the student. In college internship courses, a faculty advisor is a member of the team to ensure the success of the internship and to evaluate the experience. Internships often result in job placements for students who use the opportunity to demonstrate their knowledge and skills as well as to network with librarians.

Professional Literature

Finally, LSS benefit from reading professional journals that inform us about trends, issues, and new practices in all types of libraries. Some journals, like *Library Journal*, *Booklist*, and *School Library Journal*, also review new materials. LSS can ask to be on the circulating list of print copies of their library's professional journals, or if they prefer, view current journals, often for free, online. Their library may also have databases with current and archived issues. Table 5.5 contains a beginning list of professional literature LSS can find online.

Table 5.5. Professional Literature of Interest to LSS

American Libraries	National news publication for professional librarians and library workers.
Book Links	A magazine designed for teachers, librarians, booksellers, parents, and other adults interested in connecting children with books. Focuses on articles that target those people that educate children from preschool through eighth grade.
Children & Libraries: The Journal of the Association for Library Service to Children	Provides continuing education of librarians working with children, showcases current scholarly research and practice in library service to children, and spotlights significant activities and programs of the Association for Library Service to Children.
Library Journal	A full-service magazine/working tool tailored to the information needs of librarians and managers in public, academic, and corporate libraries.
Library Trends	A thematic journal focusing on current trends in all areas of library practice; each issue explores topics of interest primarily to practicing librarians and information scientists and secondarily to teachers and students.
School Library Journal	The most complete provider of news, information, and reviews for librarians and media specialists who serve children and young adults in school and public libraries.
School Media Connection	Publishes articles dealing with the operation of secondary school libraries and reviews of books and other media. A journal for junior and senior high school librarians.

In addition to these journals being online, many are published by professional organizations whose websites contain news and announcements. Develop a habit of perusing one professional issue per week to become informed and proactive for libraries and the people they serve.

CHAPTER SUMMARY

In this chapter, two important topics were explored: (1) basic leadership principles and (2) how LSS can plan, implement, and participate in professional learning. The relationship between these two competencies is well established in that library leaders promote and support professional development of their staff. Likewise, LSS who desire to be leaders need to be continuous learners of new library practices, trends, and issues. There are many opportunities for both leadership and learning for motivated LSS.

DISCUSSION QUESTIONS

1. What is situational leadership and how can LSS prepare to lead in times of crisis or unpredicted events?
2. What is the difference between transactional and transformational leadership?
3. Rank the nine attributes of leadership discussed in this chapter on a scale of 1 to 9. Why did you rank them in this priority order?

4. What are five major differences between traditional learning and adult learning? Why do adults learn differently than young people?
5. What ways can LSS extend their learning? Which ways would you prefer and why?

ACTIVITIES

1. Nine attributes of transformational leadership were introduced in this chapter along with three ways or strategies LSS can begin to develop these attributes. For each of the nine attributes, add a fourth strategy that you could apply in your own work situation to develop this trait. After each strategy, add a paragraph explaining why you think this would be an effective way for LSS to develop their leadership capabilities.
2. There were many suggestions made for LSS to enhance their skills and learning in this chapter. Using the example in table 5.2, select another professional library organization (other than the Public Library Association—PLA) such as the American Association of School Librarians (AASL), ALA-Allied Professional Association, or even your state library association or affiliates that you are interested in. Research this organization and create a chart similar to table 5.2 of its social media channels. Explore each of the channels. Add a third column where you will evaluate each of the channels you explored. Tell if this would be a credible learning source and why.

NOTES

1. Nuah Tarigan, "Managing the Nonprofit Organization vs. the Theory and Practice of Leadership," *International Journal of Humanities and Applied Sciences* 1, no. 4 (2012): 119, accessed June 14, 2017, journalsweb.org/siteadmin/upload/95623%20IJHAS014027.pdf.

2. Ruth Taylor, "Leadership Theories and the Development of Nurses in Primary Health Care," *Primary Health Care* 19, no. 9 (November 2009): 41–44, search.ebscohost.com/login.aspx?direct=true&db=aph&AN=45391474&authtype=cookie,cpid&custid=csl&site=ehost-live&scope=site.

3. Pamela Spahr, "What Is Situational Leadership? How Flexibility Leads to Success," St. Thomas University Online, last modified 2017, accessed June 19, 2017, online.stu.edu/situational-leadership/.

4. Matthew Miragilia, "Crisis Management in Schools," *Journal of Management and Innovation* 1, no. 1 (Spring 2015): 6–8, accessed June 19, 2017, jmi.mercy.edu/index.php/JMI/article/download/4/25.

5. Spahr, "What Is Situational Leadership?"

6. Taylor, "Leadership Theories," 42–43.

7. Veysel Okcu, "Relation between Secondary School Administrators' Transformational and Transactional Leadership Style and Skills to Diversity Management in the School," *Educational Sciences: Theory and Practice* 14, no. 6 (December 2014): 2164, search.ebscohost.com/login.aspx?direct=true&db=aph&AN=100647140&authtype=cookie,cpid&custid=csl&site=ehost-live&scope=site.

8. Okcu, "Relation between Secondary School Administrators," 2164–65.

9. Fareena Nazim, "Principals' Transformational and Transactional Leadership Style and Job Satisfaction of College Teachers," *Journal of Education and Practice* 7, no. 34 (2016): 21, www.science.gov/topicpages/t/transactional+leadership+style.html.

10. Taylor, "Leadership Theories," 43.

11. American Library Association, "Library Support Staff Resource Center," last modified 2017, accessed June 25, 2017, www.ala.org/offices/hrdr/librarysupportstaff/library_support_staff_resource_center.

12. Christoforos Pappas, "The Adult Learning Theory—Andragogy—of Malcolm Knowles," eLearning Industry, last modified 2017, accessed June 25, 2017, elearningindustry.com/the-adult-learning-theory-andragogy-of-malcolm-knowles.

13. Saul McLeod, "Kolb—Learning Styles," Simply Psychology, accessed June 25, 2017, www.simplypsychology.org/learning-kolb.html.

14. Infed, "Self-Directed Learning," accessed June 25, 2017, infed.org/mobi/self-directed-learning/.

15. Instructional Design, "Transformative Learning (Jack Mezirow)," accessed June 25, 2017, www. instructionaldesign.org/theories/transformative-learning.html.

16. University of Connecticut, "Trio Model," Department of Educational Leadership Adult Learning Program, last modified 2017, accessed June 25, 2017, adult.education.uconn.edu/triomodel/.

17. American Library Association, "Library Support Staff Resource Center."

18. University of Illinois, "Professional Organizations and Listservs," School of Information Sciences, last modified 2017, accessed June 25, 2017, ischool.illinois.edu/careers/proforgslists.

19. Public Library Association, "Official PLA Social Media Channels," American Library Association, last modified 2017, accessed June 25, 2017, www.ala.org/pla/about/connect.

20. American Library Association, "Library Support Staff Resource Center."

REFERENCES, SUGGESTED READINGS, AND WEBSITES

American Library Association. "Library Support Staff Resource Center." Last modified 2017. Accessed June 25, 2017. www.ala.org/offices/hrdr/librarysupportstaff/library_support_staff_resource_center.

———. "LSSC Home." Last modified 2017. Accessed June 25, 2017. ala-apa.org/lssc/.

Choi, Suk Bong, Kihwan Kim, and Seung-Wan Kang. "Effects of Transformational and Shared Leadership Styles on Employees' Perception of Team Effectiveness." *Social Behavior and Personality: An International Journal* 45, no. 3 (2017): 377–86. search.ebscohost.com/login.aspx?direct=true&db=aph&AN=122406754&authtype=cookie,cpid&custid=csl&site=ehost-live&scope=site.

Infed. "Self-Directed Learning." Accessed June 25, 2017. infed.org/mobi/self-directed-learning/.

Instructional Design. "Transformative Learning (Jack Mezirow)." Accessed June 25, 2017. www.instructionaldesign.org/theories/transformative-learning.html.

LibrarySupportStaff.com. "Support Staff Sites for Library Technicians, Paraprofessionals Library Assistants, Clerks and Associates." Accessed June 25, 2017. www.librarysupportstaff.com/staffsites.html#colt.

McLeod, Saul. "Kolb—Learning Styles." Simply Psychology. Accessed June 25, 2017. https://www.simplypsychology.org/learning-kolb.html.

Miragilia, Matthew. "Crisis Management in Schools." *Journal of Management and Innovation* 1, no. 1 (Spring 2015): 1–18. Accessed June 19, 2017. jmi.mercy.edu/index.php/JMI/article/download/4/25.

Nazim, Fareena. "Principals' Transformational and Transactional Leadership Style and Job Satisfaction of College Teachers." *Journal of Education and Practice* 7, no. 34 (2016): 18–22. www.science.gov/topicpages/t/transactional+leadership+style.html.

Okcu, Veysel. "Relation between Secondary School Administrators' Transformational and Transactional Leadership Style and Skills to Diversity Management in the School." *Educational Sciences: Theory and Practice* 14, no. 6 (December 2014): 2162–74. search.ebscohost.com/login.aspx?direct=true&db=aph&AN=100647140&authtype=cookie,cpid&custid=csl&site=ehost-live&scope=site.

Pappas, Christoforos. "The Adult Learning Theory—Andragogy—of Malcolm Knowles." eLearning Industry. Last modified 2017. Accessed June 25, 2017. elearningindustry.com/the-adult-learning-theory-andragogy-of-malcolm-knowles.

Public Library Association. "Official PLA Social Media Channels." American Library Association. Last modified 2017. Accessed June 25, 2017. www.ala.org/pla/about/connect.

Sheckley, B., M. Kehrhahn, S. Bell, and R. Grenier. "Trio: An Emerging Model of Adult Professional Development." *Proceedings of the 49th Annual Education Research Conference.* University of Missouri–St. Louis, June 2008.

Spahr, Pamela. "What Is Situational Leadership? How Flexibility Leads to Success." St. Thomas University Online. Last modified 2017. Accessed June 19, 2017. online.stu.edu/situational-leadership/.

Tarigan, Nuah. "Managing the Nonprofit Organization vs. the Theory and Practice of Leadership." *International Journal of Humanities and Applied Sciences* 1, no. 4 (2012): 117–25. Accessed June 14, 2017. journalsweb.org/siteadmin/upload/95623%20IJHAS014027.pdf.

Taylor, Ruth. "Leadership Theories and the Development of Nurses in Primary Health Care." *Primary Health Care* 19, no. 9 (November 2009): 40–46. search.ebscohost.com/login.aspx?direct=true&db=aph&AN=45391474&authtype=cookie,cpid&custid=csl&site=ehost-live&scope=site.

University of Connecticut. "Trio Model." Department of Educational Leadership Adult Learning Program. Last modified 2017. Accessed June 25, 2017. adult.education.uconn.edu/triomodel/.

University of Illinois. "Professional Organizations and Listservs." School of Information Sciences. Last modified 2017. Accessed June 25, 2017. ischool.illinois.edu/careers/proforgslists.

CHAPTER 6

Policies and Procedures

LSS know the value of written, approved policies and procedures and the difference between policies and procedures and are able to develop policies and procedures for review. (ALA-LSSC Supervision and Management Competency #7)

Topics Covered in This Chapter:

- Policies and Procedures
  - o Policies
  - o Procedures
  - o Rules
- Policy Examples
  - o Library Use and Borrower Policy
  - o Rules of Conduct Policy
  - o Material Selection/Collection Development Policy
  - o Internet Use Policy
  - o Meeting Room Policy
  - o Displays and Exhibits Policy
  - o Other Policies
- Policy Change That Impacts Public Service in a Library

Key Terms:

Displays and exhibits policy: Libraries must determine what displays and exhibits they can host. Depending on wall, floor, and bulletin board space, libraries can offer a wide range of material to their constituents.

Employment laws: Employment laws and regulations seek to protect employees from discrimination and harassment. Employment legislation is important because it provides protection and job security for employees against malpractices in all work-places, including libraries.

Internet use policy: Because the Internet is an unmonitored global network, libraries cannot control or monitor content; they must establish guidelines for proper use so patrons are not in violation of federal, state, and local laws.

Library use and borrower policy: A library use and borrower policy refers to borrowing privileges that are restricted to residents of a town or students of a school or college. This relates to the library and its funding structure and is solved by issuing library cards. Library cards identify eligible users and their level of access to services.

Material selection policy: A collection policy, also known as a material selection policy, is a document that provides guidance for the librarians or LSS who do collection develop-ment. It follows a set of guidelines to consider when choosing materials and includes such criteria as positive reviews, reputation of the author, local interest, demand, and budget limitations.

Meeting room policy: Libraries that have meeting rooms must have a policy that clearly outlines who may use the room and for what purpose.

Policies: Policies are clear, simple statements of how your organization intends to conduct its services or business. In libraries, policies determine who can use the library, patron behavior, and material selection.

Policy and procedural manual: A policy and procedural manual is a book or a binder of all of the library's policies and procedures that can be easily accessed and is helpful for all LSS.

Procedures: Procedures are the step-by-step tasks that support the policy—the action plan. Procedures describe how each policy will be put into action in your organization.

Rules: Rules are an accepted principle or instruction that states the way things are or should be done and tells you what you are allowed or are not allowed to do.[1]

Rules of conduct policy: Rules of conduct, patron responsibility, code of conduct, and other terms describe a policy that explains what is expected of the patron. They begin with a statement of inclusion—that everyone has the right to use the library

The USA PATRIOT Act: This is the acronym made by the Uniting and Strengthening Amer-ica by Providing Appropriate Tools Required to Intercept and Obstruct Terrorism Act. Created by Congress in the wake of 9/11, it substantially expanded the authority of U.S. law enforcement for the stated purpose of fighting terrorism in the United States and abroad. It expanded the authority of the FBI to gain access to library records, including stored electronic data and communications.

The objective of any library is to serve the information needs of its users. According to the American Library Association, when developing policies, each library needs to consider the community that it serves. Who these users are will depend on the library's demographics—the statistics of a given population by age, sex, race, and income. This is important for libraries so they can know whom they are serving and for whom they can provide the appropriate resources.

Policies have several functions in today's complex organizations. They help define the values of the organization, and they help managers and staff translate those values into service priorities. Policies establish a standard for services that can be understood by users of the service and providers. Policies ensure equitable treatment for all, and polices provide a framework for delivery of services. When policies have been adopted by a library's governing agents in a formal process and are consistent with local, state, and federal laws, they will be enforceable.[2]

POLICIES AND PROCEDURES

Policies

Policies are clear, simple statements of how your organization intends to conduct its services, actions, or business. They provide a set of guiding principles to help with decision making.[3] They guide the actions of employees and employers alike, and they provide consistency. For example, telling a disruptive patron to quiet down may be taken personally, as if that person is the only one who has ever been singled out. Having a library behavior policy to show to that patron takes the spotlight off the patron.

Policies govern the way in which staff members interact with an organization and with one another. They protect both the workers and the organization and set the tone for what it's like to work in a particular place. How well policies are written can make or break the work experience for everyone involved. The clearer policies are, the more closely they are tied to the philosophy and mission of the organization, the more carefully drawn, and the more they directly address the situations they are meant to govern, the more effective they will be.[4]

Policies also serve to set boundaries for individual action, defining how managers interact with staff and coworkers. If there were no policies in place, then anyone could act however they want, creating not only chaos but anarchy! Library policies also provide protection from harassment, bullying, inappropriate use of the Internet and social media, to name a few. We saw the list of eight advantages to workplace policies in chapter 1; it bears repeating for its relevance to this chapter. These eight advantages of having workplace policies are:

1. They help employees know what is expected of them with respect to standards of behavior and performance.
2. They set rules and guidelines for decision making in routine situations so that employees and managers do not need to continually ask senior managers what to do.
3. They help you to adopt a consistent and clear response across the library to continually refer to situations involving employee interaction.
4. They allow you to demonstrate good faith that employees will be treated fairly and equally.
5. They allow you to have an accepted method of dealing with complaints and misunderstandings in place to help avoid favoritism.
6. They set a framework for delegation of decision making.

7. They give you a means of communicating information to new employees.
8. They offer you protection from breaches of employment legislation, such as equal opportunity laws.[5]

Policies in libraries of all types—public, academic, school, and special—are designed to guide how decisions are made in many areas: material selection, collection development, circulation, Internet use, meeting room use, and patron behavior, for example. It is necessary that the library have well-worded policies available, particularly if the library, or a policy, is challenged. This is especially important in matters of civil rights and censorship. These concepts are examined more fully in chapter 1 of this text.

Ultimately, polices are the *"what"*—the principles and guidelines of a library to reach its goals. Policies are essential to back you up when a problem arises or you, as manager, are questioned about procedure or decisions.

Figure 6.1.   Policies graphic. *istock/castillodominici*

Procedures

If policies are the what, the **procedures** are the *"how."* Procedures are the step-by-step tasks that support the policy—the action plan. Procedures describe how each policy will be put into action in your organization. Each procedure should outline:

- who will do what,
- what steps they need to take, and
- which forms or documents to use.

Procedures might just be a few bullet points or instructions. Sometimes they work well as forms, checklists, instructions, or flowcharts. Policies and their accompanying procedures will vary between workplaces because they reflect the values, approaches, and commitments of a specific organization and its culture; however, they share the same role in guiding your organization.[6]

The University of California Policy Office provides a policies and procedures chart that illustrates these functions.[7]

Table 6.1.   Policies vs. Procedures

Policies	Procedures
Policies are widespread applications.	Procedures have a narrower focus.
They are nonnegotiable and change infrequently.	They are subject to change and improvement.
They are expressed in broad terms.	They are more detailed.
They are statements of what or why.	They are statements of how, when, who, and why.
They address major operational issues.	They detail a process.

When someone new is hired at the library, they must learn it all—the policies and the procedures. This can take some time to learn. One very good method for a new staff member is to give them a small notebook to take notes. Encourage them to write down the procedures as they learn them and to study and refer to them often. The LSS who follows along without taking notes, who says, "It's all right; I've got it" is the one to worry about. No one can possibly understand all the nuances of a library's procedures, from circulation to interlibrary loan to materials repair. An experienced worker may be familiar with the procedures in general, but libraries will differ in how they are carried out.

Therefore many libraries will have policy and procedural manuals. If you as a new employee aren't told about one, then ask. You, as manager, may want to routinely make, and update, procedures to share with staff. Providing a binder of policies and procedures that can be easily accessed is helpful for all LSS; even seasoned employees should periodically review them as they can be subject to change.

Rules

Then there are **rules**. While the characteristics among policy, procedures, and rules may on occasion overlap, there are differences. The policy is a statement of belief or values; procedures are the step-by-step tasks that support the policy—the action plan. Rules are an accepted principle or instruction that states the way things are or should be done and tells you what you are or are not allowed to do. For example, the library's policy is to charge fines for overdue materials. The procedure is that overdue items are charged at the rate of ten cents per item per day up to a preestablished amount. The rule then allows the LSS to be flexible if perhaps a child owes fifty cents but only brings a quarter. He could certainly expect the child to come up with the additional quarter the next time she visits, or he can forgive it. Rules allow for individual interpretation depending on the circumstances.

POLICY EXAMPLES

Libraries of every kind adopt administrative policies and procedures regulating the library and the use of its materials, services, and facilities. In chapter 1, we examined **employment law** and related policies, such as personnel. Personnel policies define the rights, obligations, treatment, and relations of people in a workplace. Personnel policies can vary from library to library but generally cover the hours worked, schedules, vacation and sick time, and rules for dealing with issues and obstacles. They also cover fairness, discrimination, and harassment. Let's look at some other policies that a library would have in place.

Library Use and Borrower Policy

Public, school, and academic libraries by nature provide free, equal, and unfettered access to all residents of a community and the library system. Service is not denied due to religious, racial, socioeconomic, or political reasons; neither can it be denied to those with mental, emotional, or physical conditions or due to age or sexual orientation. According to the Library Bill of Rights,

> The American Library Association affirms that all libraries are forums for information and ideas, and that the following basic policies should guide their services.
>
> I.   Books and other library resources should be provided for the interest, information, and enlightenment of all people of the community the library serves. Materials should not be excluded because of the origin, background, or views of those contributing to their creation.
> II.   Libraries should provide materials and information presenting all points of view on current and historical issues. Materials should not be proscribed or removed because of partisan or doctrinal disapproval.
> III. Libraries should challenge censorship in the fulfillment of their responsibility to provide information and enlightenment.
> IV.   Libraries should cooperate with all persons and groups concerned with resisting abridgment of free expression and free access to ideas.
> V.   A person's right to use a library should not be denied or abridged because of origin, age, background, or views.
> VI.   Libraries which make exhibit spaces and meeting rooms available to the public they serve should make such facilities available on an equitable basis, regardless of the beliefs or affiliations of individuals or groups requesting their use.[8]

So why do we need a policy about **library use**? After all, the Library Bill of Rights says that libraries are available to all. However, while use is guaranteed, borrowing privileges are restricted to residents of a town or students of a school or college. This relates to the library and its funding structure and is solved by issuing library cards. Library cards identify eligible users and their level of access to services. Nonresident borrowers may be eligible if the person has a valid card from their hometown library—provisions are made through regional or state reciprocal borrowing arrangements. Incidentally, a statement of confidentiality is a required element. According to the ALA Code of Ethics, "We protect each library user's right to privacy and confidentiality with respect to information sought or received and resources consulted, borrowed, acquired or transmitted."[9]

Some libraries will have a separate circulation policy that addresses loan periods, fines and fees, renewals, overdues, lost cards, proof of residency, proof of age (children often need a parent's signature), expiration date, the availability of temporary cards, and reserves. In fact, some libraries may even have separate polices for individual elements, such as reserves or overdue fees. For the sake of expediency, they will be grouped together.

Sample Outline of Library Use and Borrower Policy

1. Registration (Cards will be issued to residents upon proof of identity)
2. Loan periods/renewals
3. Reserves
4. Fines and fees
5. Damaged materials
6. Lost cards
7. Confidentiality statement

Rules of Conduct Policy

Rules of conduct, patron responsibility, code of conduct, and other terms describe a policy that explains what is expected of the patron. They begin with a statement of inclusion—that everyone has the right to use the library—then list behaviors that are not acceptable.

Sample Outline of Rules of Conduct

Statement: All persons have the right to use the library as long as doing so does not infringe on another's rights. Any patron of the library who causes disruption of the library's operation in any of the following ways will be approached by a staff member, informed of the infraction, and asked to stop. If the situation becomes threatening or dangerous, police will be called. Disruptive situations include:

1. Disruptive, threatening, offensive, or abusive language or behavior
2. Drunkenness
3. Smoking
4. Food and drink
5. Shirts and shoes
6. Cell phone use
7. Responsibility for children

These elements and others are included at the discretion of the library in varying detail. Some libraries will have separate policies for unattended children.

Material Selection/Collection Development Policy

A collection policy, also known as a **material selection policy**, is a document that provides guidance for the librarians or LSS who do collection development. It follows a set of guidelines to consider when choosing materials and includes such criteria as positive reviews, reputation of the author, local interest, demand, and budget limitations.

A collection development policy follows a set of guidelines to consider when choosing materials. The American Library Association defines collection development policies (CDP) as "documents which define the scope of a library's existing collections, plan for the continuing development of resources, identify collection strengths, and outline the relationship between selection philosophy and the institution's goals, general selection criteria, and intellectual freedom."[10]

Sample Collection Policy Elements

- Library mission statement
- Purpose of policy
- Intellectual freedom statement
- Collection development objectives
- Statement of responsibility
- Gifts
- Withdrawals
- Challenged materials
- Reconsideration
- Confidentiality of circulation records
- Freedom to Read statement
- Library Bill of Rights

In addition, it should include:

- A statement regarding who has the authority to select
- A statement regarding who is responsible for selection
- A statement regarding the library's goals and objectives
- A list of criteria for selection
- A list of review sources used
- A procedure for handling problems
- Guidelines for allocating funds

A collection development policy for a school media center would be similar but include a statement about materials chosen to support the educational goals and curriculum on all levels of difficulty and variety of viewpoints and formats. For an academic library, the policy follows a similar format but would include criteria for electronic subject guidelines and possibly interdisciplinary indexes.

Finally, the one thing that libraries agree on is the inclusion in the CDP of the Library Bill of Rights[11] and the Freedom to Read[12] statements provided by the American Library Association.

Internet Use Policy

Libraries provide free access to the **Internet** for their patrons and often have multiple computers for their use. Because the Internet is an unmonitored global network, libraries cannot control or monitor content; they must establish guidelines for proper use so patrons are not in violation of federal, state, and local laws. Parents are required to assume responsibility for the Internet use of their minor children. To ensure appropriate and effective use, the library will create a policy such as the following:

Sample Internet Use Policy

The _____ Library is providing access to the Internet as a means to enhance the information and learning opportunities for the residents of the library's service area. The governing board has established the Internet use policy to ensure appropriate and effective use of this resource.

Guidelines:

- Users may use the Internet for research and the acquisition of information to address their educational, vocational, cultural, and recreational needs.
- Users may use the Internet for the transmission and receipt of e-mail as long as they establish their own free account.
- Internet use is offered in one-hour sessions on a first-come, first-served basis. If no one else is waiting, the user may have another one-hour session; they must give it up if someone requests its use.
- Users will respect and uphold copyright laws; they will not use it for illegal purposes.
- Users will respect the rights and privacy of others.
- Users will agree to pay for all items generated on library printers.
- Users will not create or distribute viruses.
- Users will not willfully or deliberately cause damage to computer equipment or software.[13]

For a school library, the policy might add that accessed material must support classroom learning and Internet safety measures be followed that include blocking or filtering software. Since users of the Internet in academic libraries are over eighteen, those additional policies will not apply.

Meeting Room Policy

Libraries that have **meeting rooms** must have a policy that clearly outlines who may use the room and for what purpose. They can specify that the room is only used for library-related programs or that the meeting room can be reserved by outside groups. These may then be limited to only nonprofit groups or may be open to all including for-profit and political groups. According to the Library Bill of Rights,

Written policies for meeting room use should be stated in inclusive rather than exclusive terms. For example, a policy that the library's facilities are open "to organizations engaged in educational, cultural, intellectual, or charitable activities" is an inclusive statement of the limited uses to which the facilities may be put. This defined limitation would permit religious groups to use the facilities because they engage in intellectual activities, but would exclude most commercial uses of the facility.[14]

Figure 6.2.   Meeting room audience. *istock/Rawpixel*

Sample Meeting Room Use Policy

1. The room is available to individuals or organized groups in the library service area. Exceptions may be made if the library board deems extenuating circumstances are involved.
2. Use of the room does not constitute an endorsement of the group's beliefs or policies by the library board or staff.
3. The room may be reserved no more than ninety days in advance.
4. It is understood that library programming has first priority for room use.
5. There will be no charge for use of the meeting room.
6. No admission may be charged.
7. Refreshments may be served and shall be provided by the group.
8. No alcohol and no smoking is allowed.
9. Those using the room will leave it in neat, orderly condition; if not, the group will be given notice that continued offense may result in denied access in the future.
10. The library is not responsible for any equipment, supplies, materials, or other items brought into the library by groups or individuals attending a meeting.
11. The library board and staff do not assume any liability for groups or individuals attending a meeting in the library.[15]

While the Library Bill of Rights says that "libraries which make exhibit spaces and meeting rooms available to the public they serve should make such facilities available on an equitable basis, regardless of the beliefs or affiliations of individuals or groups requesting their use,"[16] conflicts can and do arise. Adherence to policy doesn't guarantee there will not be conflict. Matt Hale, the white supremacist leader of the World Church of the Creator, took advantage of these policies to book library meeting rooms around the country in the early 2000s. While there were no problems in Salt Lake City, Utah, or Peoria, Illinois, in two cases (Wallingford, Connecticut, in 2001[17] and Wakefield, Massachusetts, in 2002[18]), advance publicity brought in protestors, riots, and the police. Physical damage to the properties occurred, and people were hurt. In cases where a known group causes damage and incites confrontation, Judith Krug, then head of the American Library Association's Office for Intellectual Freedom, said that, "given the record of violent demonstrations, libraries are justified in closing the public spaces."[19] As recently as 2016, a meeting of a Black Lives Matter group in Nashville Public Library excluded non-black participants from attending; the group was told that they would not be able to continue hosting meetings in the library, as their policy of excluding non-black participants conflicts with the library's meeting room policies.[20] (This did not result in any protests.) Libraries can choose to restrict their meeting spaces to only library-related activities if they feel that a wider policy would invite conflict. Libraries that offer meeting rooms to the public must be aware of potential conflicts and understand the interpretations and limitations of their policies.

Displays and Exhibits Policy

As with meeting room policies, libraries must determine what **displays and exhibits** they can host, again on an equitable basis. Depending on wall, floor, and bulletin board space, libraries can offer a wide range of material to their constituents. Library-related exhibits and displays usually take priority and can include, for example, those thematically linked to a holiday, season, or subject. School library displays can "sell" books. Using—or reusing—items found in the classroom or library can create excitement.

There are also non-library-related displays: most libraries will have a community bulletin board or shelving with a variety of local events information and resources. Personal collections are popular in many libraries and run the gamut from antique dolls to military paraphernalia. Libraries are the go-to place for tax forms and voter registration cards. If they have the space, many libraries will also host art exhibits of local artists or schoolchildren.

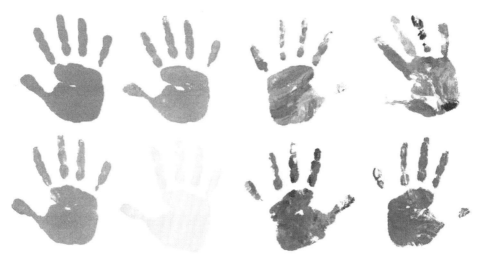

Figure 6.3.　Children's artwork graphic. *istock/Picsfive*

Bulletin boards have a variety of uses for library-related postings, displays, and signage. Additionally, the bulletin board is the perfect place for public or community notices relating to civic, cultural, or educational events in the community. Anything posted to a bulletin board must be approved in advance, conform to an acceptable size, and be dated.

Policies must be inclusive of the variety of displays the library will accept and may resemble the sample policy following:

Sample Display and Exhibit Policy

The library provides space for displays and exhibits of items from the library's own collections, as well as exhibits and displays sponsored by other community agencies or individuals.

1. Exhibits should:
   - Contribute positively to the library's environment.
   - Enrich the life of the community.
   - Create a means of strengthening partnerships between the library and the wider community.
   - Highlight, whenever possible, the collections, resources, and services of the library.
2. Displays may include:
   - Handiwork, historical material, nature works, or other materials of general interest and are subject to approval by the director.
   - The library assumes no responsibility or liability for damage or theft. All items are placed at the owner's risk.
3. Bulletin board postings:
   - Notices from individuals and from business organizations will not be accepted for posting at the library.
   - All postings should be delivered to the library's administrative assistant who will post them as space permits, depending on the number of requests on file at any one time.
   - All postings must be dated.
   - The library reserves the right to remove postings as necessary, to make space for new postings requested by the library, the town, or other nonprofit community organizations.
   - With limited space available, postings on library programs, resources, and other notices will take priority over all other requests for postings.
   - In addition, agendas for meetings of the Town Council and other town departments, boards, agencies, and commissions will receive priority over postings from local nonprofit organizations.

Other Policies

So far, we have looked at a handful of policies that are common to most libraries; there are dozens more that may be adopted depending on the size, scope, or type of library. Myriad policies fall under the umbrella of ALA's Office of Intellectual Freedom on their Intellectual Freedom Statements and Policies page[21] and are too numerous to list. In addition to a personnel policy (found in chapter 1) and those listed above, here is a list of other policies that libraries frequently adopt. No one policy is more important than any other; they all have a place in the public, school, and academic library. Such policies may include:

1. copyright
2. emergency response policy
3. equipment use
4. lending e-readers
5. programming
6. public relations
7. reference service
8. responsibilities of the library board
9. services of the library
10. unattended children
11. use of electronic resources
12. volunteers and friends

For more information and examples on these and other policies for all types of libraries, visit WebJunction,[22] Eduscapes,[23] or a specific library of your choice.

POLICY CHANGE THAT IMPACTS PUBLIC SERVICE IN A LIBRARY

"The more things change, the more they stay the same" is an age-old adage about the appearance of change while acknowledging that basically, nothing really does. But is it true about libraries today? The opening statement of the 2017 State of American Libraries report says, "In the 21st century, libraries of all types are responding to the changing social, economic, and political impacts of living in a digital society. Academic, school, and public libraries provide services that empower people for change. Library workers' expertise, combined with dynamic collections and digital resources, help individuals develop new skills, communicate with others through new technologies, and help make their communities better places to live."[24]

Libraries are doing a great job of keeping up even as social and economic changes are nipping at our heels. Libraries have evolved from institutions perceived primarily as the domain of the book to institutions that users clearly perceive as providing pathways to high-quality information in a variety of media and information sources.[25]

Policy changes that impact social, technological, economic, and political factors are major drivers of library change—for better or for worse. In the positive column, technology is ubiquitous in all types of libraries, and social media is now a fixture as well, from Facebook pages to Twitter feeds. Technology and social media bring the patron into the library even when she is not physically there. Libraries have learned to embrace change and have adjusted their service model to reflect it.

But how does that help the rural community that does not have the infrastructure in place to provide digital services? In times of economic distress, libraries are often last to the table for adequate funding—and yet these services are of the utmost importance to the underserved. When policy affects adequate library funding, those who can least afford it are the ones who are left behind.

Changing demographics often require that libraries provide service to patrons for whom English is not the native language, such as materials in the languages of the library's changing target area. Picture books featuring characters of multiple races and ethnicities should be the norm in all libraries. Changing to meet the needs of the library's demographic—as well as that of society in general—benefits all the library's constituents.

Historically, through the latter part of the nineteenth century and well into the twentieth, society expected the new library profession to exercise censorship. This represented the "community standards" of the time. Fast-forward to these standards in 2017, we find that libraries have a role to play in sanctuary cities, as libraries have always been free and open to the public—the ultimate sanctuary.[26] Also, in the wake of the events of 9/11 and the ensuing years, federal policy changes that have trickled down have had a major impact on library policy and services. These changes are for the safety of the library patron and the public, and some are indisputable. No longer can a parent, or anyone for that matter, walk into their child's school media center before strict security screening even gets them through the front door. However, Internet search records on a public library computer may be subject to seizure under the rules of **the USA PATRIOT Act**,[27] which has been met with considerable controversy. The list goes on, as does the discussion.

Changing expectations of the constituency have an impact on public service—but that is what has been driving public service all along. Regardless of policy—or, perhaps, despite it—libraries change and adapt, however needed, to continue to provide excellent public service.

CHAPTER SUMMARY

Policies and procedures are necessary to regulate library operations. They serve to set guidelines in many areas—the policies are the *what*, and the procedures are the *how*. Policies range from patron registration to patron Internet use; they provide a set of guiding principles to help with decision making. Several policies were examined, as was the effect of policy change on public service.

DISCUSSION QUESTIONS

1. What is a policy, and why is it used?
2. How does a policy differ from a procedure—or does it?
3. Name several ways that policies are useful in the workplace.
4. If the ALA Bill of Rights guarantees library use, why does a library need a library use policy?
5. Explain how, or why, policy changes can impact public service.

ACTIVITIES

1. Choose two policies from the "Other Policies" list, and create a sample policy for a library of your choice.

2. Visit a library of your choice and ask to see their policy manual. Choose one that is outlined in this chapter and compare it. Are the elements similar? If not, explain the differences.

NOTES

1. Cambridge Dictionary, "Rule," last modified 2017, accessed August 12, 2017, dictionary.cambridge.org/dictionary/english/rule.

2. American Library Association, "Library Policy Development: General," last modified May 26, 2017, accessed August 10, 2017, libguides.ala.org/librarypolicy.

3. Department of Health & Human Services, Melbourne, Victoria, "What's the Difference Between Policies and Procedures?" I Can Do That, last modified September 15, 2014, accessed August 10, 2017, www.volunteer.vic.gov.au/manage-your-volunteers/policies-and-procedures/whats-the-difference-between-policies-and-procedures.

4. University of Kansas, "Section 5. Developing Personnel Policies," Community Tool Box, last modified 2017, accessed August 12, 2017, www.ctb.ku.edu/en/table-of-contents/structure/hiring-and-training/personnel-policies/main.

5. Charles Power, "8 Advantages of Having Workplace Policies," *Employment Law Practical Handbook*, last modified June 13, 2012, accessed May 23, 2017, www.employmentlawhandbook.com.au/8-advantages-of-having-workplace-policies/.

6. Department of Health & Human Services, Melbourne, Victoria, "What's the Difference?"

7. University of California, "Determining Whether a Statement Is a Policy or a Procedure," UCOP, Ethics, Compliance and Audit Services, Universitywide Policy Office, last modified 2015, accessed August 12, 2017, ucop.edu/ethics-compliance-audit-services/policy/.

8. American Library Association, "Library Bill of Rights," last modified January 23, 1996, accessed August 14, 2017, www.ala.org/advocacy/intfreedom/librarybill.

9. American Library Association, "Code of Ethics," last modified January 28, 2008, accessed August 14, 2017, www.ala.org/tools/ethics.

10. Hali R. Keeler, *Working with Library Collections: An Introduction for Support Staff*, Library Support Staff Handbooks 4 (Lanham, MD: Rowman & Littlefield, 2017), 15.

11. American Library Association, "Library Bill."

12. American Library Association, "The Freedom to Read Statement," last modified June 2004, accessed August 14, 2017, www.ala.org/advocacy/intfreedom/freedomreadstatement.

13. Outagamie Waupaca Library System, "Sample Library Policies for the Small Public Library," accessed August 12, 2017, www.owlsweb.org/l4l/sample-library-policies-small-public-library.

14. American Library Association, "Library Bill."

15. Outagamie Waupaca Library System, "Sample Library."

16. American Library Association, "Library Bill."

17. Paul Zielbauer, "Shouts and Scuffles at White Supremacy Rally," *New York Times*, March 11, 2001, last modified April 11, 2001, accessed August 17, 2017, www.nytimes.com/2001/03/11/nyregion/shouts-and-scuffles-at-white-supremacy-rally.html?mcubz=0.

18. Norman Oder, "Racist Group Takes Advantage of PL Meeting Room Policies," *Library Journal* 127, no. 17 (October 15, 2002).

19. Ibid.

20. Mark Troknya, "Library Meeting Room Conflicts," Public Libraries Online, last modified April 26, 2016, accessed August 17, 2017, publiclibrariesonline.org/2016/04/library-meeting-room-conflicts/.

21. American Library Association, "Intellectual Freedom Statements and Policies," last modified 2017, accessed August 18, 2017, www.ala.org/Template.cfm?Section=censorship&template=/ContentManagement/ContentDisplay.cfm&ContentID=114327.

22. OCLC, "Policies," WebJunction, last modified 2017, accessed August 24, 2017, www .webjunction.org/explore-topics/policies-procedures.html.

23. Eduscapes, "Information Access & Delivery: Policies and Procedures: The School Library and Media Specialist," last modified 2013, accessed August 24, 2017, eduscapes.com/ sms/access/policies.html.

24. Kathy Rosa, ed., "The State of American Libraries 2017," American Library Association, last modified April 2017, accessed August 18, 2017, www.ala.org/news/sites/ala.org.news/ files/content/State-of-Americas-Libraries-Report-2017.pdf.

25. American Library Association, "Changing Roles of Academic and Research Libraries," Association of College and Research Libraries, last modified February 13, 2007, accessed August 18, 2017, www.ala.org/acrl/issues/value/changingroles.

26. Elizabeth Reilly, "Libraries as Sanctuary Spaces," *Unbound*, last modified January 30, 2017, accessed August 18, 2017, slis.simmons.edu/blogs/unbound/2017/01/30/libraries-sanctuary-spaces.

27. American Library Association, "Analysis of the USA Patriot Act Related to Libraries," accessed January 24, 2015, www.ala.org/offices/oif/ifissues/issuesrelatedlinks/usapatriotact analysis.

REFERENCES, SUGGESTED READINGS, AND WEBSITES

American Library Association. "Analysis of the USA Patriot Act Related to Libraries." Accessed January 24, 2015. www.ala.org/offices/oif/ifissues/issuesrelatedlinks/usapatriotactanalysis.
———. "Changing Roles of Academic and Research Libraries." Association of College and Research Libraries. Last modified February 13, 2007. Accessed August 18, 2017. www.ala .org/acrl/issues/value/changingroles.
———. "Code of Ethics." Last modified January 28, 2008. Accessed August 14, 2017. www.ala .org/tools/ethics.
———. "The Freedom to Read Statement." Last modified June 2004. Accessed August 14, 2017. www.ala.org/advocacy/intfreedom/freedomreadstatement.
———. "Guidelines for the Development and Implementation of Policies, Regulations and Procedures Affecting Access to Library Materials, Services and Facilities." Last modified 2017. Accessed August 12, 2017. www.ala.org/advocacy/intfreedom/guidelinesforaccesspolicies.
———. "Intellectual Freedom Statements and Policies." Last modified 2017. Accessed August 18, 2017. www.ala.org/Template.cfm?Section=censorship&template=/ContentManagement/ ContentDisplay.cfm&ContentID=114327.
———. "Library Bill of Rights." Last modified January 23, 1996. Accessed August 14, 2017. www.ala.org/advocacy/intfreedom/librarybill.
———. "Library Policy Development: General." Last modified May 26, 2017. Accessed August 10, 2017. libguides.ala.org/librarypolicy.
Becker, Samantha, Michael D. Crandall, Karen E. Fisher, Rebecca Blakewood, Bo Kinney, and Cadi Russell-Sauvé. *Opportunity for All: How Library Policies and Practices Impact Public Internet Access*. Washington, DC: Institute of Museum and Library Services, 2011.
Cambridge Dictionary. "Rule." Last modified 2017. Accessed August 12, 2017. dictionary .cambridge.org/dictionary/english/rule.
Department of Health and Human Services, Melbourne, Victoria. "What's the Difference Between Policies and Procedures?" I Can Do That. Last modified September 15, 2014. Accessed August 10, 2017. www.volunteer.vic.gov.au/manage-your-volunteers/poli cies-and-procedures/whats-the-difference-between-policies-and-procedures.

Eduscapes. "Information Access & Delivery: Policies and Procedures: The School Library and Media Specialist." Last modified 2013. Accessed August 24, 2017. eduscapes.com/sms/access/policies.html.

Giesecke, John, and Beth McNeil. *Fundamentals of Library Supervision*. 2nd ed. ALA Fundamentals. Chicago, IL: American Library Association, 2010.

Jaeger, Paul T. "Describing and Measuring the Value of Public Libraries: the Growth of the Internet and the Evolution of Library Value." *First Monday*. Last modified November 7, 2011. Accessed August 18, 2017. journals.uic.edu/ojs/index.php/fm/article/view/3765/3074.

Keeler, Hali R. *Working with Library Collections: an Introduction for Support Staff*. Library Support Staff Handbooks 4. Lanham, MD: Rowman & Littlefield, 2017.

OCLC. "Policies." WebJunction. Last modified 2017. Accessed August 24, 2017. www.webjunction.org/explore-topics/policies-procedures.html.

Oder, Norman. "Racist Group Takes Advantage of PL Meeting Room Policies." *Library Journal* 127, no. 17 (October 15, 2002).

Outagamie Waupaca Library System. "Sample Library Policies for the Small Public Library." Accessed August 12, 2017. www.owlsweb.org/l4l/sample-library-policies-small-public-library.

Power, Charles. "8 Advantages of Having Workplace Policies." *Employment Law Handbook*. Last modified June 13, 2012. Accessed August 10, 2017. www.employmentlawhandbook.com.au/8-advantages-of-having-workplace-policies/.

Reilly, Elizabeth. "Libraries as Sanctuary Spaces." *Unbound*. Last modified January 30, 2017. Accessed August 18, 2017. slis.simmons.edu/blogs/unbound/2017/01/30/libraries-sanctuary-spaces/.

Rosa, Kathy, ed. "The State of American Libraries 2017." American Library Association. Last modified April 2017. Accessed August 18, 2017. www.ala.org/news/sites/ala.org.news/files/content/State-of-Americas-Libraries-Report-2017.pdf.

Troknya, Mark. "Library Meeting Room Conflicts." Public Libraries Online. Last modified April 26, 2016. Accessed August 17, 2017. publiclibrariesonline.org/2016/04/library-meeting-room-conflicts/.

University of California. "Determining Whether a Statement Is a Policy or a Procedure." UCOP, Ethics, Compliance and Audit Services, Universitywide Policy Office. Last modified 2015. Accessed August 12, 2017. ucop.edu/ethics-compliance-audit-services/policy/.

University of Kansas. "Section 5. Developing Personnel Policies." Community Tool Box. Last modified 2017. Accessed August 12, 2017. www.ctb.ku.edu/en/table-of-contents/structure/hiring-and-training/personnel-policies/main.

Zielbauer, Paul. "Shouts and Scuffles at White Supremacy Rally." *New York Times*. March 11, 2001. Last modified April 11, 2001. Accessed August 17, 2017. www.nytimes.com/2001/03/11/nyregion/shouts-and-scuffles-at-white-supremacy-rally.html?mcubz=0.

CHAPTER 7

Budgeting and Fiscal Management

LSS know the basic purposes and concepts of budgeting and are able to request, defend, and follow a budget for library activities. (ALA-LSSC Supervision and Management Competency #8)

Topics Covered in This Chapter:

- Budget Basics
  - o Collapsed and Expanded
  - o Income Sources
  - o Operating Expenses
  - o Capital Costs
  - o Balance Sheet—Assets and Liabilities
  - o Balanced Budgets
- Budget Planning and Presentation Processes
- Line Items and Cost Centers
- Monitoring the Budget
  - o Audit
- Examples of School and Public Library Expenditure Functions and Codes

Key Terms:

Assets: These items are the investment funds, real estate, and financial resources the library may use to meet future operating costs, expenditures, building projects, or other commitments.

Audit: In this formal process, a certified accountant who does not work for the library or parent institution is contracted annually to review the library's income and expenditures to ensure all financials are in order.

Balanced budget: In any library budget, the income is expected to equal the amount of expenditures. In other words, the amount of funds taken in each year by a library must be expended on personnel, operating expenses, or investments.

Budget: This is an annual process of planning the income and expenditures required to operate the library for the coming year.

Budget narrative: This is an amount of detail, description, or justification written by the library director to explain what the numbers in the budget spreadsheet represent, how the costs were arrived at, and how the library objective will be achieved if the budget is approved.

Calendar year: This is a twelve-month period that begins January 1 and ends December 31.

Collapsed budget: This type of budget document or presentation is a summary of the main income and personnel and operating expenses for the library.

Cost center: This is the library department, service, or other unit to which annual expenses are estimated in the annual budget or charged for accounting purposes.

Diversification: This is a strategy used to avoid extreme financial risks whereby the library endowment is invested in multiple ways, such as mutual funds, bonds, income property, and so on.

Endowment: A library endowment is an income or property given to the library to help sustain its operation. An endowment fund can be made up of past and current donations or bequests by individuals or estates for sustained support of the library.

Fiscal year: This is a twelve-month period used for accounting purposes and preparing financial statements, such as the library budget. A common fiscal year many libraries use begins July 1 and ends June 30.

Level services: This type of budget is a funding plan that allows for providing current services "as is" in the next budget cycle. Libraries that are funded for level services typically only receive an increase for personnel contracts and anticipated inflationary costs for materials, supplies, or equipment. New library initiatives or services are not budgeted.

Liabilities: The opposite of assets, liabilities are financial obligations that are reported on the library balance sheet. Liabilities must equal or total the same amount as the assets in a budget. They account for how the assets are being used for library expenditures, operating costs, or investments.

Line item: This is a line that appears on a separate entry in a fiscal budget, balance sheet, or accounting ledger.

Operating expenses: In addition to staff, these are the items such as postage, utilities, fuel, maintenance, materials and supplies, vehicle replacement, and so forth required to open the library and provide its services each year.

Reconcile: This is an accounting process whereby the library director and other staff review line items during the year to ensure transactions are complete and review spending and income accounts to be certain they are consistent with the approved budget.

Preparing a library **budget** is an annual process that involves planning for acquiring the income and matching it to the anticipated expenditures needed to run the library for the coming year. There are many steps in budgeting, such as securing quotes and estimating costs for future purchases of materials and databases and allocating sufficient funds for staff salaries, benefits, and other compensation. Budgeting also includes capital expenses for the building and equipment, maintenance and replacement of technology, and many other predictable—and unpredictable—costs for maintaining library staff and services.

This chapter will explain how library boards and library directors create budgets and the role LSS have in many of the steps. The processes school, public, academic, and special libraries may use to request, defend, and follow the budget in the annual cycle will also be explored.

BUDGET BASICS

Budgets for all types of libraries typically follow the **fiscal year** rather than the **calendar year**. The calendar year is familiar, with the year beginning January 1 and ending December 31. A fiscal year is a twelve-month period used for accounting purposes and preparing financial statements, such as the library budget. The majority of government, academic, school, and other institutions do not budget on the calendar year but rather on the fiscal year, which most often begins July 1 of the current year and ends June 30 of the following year. A less popular fiscal year begins on October 1 and ends the following September 30. For municipalities and educational institutions, July 1 through June 30 is the most common fiscal year.

The fiscal year is split between two calendar years and is often written like this: FY 18–19.

TEXTBOX 7.1: EXPLANATION OF FY 18–19

FY stands for Fiscal Year
18 represents 2018
19 represents 2019
FY 18–19 will begin on July 1, 2018, and end June 30, 2019

What the fiscal year means for librarians is that they often must begin planning for the budget long before July 1. It is not uncommon to begin the process six to nine months ahead. Public school and town libraries that receive funding from local taxpayers go through a budget planning process similar to the police, public works, and other town agencies or departments.

Collapsed and Expanded

Budgets are often presented in two forms: collapsed or expanded. A **collapsed budget** is a summary of the main personnel and operating expenses. Depending upon the library, it may have more detail than the cost centers shown in table 7.1.

Table 7.1.   Collapsed vs. Expanded Professional Development Budget Item

Collapsed		Expanded	
Professional Development	$8,515.00	Dues and Subscriptions	$1,200.00
		Transportation and Hotel	$4,410.00
		Registration	$1,935.00
		Books and Materials	$200.00
		Meals	$770.00
			$8,515.00

The idea of a collapsed budget is to give the community a summary breakdown of the budget.

An expanded budget is primarily for the decision makers who will present, approve, use, and monitor the budget. Such decision makers are the library board, library director, town manager, and town or institution finance committee. An expanded budget has a budget narrative or other details that explain why the expense is necessary. Table 7.1 shows a comparison of an expense, professional development, in a collapsed vs. expanded budget for a library with three professional librarians who will be attending state and national conferences.

Income Sources

All budgets are composed of two main parts: income and expenses. Income or revenue is the funds that will be available to support the operation and staffing of the library in the coming year. Income for libraries come from many places. In public libraries, whether they are municipal, school, or academic, the primary source of funding is tax dollars. A recent national survey of public libraries by *Library Journal* found that funding for most municipal libraries has increased from the 2006–2009 recession with total operating budgets averaging a 3.4 percent increase.[1] In the same survey, two-thirds of the libraries relied on annual funding from their local governments. Public school libraries also rely heavily on taxpayer funding for their operations. Academic libraries are primarily funded by tuition. If they are public universities, they also receive state support.

Donations made up nearly 2 percent of public library budgets in 2016 with the larger libraries typically receiving the most where there could be a stronger outreach for philanthropy.[2] Donations may come unexpectedly from patrons, community agencies, or businesses. It is important for libraries to work with accounting experts to be sure they can receive donations without penalty. One way to do this is to establish a friends group.

Friends groups are always so helpful for their volunteering as well as fundraising. Friends groups that have established legal status to be a nonprofit by formally obtaining 501(c)(3) federal tax exemption status as well as their state income tax exemption may accept donations without penalty or obligation of taxes. In the majority of states that have a state income tax, the process would be similar as that found in textbox 7.2.

LSS often serve as contacts with friends groups or may even be members. Because LSS have direct contact with the public and are often the face of the library, it is

Figure 7.1. Library fundraiser. *istock/Thinglass*

important for LSS to know the patrons who are supporters of the library and to welcome them accordingly.

Another 2 percent of budgets came from grants, again with larger libraries receiving more of a significant share. This is most likely because larger libraries may have the staff required for the often extensive process of applying and monitoring grants. With many states in dire financial straits, there are fewer grants available to support the work of libraries. This shifts the burden back onto local taxpayers and fundraising efforts of libraries. The following chapter will be about how libraries can maximize their efforts in the areas of grant writing and fundraising.

Another source of funding, particularly for private libraries, is the income from **endowments** and investments. A library endowment is an income or property given to the library to help sustain its operation. An endowment fund can be made up of past and current donations or bequests by individuals or estates for sustained support of the library. Libraries with endowment funds typically have a board-approved

---

TEXTBOX 7.2: STEPS FOR LIBRARY FRIENDS GROUPS TO BECOME NONPROFITS IN CONNECTICUT[3]

1. Incorporate as an organization in Connecticut.—State
2. Obtain an employee identification number (EIN).—Federal
3. Obtain tax-exempt status (501[c][3]).—Federal
4. Obtain Connecticut Income Tax exemption.—State
5. Obtain Connecticut Sales and Use Tax exemptions.—State
6. Register as a charitable organization.—State

investment policy. For example, the Kalamazoo Public Library states on its website key goals of its investment policy, which are:

1. To provide funds to support projects as designated by the donor or as identified by the Library Board; and
2. To ensure the continuing availability and growth of such funds in the future.[4]

Libraries with endowments work with qualified financial experts to ensure the holdings of the portfolio are both diverse and invested in blue chip or other instruments that ensure growth at a minimum of risk. The library board should be informed at regular intervals about the return on the investment, and they should formally review their investment strategy every two to five years, depending upon the market. **Diversification** is also very important to ensure a library endowment is not heavily invested in just one or two instruments that may suddenly tank and lose their value.

Finally, there are other sources of income a library may have from patron services such as the copier, rental of rooms, fines for overdue or lost or damaged books, and so forth. All income must be carefully recorded and deposited and accounted for in the budgeting process. Schools and academic libraries, depending on whether they are public or private, may have similar sources of income as discussed above. Corporate libraries are in institutions that are for profit and receive their funding from the profits of the parent company.

Operating Expenses

We have so far talked about the income or funding of the library. Libraries must budget for all of the money they need to operate during the year, thus the term "operating expenses." Library directors and boards must plan for the expenses of the coming year. This side of the budget often involves many staff, including LSS who work with patrons and materials and often have excellent suggestions for new acquisitions to improve the library environment and services. Operating expenses are the obligations a library has to provide services during the year. They recur regularly and can be anticipated year to year.[5] Here are some of the typical operating expenditures libraries budget for each year:

Personnel: These are the salaries and benefits for all full- and part-time staff. Some budgets will specify professional librarians from other categories of library support staff. In the budget will be a line for overtime, longevity pay, and other salary adjustments for sick leave or expected promotions. New staff to be hired during the upcoming year must be budgeted for. From the personnel part of the budget will also come Social Security and any other employer contribution on wages that will be due state or city governments.
Professional development: Budgeted are the expenses of professional meetings, workshops, membership dues, travel, training, and other supports for library staff to enhance their skills and learning.
Maintenance of facilities: Annual maintenance of facilities includes small repairs and janitorial and grounds maintenance. Any large or planned projects should be budgeted under capital costs.

Utilities: Most libraries, unless they are being covered by public works, a board of education, or a larger university or college, budget for electricity, heating fuel, water, air conditioning, cable, Internet service, phone, and so forth. As in our homes, libraries must pay for the utilities they use.

Materials and supplies: In this category are the cost of library books, DVDs, e-books, media, and other items that circulate to patrons. In addition, materials include supplies used for processing, children's services, marketing, and so forth. Materials are a very important part of a library budget. LSS may make suggestions to supervisors for this category as they have firsthand knowledge of the collections and the type of materials most popular with patrons as well as the supplies they need in their work.

Software fees: The acquisition of library software and the annual leasing of databases account for this operating expense category. Some libraries budget their integrated library system (ILS) here as well as their website support.

Computer replacement and technology: Large investments in technology are budgeted under capital costs; however, annual leases on printers, copiers, or other devices are listed under operating expenses. Inexpensive technology or single units may be acquired here.

Equipment: Small equipment is required to maintain services and provide a safe environment for library patrons including security cameras, book carts, vacuum cleaners, and so forth that can be planned for in operating expenses. While the same items are not purchased each year, an amount budgeted in this line item allows the library director to acquire or replace a variety of small equipment annually.

Maintenance: LSS can support the budget process by recommending maintenance of equipment they observe is in need of cleaning or repair.

Vehicle usage: While the purchase of a car or bookmobile is a capital cost, a vehicle's annual ongoing expenses, including fuel, insurance, and maintenance, are budgeted in the operating budget. If the library has access to an institution car, such as from the university's or company's fleet, it may have to reimburse usage expenses.

Capital Costs

Capital costs appear separately on the budget spreadsheet because they occur irregularly and often require special funding efforts, such as applying for grants or additional appropriations from the town or funding source.[6] Capital costs are also the location in a library budget for a new building, renovation, or other major campaign. Here are examples of common capital costs:

Facilities: Remodel of the existing library, building additional rooms, or new construction that replaces the current library all are budgeted for in the capital budget as they are extraordinary expenses that cannot be absorbed in the operating budget. Often it may take multiple years of capital planning and fundraising to see a building project through its completion. Each year capital costs are accounted for in the budget separately from operating expenses.

Figure 7.2.   Library renovation. *istock/Supamon R*

Furniture: Furniture and furnishings require budgeting for both new items and replacement or repair. This includes tables, chairs, carpeting, shelving, and so on.

Equipment: There are many kinds of costly equipment required to maintain services and provide a safe and comfortable environment for library patrons including security systems, self-checkout equipment, video production studio equipment, heating or cooling units, and so forth.

Computer replacement and technology: Libraries commonly provide a variety of computing options for patrons that include desktops, tablets, and Wi-Fi support for personal devices. In this category, audio and video equipment, makerspace equipment, and any major hardware or network acquisition are budgeted. Many libraries have a multiyear replacement plan for staff and patron computers. LSS who work with technology may suggest when a unit is in need of replacement.

System upgrades: Major integrated library system (ILS) upgrades or replacement can be considered capital costs if they cannot be absorbed as an operating expenditure.

Vehicles: If a vehicle is to be owned, its purchase is budgeted here. Libraries may lease a vehicle rather than own it.

Later in this chapter are templates of how income, operating expenses, and capital costs are presented in school, academic, special, and public library budgets.

Balance Sheet—Assets and Liabilities

Some libraries, particularly private institutions with endowments that are not part of an educational institution or municipality, rely heavily on investments for future projects and operations. These investments are called **assets**. Assets are funds, property, and other financial resources that can be used to meet future debts or commitments. Library directors and boards work with accounting experts to be sure assets are restricted in a way that they are only to be used by the library and will be nontaxable. Examples of library assets could be a donated building used as a rental property or savings, checking, and money market accounts.

The opposite side of assets are **liabilities**. A liability is a financial obligation. Liabilities are reported under or on the second half of the library balance sheet. Liabilities must equal or total the same amount of the assets in a budget, and they account for how the assets are being used for library expenditures, operating costs, or investments. For example, a library may have an asset of $100,000 in its board-restricted money market account. The liability of this asset is its continued equity investment in the money market account where it is anticipated to make income through dividends and interest. See figure 7.3 for an example of a balance sheet of assets and liabilities.

Assets and Liabilities Balance Sheet

	August, 2017
ASSETS	
Current Assets	
Checking/Savings	
1010 · TD Bank Checking Account	5,000.00
Total Checking/Savings	5,000.00
Accounts Receivable	
1030 · Accounts Receivable	500.00
Total Accounts Receivable	500.00
Other Current Assets	
1040 · Board Restricted Assets	
1042 · Morgan Stanley Investment	10,000.00
1043 · M Stanley Change in Mkt Value	100,000.00
Total 1041 · Morgan Stanley Investment	110,000.00
Total 1040 · Board Restricted Assets	110,000.00
Total Other Current Assets	110,000.00
Total Current Assets	115,500.00
TOTAL ASSETS	115,500.00
LIABILITIES & EQUITY	
Liabilities	
Current Liabilities	
2010 · Accounts Payable	500.00
Total Accounts Payable	500.00
Other Current Liabilities	
Total Other Current Liabilities	0.00
Total Current Liabilities	500.00
Total Liabilities	500.00
Equity	
3010 · Beginning Balance Equity	100,000.00
32000 · Unrestricted Net Assets	5,000.00
Net Income	10,000.00
Total Equity	115,000.00
TOTAL LIABILITIES & EQUITY	**115,500.00**

Figure 7.3. Assets and liabilities balance sheet. *Courtesy of the author*

LSS can be better informed about the budgeting process of the library by becoming familiar with the balance sheets of their library and other nonprofit organizations. These can often be found online at the library or organization's website, especially if they are public institutions. Discuss with supervisors your role in the budget process and seek areas where you can be supportive such as researching current costs for maintenance or replacement of equipment, technology, or needed furnishings. Talk with others who also work with budgets to learn how both municipal and for-profit businesses develop their annual financial plans.

Balanced Budgets

As we saw on the balance sheet in figure 7.3, the assets are required to equal the amount of the liabilities. In any budget the expected income is to equal the amount of the annual expenditures. In other words, in a **balanced budget**, the amount of funds taken in each year by a library must be expended on personnel, operating expenses, or investments. As we also saw in figure 7.3, investing endowment or other funds is an expenditure. All budgets must be balanced, and the amount libraries may set aside for investments must follow the legal guidelines of their charters and incorporation documents so as not to incur tax penalty. Accountants will guide library boards and directors as to the amount they may set aside in assets to keep nonprofit status.

BUDGET PLANNING AND PRESENTATION PROCESSES

The library director is responsible for developing its budget and presenting it to the next level of decision makers. In school libraries, most likely this would be the building principal, who will accept the budget as is or will ask for changes in line items. In special or corporate libraries, the next level of management may be a division head or vice president. Large academic library directors are often supervised by a dean or, if the college is small, a vice president or similar level administrator. Directors of public libraries that are a department of the town or city and primarily funded by taxpayers report to a town manager, mayor, or other town official who reviews and forwards the budget to the next level of decision makers. Public libraries that are not fully funded by taxpayers or not town departments most often have their budgets approved by their library board, who function as both a management and finance committee with final say.

There are numerous approaches to planning a library budget, but all involve some similar steps:

TEXTBOX 7.3: STEPS IN PLANNING THE ANNUAL LIBRARY BUDGET

1. Keep notes, including a "wish list" during the year in preparation.
2. Six to nine months prior to formal budget adoption, begin drafting a library budget. Supervisors may seek input from LSS for recommendation or LSS can suggest materials, equipment, and maintenance needs they encounter on the job.
3. Library director obtains guidelines from his or her supervisor to create one or more budgets: a percentage increase budget, a percentage decrease budget, or a zero-increase budget.

4. LSS can help and support supervisors by researching costs, vendors, and other information for accurate pricing.
5. Library director meets with supervisor frequently to develop the budget, answer questions, and make revisions.
6. Five to six months prior to formal budget adoption, library director finalizes budget and presents it to library board, principal, or direct supervisor for approval. In a large institution, the library budget is incorporated as a function or department in the overall budget document.

Library directors work with their staff and supervisors to find efficiencies in the budget. For example, database contracts can be reviewed and, if possible, renegotiated or purchased through consortium bidding for best pricing. In today's financial climate, librarians need to be sharp shoppers for both value and cost savings in order to get the most for each allocated dollar. LSS can greatly support this process in their own research and contacts.

After the budget is prepared by the library director, there are many more steps and meetings before it is adopted. Depending upon the town, educational institution, or parent entity, the process will vary. Below are three scenarios of the budget adoption process for a public library, a private library, and a K–12 school.

1. Public Library: Mayflower Public Library, located in a New England state, has a multilevel budget adoption process. The library is a town department, and the director reports to the town manager, who presents all town department budgets in one document to the town finance committee in early March. (a) The finance committee reviews each department budget in a series of evening meetings. On the night of the library budget review, the library director and board members are on hand to answer questions of committee members. After deliberations, the committee votes on a budget that they will forward to the town council. (b) It is early April when the library director and board meet with the manager and town council who carefully examine the finance committee's recommendation. The council may accept the recommendation or vote their own changes. The library budget the council approves will be included in the full town budget for adoption by the taxpayers. (c) It is now May and time for a town meeting where all property owners of Mayflower are invited to vote on the proposed annual budget for the coming year. With approval, the library has its income, operating expenses, and capital improvement plan for the next twelve months beginning July 1.
2. Private Library: The Butler Memorial Library is a small library located in a southern state that was donated by a wealthy family more than one hundred years ago. The library director reports to the board, who has both financial and management authority. The library has an endowment of $5 million with donations each year of approximately $50,000. The library board asks the director to present the annual budget to them three months before the fiscal year. (a) In April the director presents a budget that will use 5 percent income from the endowment. However, there is need for capital improvements as the roof, windows, and heating systems are in dire need of replacement. The library director presents several options to the board on how to accommodate these expenses. The finance subcommittee of the board is charged to work with the

director to find efficiencies in the budget that may have been overlooked and to review the library investments. (b) At the May meeting, the library board hears the report from the board finance committee about investments and expenditures. The finance committee has a few small changes to the director's budget that he agrees with. A vote is taken and approval of the budget is acquired.

3. K–12 School: The building principal asks the library media specialist to prepare the department budget and present it to him at the end of October using the guidelines she has from the district schools superintendent. (a) Meetings occur with principal and others prior to the presentation. At the presentation, the library media specialist proposes three budgets that follow the superintendent's guidelines for new spending, less spending, and **level services**. (b) Principal accepts library budget and includes it in her building budget that is presented to superintendent in December. (c) In January, superintendent presents school district budget to board of education. Many meetings occur over the drafting of district budget. (d) In March board of education presents budget to town finance committee. (e) Finance committee presents budget to town council in April, when the town also reviews other town departments, including the public library. (f) Budget of town council goes to taxpayers for a town meeting approval vote in May. (g) If budget fails, a referendum vote will occur several weeks later and will continue to do so until a budget is approved.

Regardless of the process, it is prudent of the library director, board, and staff to follow the budget approval process. At certain intervals, there is opportunity for staff and the public to speak for or against a budget. The more community support and interaction with decision makers, the greater the likelihood the library budget will be approved. LSS can do much to encourage patrons to support their libraries as well as to individually speak or otherwise communicate their opinions during the process.

LSS Support the Budget Process

1. Become informed about the financial situations of your state, town, and institution that will affect the library.
2. Formulate your opinion about library funding. LSS have great insight about the needs and expenditures of the library.
3. Speak with others including family members, friends, patrons, and community members whose support is needed to approve the library budget.
4. Plan to speak at public hearings about the library. Your insights are invaluable!
5. Use social media and print media to convey your feelings. You may want to talk with your supervisor if you choose to speak or write to help you formulate your approach.
6. Follow the budget process in all of its steps. Attending meetings as a member of the public does make a difference to decision makers who see people who make the effort to show their support for the library.

LINE ITEMS AND COST CENTERS

Budgets are constructed of many **line items** that add up to a total or final amount. Line items identify unique categories of funding, such as library print books (643)

Table 7.2. Examples of the Line Items for 600 Elementary School Library Materials

Code	Category	Amount
610	Library Supplies	
	Laminating supplies for second-grade book project	$200
	Printer cartridges for writing center	$300
	General supplies (transparency film, pens, library supplies)	$200
643	Books	
	Titles for new science curriculum: weather, geology, astronomy	$900
	Collection development schedule (900s); support of social studies units: American history, countries, geography	$2,000
	Professional books: brain research faculty study group	$200
	Software/Non-Print	
	Iowa Children's Choice titles	$400
644	Periodicals	
	Paper and online subscriptions	$400
650	Computer Software	
	Assistive technology requested by SCI classes	$200
	Additional Kidspiration licenses	$400
660	Audiovisual/Non-Print	
	DVDs for General Music	$148
	Audio book downloads for third grade	$380

or library periodicals (644). Table 7.2 gives examples of other common library line items in the 600 materials category with brief explanations for each line. Later in this chapter, we will examine all of the codes 100 through 900 and the accompanying categories schools and academic libraries use in line item budgeting.

Public schools and public academic libraries adopt a budgeting format according to their state statutes. In addition to line item budgeting, there is another type of budget format with **cost centers**. Cost center budgeting uses broader categories than line item budgeting; however, the goal is similar in that like expenditures are grouped together either by material type or subdepartment. Cost centers also use codes. There is not the detail specificity or as much descriptive **budget narrative** in cost centers as in line item budgeting. Budget narrative is accompanying detail, description, or justification written by the library director that explains what the numbers in the budget spreadsheet represent, how the costs were arrived, and the library objective to be achieved if the budget is approved. LSS who work in a public or private library will find it more likely uses cost centers in presenting its income and expenditure budget plan. A municipal library will have a budget function code that distinguishes it from other town departments. The Groton Public Library in Connecticut has the function code of 1063 with four cost centers as shown in table 7.3.[7]

Table 7.3. Excerpt of Cost Center Budgeting

Cost Center	Category
10630	Leadership and General Support
10631	Circulation and Technical Services
10632	Audiovisual and Video Services
10635	Public Services

The cost center codes for the Groton Public Library are a combination of the library function code 1063 plus the broad category single digit. Thus the cost center code 10635 is composed of 1063 for the function "Library" and the digit 5 that represents "Public Services." At a glance people can get a summary idea of how much expense is associated with each cost center. The sum of the cost center expenditures add up to the total amount of the budget requested.

After the cost centers are introduced, the library budget is broken down into two categories: personnel expenses and **operating expenses**. Personnel is the highest expense for a library, with 85 percent of the budget for staffing. The remaining 15 percent is for materials, building, technology, and so forth. In a cost center budget, there will be the annual expense of all of the library staff categories—not names of the people—listed. Under operating expenses, or what it takes to operate the library in addition to staff, there could be a long list of items such as postage, utilities, fuel, maintenance, materials and supplies, vehicle replacement, and so forth. The library director has to project all of the operating needs for the coming year with their accurate prices.

MONITORING THE BUDGET

Once the budget is approved, LSS may be involved with the expenditures that relate to their work. It is a good idea to keep a spreadsheet of the real cost of expenditures and the current balance. The library bookkeeper will also monitor the spending of the budget, and it is helpful to regularly **reconcile** your figures with his to find agreement or discrepancies.

Audit

The **audit** is a formal process whereby a certified accountant who does not work for the library or parent institution annually does a complete review of income and expenditures.

An IRS audit is a review/examination of an organization's or individual's accounts and financial information to ensure information is reported correctly according to the tax laws and to verify the reported amount of tax is correct.[8] As libraries are nonprofit, tax-exempt institutions, they are not subject to IRS audits, but they do require an audit process to ensure that all financials are in order. An "independent audit" is performed by a public accounting firm or an individual who is a certified public accountant (CPA) and who is engaged to provide an independent opinion to the management as to whether or not the nonprofit's financial statements/records comply with accounting standards known as "GAAP" or generally accepted accounting principles.[9]

If the library receives federal, state, or grant funds, most likely it is required to be audited to ensure all stakeholders—staff, board members, and others—are making sound financial and management decisions for the good of the library. Audit reports are presented to board members and, if required by the state or town, are filed with the appropriate agency as part of the financial record of the library.

An audit will also examine the percentage of funds spent each month. As we do in our personal lives, library directors and their supervisors have to plan for contingencies or unexpected interruptions to the income. If the funding agency is in crisis, such as a town or state that is in crisis and must withhold funds to the library, the director may need to be able to meet payroll with other line items such as equipment or materials. By the end of the twelve months, however, all annual funds should be expended, thus the reason why some libraries have significantly large acquisitions of materials in late spring when, with a sigh of relief, the horizon is clear to spend down the budget appropriately.

LSS can help with the audit by following all designated procedures for collecting fines and any other handling of money from patrons. They can also keep accurate records of any funds they have been given to spend and to reconcile any receipts and records with the library bookkeeper.

EXAMPLES OF SCHOOL AND PUBLIC LIBRARY EXPENDITURE FUNCTIONS AND CODES

Below are two examples of the expenditure codes of libraries, one for schools and the other for public libraries. LSS should be aware that every library could have its own variation of how it constructs its budget and the template format. Academic libraries vary greatly using internal codes and functions, depending upon if they are state institutions, grant-based, or private colleges. There is no one-sized shoe that fits all!

1. *K–12 School Library: Function 2222*
   The function describes the activity for which a service or material object is acquired. The major functions of a school district are classified into seven areas:

   1000 Instruction
   2000 Support Services
   3000 Enterprise and Community Services
   4000 Facilities Acquisition and Construction
   5000 Other Uses (Interagency/Fund Transactions and Debt Service)
   6000 Contingency
   7000 Unappropriated Ending Fund Balance

   Because school libraries are a support service, the function is in the 2000 range, specifically 2222 for libraries. Below in table 7.4 are the codes used by public school library media centers, which are similar or with slight variation for most budgets.[10]

Table 7.4.   2222—Library Media Center

Code	Category	Amount	Rationale
111	Professional salaries		
112	Classified salaries		
210	Public employee retirement		
230	Other required payroll costs		
310	Data processing and annual subscription databases		
410	Consumable supplies and materials		
411	Instructional supplies		
412	Library supplies		
430	Library books		
433	Repair and maintenance of equipment		
440	Library periodicals		
470	Computer hardware		
480	Computer software		
580	Travel		
692	Professional materials		
693	Audiovisual materials		
694	Software		
731	Instructional equipment—replacement		
732	Noninstructional equipment—replacement		
733	New instructional equipment		
734	New noninstructional equipment		
810	Memberships and dues		

2. *Public Library: Function depends on town or private accounting system.*
What type of template a public library uses depends upon its funding source. If it is a town department, it will follow the accounting practices set forth by the town and state. If it is private, it may not follow these conventions.

Table 7.5.   1063—Public Library, Town Department

Code	Service	Actual FYE 2018	Adjusted FYE 2018	Estimate FYE 2018	Request FYE 2019	Council FYE 2019	Final FYE 2019
5101	Full-time personnel						
5102	Part-time personnel						
5104	Overtime pay						
5105	Longevity pay						
5109	Salary adjustments						
5112	Sick incentive						
5116	Wage continuation						
5151	Social Security						
5201	Postage						
5210	Professional development						
5220	Utilities/fuel/mileage						
5230	Payments/contributions						
5260	Repair and maintenance						
5261	Software maintenance						
5290	Technical services						
5300	Materials and supplies						
5317	Vehicle fuel						
5318	Computer replacement						
5400	Equipment/furniture						

CHAPTER SUMMARY

Library budgeting is a complex process that requires the input of many people. At a certain point, as we saw in examples of the budget process, it is no longer in the control of the library director; rather community and other decision makers ultimately approve the library budget. The LSS who know the basic purposes and concepts of budgeting and are able to request, defend, and follow a budget for library activities provide invaluable support in the process as they enhance their own knowledge of library financials.

DISCUSSION QUESTIONS

1. What are the different types of income streams school, public, special, and academic libraries depend upon?
2. What is a library endowment and what ways may they grow and be managed?
3. What are the operating expenses of your library? What are the capital expenses of your library? Obtain your library budget document to find these.
4. What steps are in a typical library audit and why are annual audits important?
5. What are the differences between a line item budget and a cost center budget? How can LSS be helpful in identifying needs in either a line item or cost center?

ACTIVITY

Obtain a current copy of your local school, academic, or public library budget. If it is a publicly funded budget, it most likely is available online at the library website. If it is a private library, you may have to ask to see a copy.

Answer these questions about the library income from the budget:

1. What is the amount of income the library expects for the coming year?
2. What are the sources of this income?
3. What increase is anticipated from the library investments or endowments?

Answer these questions about operating costs found in the library budget:

1. What amount did the library budget for salary and wages for staff?
2. What amount did the library budget for operating expenses?
3. What is your conclusion about the cost ratio, that is, the amount of money spent on salary and wages compared to all of the operating expenses for the library?

Using the information from your analysis of income and expenditures, write a two-page paper that responds to these questions:

1. Why is it necessary for the library to develop its budget?
2. How may the library director and library board use the budget during the coming year?
3. If there was an unexpected budget cut, how could the library financially survive? Cite one article you have researched as an example.
4. Do you think the budget you analyzed is adequate for its services and expenses? Where would you increase it? Decrease it? Explain your reasoning.

5. What other sources of income do you think the library could obtain that are not already in the budget? What methods or ways could the library director and board obtain more sustained income for library operating and capital expenses?

NOTES

1. Lisa Peet, "Keeping Up," *Library Journal* 142, no. 2 (February 1, 2017), search.ebsco host.com/login.aspx?direct=true&db=aph&AN=121496779&authtype=cookie,cpid& custid=csl&site=ehost-live&scope=site.

2. Ibid.

3. Friends of Connecticut Libraries, "Handbook," last modified 2017, accessed August 15, 2017, foclib.org/handbook.

4. Kalamazoo Public Library, "Endowment Fund Investment Policy," last modified 2017, accessed August 15, 2017, www.kpl.gov/policies/endowment-fund-investment.aspx.

5. Wisconsin Department of Public Instruction, "Developing the Library Budget," *Trustee Essentials: A Handbook for Wisconsin Public Library Trustees,* last modified 2016, accessed August 22, 2017, dpi.wi.gov/sites/default/files/imce/pld/pdf/TE08.pdf.

6. Ibid.

7. Town of Groton, Connecticut, "Town of Groton Adopted FYE 2018 Budget," Welcome to the Town of Groton, last modified 2017, accessed August 14, 2017, www.groton-ct.gov/ budget/fye2018-adopted/default.asp.

8. Internal Revenue Service, "IRS Audits," last modified 2017, accessed August 22, 2017, www.irs.gov/businesses/small-businesses-self-employed/irs-audits.

9. Foundation Center, "Where Can I Learn More About Nonprofit Audits?" Grantspace, last modified 2017, accessed August 22, 2017, grantspace.org/tools/knowledge-base/Non profit-Management/Accountability/nonprofit-audits.

10. Oregon Department of Education, "Program Budgeting and Accounting Manual for School Districts and Education Service Districts in Oregon," last modified 2012, accessed August 22, 2017, /www.oregon.gov/ode/students-and-family/childnutrition/SNP/Docu ments/2012-pbam-manual.pdf.

REFERENCES, SUGGESTED READINGS, AND WEBSITES

Foundation Center. "Where Can I Learn More About Nonprofit Audits?" Grantspace. Last modified 2017. Accessed August 22, 2017. grantspace.org/tools/knowledge-base/Nonprofit -Management/Accountability/nonprofit-audits.

Friends of Connecticut Libraries. "Handbook." Last modified 2017. Accessed August 15, 2017. foclib.org/handbook.

Haigh, Craig A. "The Art of Planning." *Fire Engineering* 369, no. 8 (August 2016): 67–72. search.ebscohost.com/login.aspx?direct=true&db=aph&AN=117274873&authtype=cookie ,cpid&custid=csl&site=ehost-live&scope=site.

Internal Revenue Service. "IRS Audits." Last modified 2017. Accessed August 22, 2017. www .irs.gov/businesses/small-businesses-self-employed/irs-audits.

Iowatown School Library Budget Request 20XX-20XX. Iowa Department of Education. Accessed August 14, 2017. www.educateiowa.gov/.../0708_pk12_school-library_budget-request-template.

Kalamazoo Public Library. "Endowment Fund Investment Policy." Last modified 2017. Accessed August 15, 2017. www.kpl.gov/policies/endowment-fund-investment.aspx.

Oregon Department of Education. "Program Budgeting and Accounting Manual for School Districts and Education Service Districts in Oregon." Last modified 2012. Accessed August 22, 2017. www.oregon.gov/ode/students-and-family/childnutrition/SNP/Documents/2012-pbam-manual.pdf.

Peet, Lisa. "Keeping Up." *Library Journal* 142, no. 2 (February 1, 2017): 22–24. search.ebscohost.com/login.aspx?direct=true&db=aph&AN=121496779&authtype=cookie,cpid&custid=csl&site=ehost-live&scope=site.

Town of Groton, Connecticut. "Town of Groton Adopted FYE 2018 Budget." Welcome to the Town of Groton. Last modified 2017. Accessed August 14, 2017. www.groton-ct.gov/budget/fye2018-adopted/default.asp.

Wisconsin Department of Public Instruction. "Developing the Library Budget." *Trustee Essentials: A Handbook for Wisconsin Public Library Trustees*. Last modified 2016. Accessed August 22, 2017. dpi.wi.gov/sites/default/files/imce/pld/pdf/TE08.pdf.

CHAPTER 8

Fundraising and Grant Writing

LSS know the basics of fundraising and grant writing and are able to prepare a proposal to raise funds to support library programs. (ALA-LSSC Supervision and Management Competency #9)

Topics Covered in This Chapter:

- Fundraising Basics
- Budgets
  - o Making the Plan
  - o The Annual Appeal
  - o Planned Giving
  - o Crowdsourcing
- Writing a Grant Proposal
- Promotional Aspects of Fundraising

Key Terms:

Annual appeal: An annual appeal is a solicitation of individuals that asks for support for the library and its programs. It is carried out through a combination of direct mail (usually solicitation letters and, if available, brochures) and one-on-one individual solicitations between a volunteer for the library and the individual being solicited.

Budgets: A budget is an estimate of income and expenses over a defined period of time, usually the library's fiscal year. It is critical for libraries to keep a budget in order to determine where funds are needed for allocation and the source from which they will come.

Crowdsourcing: Crowdsourcing is the concept used to solicit goods and services from the online community instead of from traditional outlets. It is often used to raise funds for a cause or an event.

Endowment: An endowment is a sum of money that is permanently invested in equities (stocks) and fixed income (bonds and CDs, etc.) in order to increase its size annually.

Fundraising: Fundraising is the process of getting voluntary donations from individuals and businesses to benefit a specific purpose. Fundraising is also known as development.

Grants: A grant is a sum of money given by an organization to a library (or other nonprofit) for the purpose of funding a project or initiative that will improve services or otherwise benefit the organization. The library must apply for a grant and meet certain qualifications to be considered.

Planned giving: Planned giving is a program designed for donors to gift financial support to the library during their lifetimes and after their deaths. It is a form of charitable giving that is arranged through wills and estate plans.

Stewardship: Stewardship is the cultivation and maintenance of relationships and is an important aspect of fundraising. Showing appreciation for past contributions and staying in contact with donors for future donations greatly increases the chances of continued giving.

Funding is how libraries pay the bills. Local taxes financially support public schools and most public libraries through their local town or county municipalities. What they receive impacts what services they can offer and can affect the quality of their services. The funding they receive may come from their state library through various programs, but these are, in turn, dependent on how well the state is funded by its governing body. There is a disturbing trend that, when budgets get tight, the library is often the first to take the cut. Obviously less money equals fewer resources. Many libraries are treading water to stay solvent.[1]

In this chapter, we will look at various methods of fundraising that libraries can use to augment their financial situation, including grant writing, so they can continue to provide the services that their patrons rely on.

FUNDRAISING BASICS

If a town, city, or county is struggling to fund its community, the schools' and public libraries' budgets will be similarly impacted. Libraries usually have unqualified support of a community in principle, but the funding may not follow. It is often necessary for a town to take proactive measures to support library funding.

Libraries need funding for the staff, collection, technology, and myriad other expenses that go into running a library. The library must have an idea of what funding it needs to accomplish this. They do that by creating a **budget**.

BUDGETS

Chapter 7 gave us a detailed overview of the budget process. Now we will look at it from a planning perspective.

To develop a library budget, it is necessary to first determine what the library expects to accomplish. For example, if a library's plan is to replace twenty-five computers within five years at a rate of five per year, then the budget would spread out that expense over the five years. Changing priorities such as increased costs, new services, or staffing may require that some expenses be shifted within a budget—or even eliminated.

Before a budget can be created, it is helpful if the person responsible for creating it knows the amount of funding available for the coming year and the source of those funds. Depending on how a library is funded, he may be able to anticipate expected income based on recent budgets, although a percentage change up or down is common. If a library is funded by its municipality, then he can count on the budget amount that was previously approved so he knows from the start how much he has to work with, although circumstances may necessitate adjustments. In one town, the public library was asked to make mid-year cuts due to a decrease in expected funding. It was also told that their next year's budget must come in another 5 percent lower. This is always problematic, and in what amounts to almost a Faustian bargain, the library must decide whether to cut staff, materials, or services to continue operation for the good of the community.

For libraries that are funded by **endowments** or investments, income is typically derived from a percentage of the funds. (In the academic library, in some cases, collections or even the entire building can be endowed by and dedicated to a large donor.) Without going into the specifics of investment policy, the rule of thumb recommends most organizations spend between 4 and 5 percent of the value of their endowment fund each year. (While the returns on investments can vary dramatically from year to year, it is prudent to take the same amount annually as the averages generally stabilize over a period of time.[2]) These allotted amounts, from a municipal budget or an endowment, plus expected annual **grants** (from the town or state) and anticipated fundraising revenue, make up the income that the library can use to calculate the expenses of the budget.

Programs and services will vary from library to library, but the basics of budgeting will remain the same. The two main expenses will be personnel (wages and benefits) and collections; the remainder will be a proportionately smaller expense.[3]

Not surprisingly, personnel costs are typically 60 to 80 percent of library expenditures. Collections take up approximately 10 to 20 percent of expenditures and consist of printed materials that can be divided into such categories as fiction, nonfiction, juvenile, and young adult; they can be even further divided by genres into adult fiction mysteries, romance, science fiction, and so on. Electronic materials would also be further broken down into additional budget items, or lines. Finally, a budget will have an area for other operating expenditures such as utilities, maintenance, audit, professional development, postage, insurance, heating cost, and programming; these expenses account for the remaining 10 to 20 percent. While these proportions may vary by region, the three areas of personnel, collections, and other operating expenses make up the basis for the typical library budget.

Ideally the projected income and the projected expenses will equal each other. If the income side comes up short, then the library must create a plan to make up for the shortfall.

Making the Plan

As noted previously, libraries have some dedicated funding sources, but they may not cover the entire budget. This is when the library must make a **fundraising** plan. There are steps to laying out the foundation for this plan:

1. Start with the mission.
    a. Your plan should identify specific strategies that support the library's mission.
2. Identify your priorities and costs.
    a. What are your gaps, and how can they advance the mission and serve the community?
    b. What are your revenue sources, and can they support all your needs?
    c. What are your costs, and how much will you need to fund the operation?
    d. What are your goals, and where will you find the money you need?
3. Develop your rationales.
    a. Articulate the reasons you have selected your priorities.
    b. Be able to explain why, for example, the collection needs enhancement.
    c. Use the data you collect to bolster your case.
4. Identify your prospects.
    a. Who donated to and supported the library last year?
    b. How can you make it easier for donors to give?
    c. Who will make the request? This is important because donors are much more likely to give when the right person asks for a gift.
5. Grow your donor base.
    a. Encourage those who already give to give more.
    b. Have library trustees identify higher-level prospects.
    c. Have donor appeals on your website, in all advertising, and at all events.
6. Use marketing and advocacy.
    a. Marketing communicates messages that influence people's behavior, not just persuading them to use your library but to support it.
    b. Marketing lets people know that the library needs private funding and makes it easy for an individual or organization to give.
    c. Advocacy is the process of advancing a cause or course of action, often to affect public opinion (such as writing letters or handing out flyers).
7. Measure your success.
    a. Target the goal of amount to be raised vis-à-vis the actual amount raised.
    b. Target the percentage of increase in giving vis-à-vis the actual percentage.
    c. Target the number of online donors vis-à-vis the actual number of online donors.

The most important element of fundraising is to ask, and most people will give if they are asked.[4] This brings us to another concept called "the ask." A fundraising "ask" isn't always about money. While some people on your radar may in fact be ready to be asked for money, "the ask" can also be about educating people about your library before you ever get to that point. It may be inviting someone to an event or to read your newsletter. This "ask" can be for time and effort as an attempt to get them comfortable with your library and to develop a relationship that may ultimately lead to a financial commitment. There are three steps to "the ask," as shown in textbox 8.1.

When people are asked for a specific amount, or to take a specific action, they are much more likely to give and at a higher level.[5]

TEXTBOX 8.1: THE "ASK"

1. The ask must be an actual question, such as "Will you . . ." or "Would you be willing . . ."
2. The ask invites someone to make a first step, such as to attend an event or pass out flyers. It is not necessarily asking for money.
3. The ask must be specific.
4. If you are asking for money, ask for, say, $500 rather than asking "Would you be willing to contribute?"
5. If you are asking for attendance at an event, specify the event, such as "Will you come to our author event on February 3?"

The Annual Appeal

An **annual appeal**, sometimes called an annual campaign or an annual fundraiser, is a solicitation of individuals that asks for support for the library and its programs. It is carried out through a combination of direct mail (usually solicitation letters and, if available, brochures) and one-on-one individual solicitations between a volunteer for the library and the individual being solicited. The annual appeal is usually conducted in late fall when individuals are giving more consideration to year-end contributions. It will typically highlight the good works that the library has accomplished during the year and will also specify that all gifts to the annual fund will be unrestricted, that is, eligible to support any of the library's activities.[6]

An annual appeal has become a mainstay of many public libraries as a way to increase their funding. With the competition from other nonprofits at this time of the year, it is important that your letter is creative, specific, and short. Keeping it to one page is ideal, and adding a personal note is appreciated if someone on your appeal team knows the person to whom the letter is going. In fact, following the letter up with a phone call or visit can be very effective. The more personal the appeal, the more likely you are to get a donation.

In addition to highlighting the library's successes, it can be helpful to specify what the solicitation is for, whether it's general support or a specific project. While libraries will occasionally conduct a capital campaign for a big-ticket item, such as an addition or replacement of the HVAC system, the annual appeal letter can specify an upgrade to the circulation system, replacement of public access computers, the addition of a new database, and so on. Donors often like to know to what they are contributing and look forward to hearing about it in the following year's appeal letter. The following samples show excerpts of exceptional appeal letters:

Sample 1:
Given the challenges we have all recently experienced, the Yourtown Public Library is fortunate to have supporters like you. Because I know you value the library and its services to our community, please consider a year-end gift. In these trying times, it is all about continuing, and increasing, your support for the Yourtown Library, an essential service to our town and a personally important place for those who live here.

Sample 2:
Your generous past gifts have enabled the library to fund needed after-school programs and homework assistance for thousands of children. . . . Regardless of what happens to the economy in the short run, the library's long-term needs remain and must be met.

At the close of the appeal, it is important that LSS, if part of their job, assist in the acknowledgment of all gifts received. "Acknowledging gifts in a personal and timely fashion provides an important opportunity to build or enhance the connections between your library and its donors. From connections, come relationships."[7] Doing so deepens the relationship between library and donor, and staying in touch with updates about library activities and successes contributes to this relationship. Building and maintaining these relationships is called **stewardship**, an important component in the appeal process.

Planned Giving

Planned giving is the arrangement, in the present, of a contribution that will be allocated at a future date. This is commonly done through wills, trusts, and estates, and the contribution is bestowed after the donor has died. A planned gift is a future gift to a library to enhance its mission and work. It's a lot like planting a tree today so someone can enjoy its shade tomorrow.[8] Planned gifts are also called legacy gifts because they are created to benefit future generations.

Figure 8.1.   Planned giving graphic. *istock/vchal*

There are several ways to make planned gifts:

1. The Outright Gift: in which the donor makes a bequest to the library in their will. It can be cash, real estate, securities, or a percentage of the estate.
2. Life Insurance: a library can be named a beneficiary of all or part of a donor's will.
3. Retirement Plans: a donor can name the library as a full or partial beneficiary of a donor's retirement plan, which can be a major portion of one's estate.

Planned gifts are a great way to benefit the library in the future, but they must be carefully considered by the donor in conjunction with her attorney or financial advisor. Libraries that undertake this kind of fundraising should have a plan in place to advertise and implement it. Here are eight suggestions from the American Library Association:

- Clearly articulate your mission and the main functions of your organization, and identify ways large and small gifts could impact your work.
- Educate your board and staff about planned giving opportunities and the importance to the library.
- Develop or purchase informational materials for mailings to prospective donors.
- Let supporters know about planned giving opportunities through your newsletter.
- Create a web page for planned giving opportunities.
- Promote the concept of planned giving by using brochures, bookmarks, advertisements, articles, and programs.
- Prepare a response card.
- Attend seminars, workshops, or classes sponsored by other institutions to learn more about planned giving.[9]

If a library wants to consider having a program of planned giving, then it must make and follow a plan. The Fundraising Authority, a website dedicated to helping nonprofits in their fundraising efforts, suggests six steps to launch such an initiative.

Step 1: Research.
> You'll want to make sure you understand (at a basic level) how planned giving works and what basic wills look like.

Step 2: Write.
> Write up a short document explaining why people should remember your organization in their will and briefly explaining just how easy it is to do so.

Step 3: Publish.
> Create a planned giving website.
> Create planned giving brochures for distribution.

Step 4: Launch.
> Ask the library board to take the lead by remembering the library in their wills.
> Ask key donors and supporters to remember the library in their wills.
> Mail requests to your donor list.

Step 5: Recognize.
    Create a legacy or donor group.
    Stay in contact with your donors to ensure their support.
Step 6: Include.
    Include information about planned giving on your website, newsletter, and all communications.[10]

When considering a legacy giving program, in addition to the marketing outlets previously mentioned, think also about contacting estate lawyers and funeral homes to be sure they have your information available for clients who may not have previously considered a legacy gift. Many libraries have collaborated with an organization called Leave a Legacy, which was a public awareness campaign designed to inspire people to make a charitable bequest. It helped people identify a charity and set up an account that would benefit the organization. No longer active, the National Association of Charitable Gift Planners has replaced it and continues to help the public with planned giving to nonprofits.[11]

Crowdsourcing

When a library needs to raise money, it usually relies on traditional sources such as grants, donations, and fundraising campaigns. **Crowdsourcing**, powered by social media, has become a successful method. It is the practice of engaging a "crowd" or group for a common goal; technology and social media power it. Thanks to our growing connectivity, it is easier than ever for individuals to collectively contribute to a project or cause.[12]

Well-known sites with which you may be familiar include Kickstarter, GoFundMe, Indiegogo, CauseVox, RocketHub, and even AmazonSmile (which donates 0.5 percent of the purchase price of eligible products to the charitable organization of your choice), among others. Libraries are no strangers to these sites and have had varying degrees of success in funding special projects. There are charges and fees involved that can vary depending on whether the library has reached its fundraising goal. Kickstarter requires a clear end to a project and does not fund "causes." Additionally, it is not flexible: either the project is completed, or the money raised is returned to the donors. Indiegogo is more nonprofit-friendly and provides networks to helpful sites that may help fund a particular interest. Libraries in Iowa City and Santa Cruz ultimately found success for their projects through Indiegogo.[13] The Northlake Public Library District in Illinois had success through Indiegogo as well to promote their graphic novel collection by fundraising for a nine-foot-tall statue of the Incredible Hulk. The media attention was so widespread that the statue ended up being donated, and they were able use the funds for new technology, including a 3-D printer.[14] An article provided by TechSoup for Libraries gives us five tips to planning a successful crowdfunding campaign:

1. Set specific and measurable goals.
2. Advertise to your existing network by way of newsletters, flyers, and social media first, and ask them to share.
3. Use e-mail and social media to reach more people through multiple channels.

4. Tell your story to let your supporters know why you need to raise money and how it will impact your community.
5. Run a longer campaign (sixty to ninety days) so that you have time to gain momentum and support.[15]

Crowdsourcing is not a tool restricted to public libraries. It can be, and has been, used successfully by institutional archives such as the University of Maryland Libraries (for a digital data project) and for the creation of Metadata Games, a crowdsourced project for tagging photographs and collections used by the British Library, Boston Public Library, and the Digital Public Library of America.[16] Clearly, crowdsourcing is a valuable tool that should be considered as part of any library's fundraising plan.

WRITING A GRANT PROPOSAL

"Libraries" and "well-funded" are not usually words one would find together in a sentence. While some communities may be wealthier than others, libraries often have to contend with a shortfall in some area of their budget. As we saw earlier in the chapter, there is a disturbing trend that, when budgets get tight, the library is often the first to take the cut. When preparing the annual budget, libraries will often factor in what grants they can expect to be able to apply for and for which parts of the budget. Typically grants do not fund operations or personnel. A library can write a grant for funds to increase materials in certain areas of the collection such as science, travel, children and teens, graphic novels, databases, media, and so on. It cannot write a grant for copy paper, ink, or breakroom supplies. Most grants are written for a specific purpose, and after the funding runs out, the library is expected to be able to fund it from then on. For example, a middle school in Riverside, California, received a grant for the *Fuse: Algebra I* app for iPads that uses video tutorials, step-by-step examples, homework help, quizzes, tips, hints, and reviews, which resulted in students being more engaged.[17] The public library in Groton, Connecticut, used a Community Foundation grant to build a teen room within the existing library to provide teens with their own space.

Building projects for new buildings, additions, ADA accessibility, HVAC systems, and preservation of materials, for example, are often at least partially funded by local, state, national, and historic organizations such as the National Trust for Historic Preservation, the National Endowment for the Humanities, the Community Development Block Grant (CDBG) Program, and other federal sources.

Some grantors place restrictions on what kinds of proposals can be requested. For example, a scientific corporation may restrict grants to science-related projects or an art-based organization may prefer to fund projects from that field. Be sure you are aware of the criteria before you go too far.

So let's say you want to find funds to replace some of the shelving in the children's room because it is old and sagging dangerously from the weight of the books. This is not a regular budget item. Now during budget planning, this could have been identified as a capital expense, and money may have been put aside for it. But perhaps your budget doesn't have the funds to include capital expenses. You decide to find grant money. Where do you even start?

If you are a school media center, you can take advantage of ongoing fundraising such as book fairs, PTO raffles, and bake sales. Scholastic has a link to its book fair tool kit,[18] and Follett also offers key book fair ideas and support for fundraising.[19] Many school libraries work with their local bookstores for fairs. They also seek funds from local merchants, similar to what some public libraries may do.

If you are the LSS assisting with this project, you need to do some research to see what grants are available and if your project would qualify. You can do this as you already have experience finding information, answering questions, serving the community, and building relationships. Networking with colleagues is also valuable. Ask them what sources they have used and for what purpose. Let's make a list of potential grant sources.

1. Find out who has already given the library grant money in the past few years and what the relationship is between the two organizations. Can you reapply?
2. Check your local banks. They often have a foundation or community outreach component that is dedicated to sponsoring and supporting local initiatives.
3. Investigate local businesses or corporations that might be interested in investing in the community.
4. If you have a community foundation, ask them about how one goes about applying for funds.
5. Check with the Rotary, Lions, and other service groups for their donation policies.
6. Use the Foundation Directory Online, a large database of grants and grant makers. This is a public-access, free-of-charge source for researching foundation and corporate funding sources that can be found at larger libraries and colleges (which pay to subscribe).

Some grant opportunities come to you through announcements via e-mail, professional websites, and journals. Examples include the Will Eisner Graphic Novel Grant announcement in the January/February 2018 issue of *American Libraries* to support the expansion of existing graphic novel services and programs[20] or the We the People Bookshelf on "Picturing America" grant that provides libraries with a full set of books on one of a variety of themes, from ALA in collaboration with the National Endowment for the Humanities (NEH).[21]

Having used these sources to identify a potential grantor and meeting their qualifications, it's time to write the grant. The following sample "template" can be a guide to your proposal.

Project Title

I.   Cover Letter
      This can be a form to be filled out, or a standard introductory letter.
II.   Proposal Summary
      This is one paragraph (one to three lines) that includes the amount of funding and a brief general description of the project.
III. Organization Description and History
      This should be about one to four pages in length and should include the history of the organization, its structure, and information about office locations that will be involved in carrying out the activities that will be funded by the requested grant.

IV. The Background
This section, two to five pages, should provide the reader with an explanation of the problem that has created the need for the program that will be funded by the requested grant. Here you provide evidence that the problem exists and explain how the proposed project will contribute to a solution.

V. Project Description (Program Narrative)
This part can vary in length and should give a detailed description of the program that will be funded. It should explain the length of time during which the funds will support the project, the goals, how they will be achieved, how success or failure will be measured, and what results you expect to bring about.

VI. Project Timeline/Budget Timeline
Using the Project Description, provide a timeline that shows the chronological order in which the activities listed will be undertaken and/or completed. Also include information about how/when funds that are awarded will be spent to support each activity.

VII. Budget
Here you include your project budget—what it's going to cost, how much you are requesting. Be sure to include income and expenses for the project.

VIII. Accompanying Documents
You may be asked to include any or all of the following:
a. *IRS letter proving that your organization is tax-exempt,*
b. *list of your board of directors and their affiliations,*
c. *a budget for your current fiscal year,*
d. *the budget for your next fiscal year if you are within a few months of that new year,*
e. *a recent audit, and*
f. *the most recent form 990.*[22]

Be aware that grants come with deadlines: to submit the grant, to complete the grant, and to report back on the outcome. Failure to meet any of them could jeopardize your chances of getting future funding from that source.

Common reasons that a grant is not funded include that the proposal was poorly written, the budget wasn't clear, your project didn't match the funder's purpose, or simply that the guidelines were not followed. Grant writing is a process; to be successful you must carefully complete every step. Be sure you have all of the necessary information so the grant you submit meets all the requirements; it's always a good idea to have a colleague review it for accuracy before it is submitted.

PROMOTIONAL ASPECTS OF FUNDRAISING

Fundraising is about relationships. It is an interaction between LSS and other staff members, staff and management, management and trustees, and all of them with the community. Raising funds for the library is not done in a vacuum; rather it involves library personnel and the public. Making the public aware of it is the first step. Go ahead and use traditional media: direct mail, print advertising, and flyers are all useful, alongside social media. "When it comes to marketing your fundraiser, you've got a new best friend. And her name is social media."[23]

If you want your fundraising event to be a success, you've got to put in the time to make sure it happens. That's where promotion comes in. An integrated promotion approach is going to give you the most payoff. Try something different for your appeal, such as holding a contest for the best tweet or Facebook post about the library. People love to win something no matter how small the prize. Try tempting the public with intrigue or mystery, and hint about it in your promotion. It will just make them want to find out more. When one fundraiser ends, start building hype for the next one. Post pictures of the event or the results of your campaign, and tag the people in it so it shows up on their feeds.[24]

Promotion is ongoing and targets activities involved in achieving specific goals and objectives for the library. In this case, the goal is fundraising for a specific cause, be it new shelving, graphic novels, an addition to the building, or outreach to the underserved. Marketing and promotion increase the amount of attention the library will get. The public is your target market, and your fundraising appeal is the product. If your project was successful, do it again. It can't be effective if the public doesn't know about it, so be aggressive about bringing your message to where they are.

CHAPTER SUMMARY

In a perfect world, all libraries would have all the money they need to be effectively run. The reality is that libraries must anticipate the funds that will be available to prepare annual operating budgets. LSS, if in charge of a department or a small library or in conjunction with their director, need to understand the basics of budgeting and fundraising to close the inevitable gaps. They must understand the financial plan as well as the sources of additional money including annual appeals, crowdsourcing, planned giving, and grants and how to write them. LSS must be aware of the promotional aspects of fundraising as well as the library's place in the community.

DISCUSSION QUESTIONS

1. Libraries must make and follow budgets to ensure adequate funding. Name six items that a library would include in its budget and why.
2. Explain how a library would go about creating a fundraising plan.
3. How does an annual appeal differ from planned giving?
4. Explain what is meant by the word "stewardship" and why it may be important to a library.
5. Why would library fundraising be considered a promotional activity?

ACTIVITIES

1. Using the key grant-writing elements identified in this chapter, choose a new or existing library service and provide an outline of a grant proposal for this service.
2. Using the information in this chapter, write a press release for an upcoming library event. To whom will you distribute it, and why?

NOTES

1. Hali R. Keeler, *Working with Library Collections: An Introduction for Support Staff*, Library Support Staff Handbooks 4 (Lanham, MD: Rowman & Littlefield, 2017), 21–22.

2. Library Strategies Consulting, "The Power of Endowments," last modified January 15, 2017, accessed December 24, 2017, librarystrategiesconsulting.org/2017/01/the-power-of-endowments/.

3. Christine Lind Hege, *The Public Library Start Up Guide* (Chicago: American Library Association, 2004), 48.

4. American Library Association, "Laying Your Foundation: Developing a Fundraising Plan," accessed December 18, 2017, www.ala.org/advocacy/advleg/frontlinefundraising/foundation.

5. Joe Garecht, "What Is a Fundraising Ask?" The Fundraising Authority, last modified 2011, accessed December 20, 2017, www.thefundraisingauthority.com/fundraising-basics/fundraising-ask/.

6. American Library Association, "The Annual Fund: The Cornerstone of All Fundraising," accessed December 18, 2017, www.ala.org/advocacy/advleg/frontlinefundraising/annualfund.

7. American Library Association, "An Attitude of Gratitude: Acknowledgement and Stewardship," accessed December 18, 2017, www.ala.org/advocacy/advleg/frontlinefundraising/gratitude.

8. American Library Association, "Planned Giving: Encouraging People to Leave a Legacy," accessed December 18, 2017, www.ala.org/advocacy/advleg/frontlinefundraising/legacy.

9. Ibid.

10. Joe Garecht, "How to Launch Planned Giving at Your Non-Profit," The Fundraising Authority, last modified 2016, accessed December 20, 2017, www.thefundraisingauthority.com/planned-giving/launch-planned-giving/.

11. National Association of Charitable Gift Planners, "Leave a Legacy," last modified 2017, accessed December 22, 2017, info.charitablegiftplanners.org/leave-a-legacy.

12. Crowdsourcing Week, "What Is Crowdsourcing?" accessed December 18, 2017, crowdsourcingweek.com/what-is-crowdsourcing/.

13. Caroline Lewis, "Crowdfunding the Library," *Library Journal*, last modified April 17, 2013, accessed December 21, 2017, lj.libraryjournal.com/2013/04/funding/crowdfunding-the-library/#_.

14. Ginny Mies, "Crowdfunding Tips from Two Small Libraries," TechSoup for Libraries, last modified August 3, 2015, accessed December 21, 2017, www.techsoupforlibraries.org/blog/crowdfunding-tips-from-two-small-libraries.

15. Ibid.

16. Medium, "Crowdsourcing in the 21st Century Library, Museum and Archive," last modified November 18, 2015, accessed December 18, 2017, medium.com/@crowdconsortium/crowdsourcing-in-the-21st-century-library-museum-and-archive-694155df93c0.

17. School Funding Center Grant Blog, "Grants for School Libraries," accessed December 18, 2017, www.schoolfundingcenter.info/blog/grants-school-libraries/.

18. Scholastic, "Book Fairs Chairperson Tool Kit," last modified 2017, accessed December 30, 2017, bookfairs.scholastic.com/bookfairs/cptoolkit/profile/login.jsp.

19. Follett Corporation, "Follett Book Fairs," last modified 2017, accessed December 30, 2017, www.follettbookfairs.com/.

20. "Will Eisner Graphic Novel Grant Nominations are Open," *American Libraries* 49, no. 1/2 (January/February 2018): 13.

21. American Library Association, "We the People Bookshelf on 'Picturing America,'" last modified 2017, accessed December 24, 2017, www.ala.org/awardsgrants/we-people-book shelf-%22picturing-america%22.

22. Legal Action Center, "Grant Proposal Template," last modified 2014, accessed December 21, 2017, lac.org/wp-content/uploads/2014/07/Grant_Proposal_Template.pdf.

23. Lyndsey Hrabik, "How to Hype Up Your Next Fundraising Event," nonprofit Hub, accessed December 24, 2017, nonprofithub.org/fundraising/22-clever-marketing-ideas-to -promote-your-next-fundraiser/.

24. Ibid.

REFERENCES, SUGGESTED READINGS, AND WEBSITES

Ablelibrarian.org. "Financial Management in the Small Public Library." ABLE: Administering Better Libraries—Educate. Accessed December 18, 2017. ablelibrarian.org/final-docu ments/mod2/2-powerpoint.ppt.

American Library Association. "The Annual Fund: The Cornerstone of All Fundraising." Accessed December 18, 2017. www.ala.org/advocacy/advleg/frontlinefundraising/annual fund.

———. "An Attitude of Gratitude: Acknowledgement and Stewardship." Accessed December 18, 2017. www.ala.org/advocacy/advleg/frontlinefundraising/gratitude.

———. "Laying Your Foundation: Developing a Fundraising Plan." Accessed December 18, 2017. www.ala.org/advocacy/advleg/frontlinefundraising/foundation.

———. "Planned Giving: Encouraging People to Leave a Legacy." Accessed December 18, 2017. www.ala.org/advocacy/advleg/frontlinefundraising/legacy_.

———. "We the People Bookshelf on 'Picturing America.'" Last modified 2017. Accessed December 24, 2017. www.ala.org/awardsgrants/we-people-bookshelf-%22picturing-america%22.

Browning, Beverly A. "Grant Writing for Dummies Cheat Sheet." Dummies. Last modified October 2016. Accessed December 21, 2017. www.dummies.com/business/nonprofits/grants/ grant-writing-for-dummies-cheat-sheet/.

Crowdsourcing Week. "What is Crowdsourcing?" Accessed December 18, 2017. crowdsourc ingweek.com/what-is-crowdsourcing/.

Eduscapes. "School Library Media Specialist: Program Administration: Funding Sources." Last modified 2013. Accessed December 18, 2017. eduscapes.com/sms/administration/grants .html.

First. "Fundraising Toolkit." Last modified March 23, 2017. Accessed December 18, 2017. www.firstinspires.org/resource-library/fundraising-toolkit.

Follett Corporation. "Follett Book Fairs." Last modified 2017. Accessed December 30, 2017. www.follettbookfairs.com/.

Garecht, Joe. "How to Launch Planned Giving at Your Non-Profit." The Fundraising Authority. Last modified 2016. Accessed December 20, 2017. www.thefundraisingauthority.com/ planned-giving/launch-planned-giving/.

———. "What Is a Fundraising Ask?" The Fundraising Authority. Last modified 2011. Accessed December 20, 2017. www.thefundraisingauthority.com/fundraising-basics/fund raising-ask/.

Hage, Christine Lind. *The Public Library Start Up Guide*. Chicago: American Library Association, 2004.

Hrabik, Lyndsey. "How to Hype Up Your Next Fundraising Event." nonprofit Hub. Accessed December 24, 2017. nonprofithub.org/fundraising/22-clever-marketing-ideas-to-promote -your-next-fundraiser/.

Infopeople. "Easy Fundraising for Public Libraries." City of Porterville, California. Accessed December 18, 2017. www.ci.porterville.ca.us/govt/BoardsandCommissions/documents/EasyfundraisingforPublicLibraries.pdf.

Keeler, Hali R. *Working with Library Collections: An Introduction for Support Staff*. Library Support Staff Handbooks 4. Lanham, MD: Rowman & Littlefield, 2017.

Legal Action Center. "Grant Proposal Template." Last modified 2014. Accessed December 21, 2017. lac.org/wp-content/uploads/2014/07/Grant_Proposal_Template.pdf.

Lewis, Caroline. "Crowdfunding the Library." *Library Journal*. Last modified April 17, 2013. Accessed December 21, 2017. lj.libraryjournal.com/2013/04/funding/crowdfunding-the-library/#_.

Library Strategies Consulting. "The Power of Endowments." Last modified January 15, 2017. Accessed December 24, 2017. librarystrategiesconsulting.org/2017/01/the-power-of-endowments/.

Martin. "Marketing Mix | Promotion in Four P's." Cleverism. Last modified August 8, 2014. Accessed December 26, 2017. www.cleverism.com/promotion-four-ps-marketing-mix/.

Medium. "Crowdsourcing in the 21st Century Library, Museum and Archive." Last modified November 18, 2015. Accessed December 18, 2017. medium.com/@crowdconsortium/crowdsourcing-in-the-21st-century-library-museum-and-archive-694155df93c0.

Michigan State University. "Academic Fundraising Web Resources." Last modified October 13, 2017. Accessed December 18, 2017. staff.lib.msu.edu/harris23/grants/4acfrais.htm.

Mies, Ginny. "Crowdfunding Tips from Two Small Libraries." TechSoup for Libraries. Last modified August 3, 2015. Accessed December 21, 2017. www.techsoupforlibraries.org/blog/crowdfunding-tips-from-two-small-libraries.

National Association of Charitable Gift Planners. "Leave a Legacy." Last modified 2017. Accessed December 22, 2017. info.charitablegiftplanners.org/leave-a-legacy.

Nelson, Janet. "Play It Again! Grant Writing Tips for Every Library!" Ideas + Inspiration. Last modified January 14, 2015. Accessed December 18, 2017. ideas.demco.com/blog/grant-writing-tips/.

Payton, Susan. "6 Crowdfunding Sites: Which Is Best for You?" Intuit. Last modified 2017. Accessed December 21, 2017. quickbooks.intuit.com/r/crowd-funding/6-crowdfunding-sites-which-is-best-for-you/.

Scholastic. "Book Fairs Chairperson Tool Kit." Last modified 2017. Accessed December 30, 2017. bookfairs.scholastic.com/bookfairs/cptoolkit/profile/login.jsp.

School Funding Center Grant Blog. "Grants for School Libraries." Accessed December 18, 2017. www.schoolfundingcenter.info/blog/grants-school-libraries/.

"Will Eisner Graphic Novel Grant Nominations Are Open." *American Libraries* 49, no. 1/2 (January/February 2018): 13.

CHAPTER 9

Community Demographics and Customer Service

LSS plan library services based on community demographics, data analysis, and needs and are able to evaluate these services. (ALA-LSSC Supervision and Management Competency #10)

LSS apply concepts of user-oriented customer service to build positive relationships between staff and users. (ALA-LSSC Supervision and Management Competency #14)

Topics Covered in This Chapter:

- Demographics of the Community
  - o Community Assessment
  - o Needs Assessment
  - o Data Analysis
- The Academic and School Environment
- Elements of Customer Service
  - o Customer Service to a Variety of Patrons
  - o Communication Skills

Key Terms:

Communication skills: Communication is the act of exchanging information between two or more people. It can be done verbally, using words, or nonverbally, using gestures. There are specific skills that staff can use to show the patron that they are approachable and ready to help with all of their information needs.

Community: A community is usually considered to be all the people who live in a particular area or place.

Community assessment: Community assessment is the analysis of the demographics of a community. This information informs library services.

Customer service: Customer service means assisting patrons (users, customers) with their needs in person, by phone, or electronically by providing high-quality service. Library

---

support staff and management do this to achieve a goal or complete a transaction while showing respect, courtesy, and interest in the patron.

Demographics: Demographics are the statistics of a given population by age, sex, race, and income. This is important for libraries, so they can know whom they are serving and for whom they can provide the appropriate resources.

Needs assessment: A needs assessment is a systematic process for determining and addressing needs, or "gaps" between current conditions and desired "wants." The discrepancy between the current condition and wanted condition must be measured to appropriately identify the need.[1]

For a library to service its community, it must know who, and what, a community is. A **community** is usually considered to be all the people who live in a particular area or place. It comes from the Latin word *communis*, meaning "common, public, shared by all or many."[2] While the members of a community could share characteristics, it is made up of a variety of people of different races, ages, incomes, and tastes. Learning who is in the library's community is important so the library can understand and best serve their needs. Library staff also need to serve this population with the best customer service they can provide. In this chapter, we will look at the demographics of a community and elements of customer service.

DEMOGRAPHICS OF THE COMMUNITY

Who uses a library depends on the kind of library and on the library's **demographics**. The Merriam-Webster Online Dictionary defines this as "the qualities (such as age, sex, and income) of a specific group of people."[3] According to a Pew Research study of 2013, 54 percent of Americans have used a public library in the past twelve months, and 72 percent live in a "library household" (age sixteen and over).[4] Those aged thirty to sixty-four find library services are very important, and in general more women than men use library services.[5] These statistics will vary according to the library, specific services, and the particular community, but the results present an overall pattern.

In a follow-up survey conducted by Pew in 2016, most Americans viewed public libraries as important parts of their communities, with a majority reporting that libraries have the resources they need and play at least some role in helping them decide what information they can trust.

As in past Pew Research Center surveys of library use, the April 2016 survey also measured Americans' usage of and engagement with libraries. Overall, 53 percent of Americans age sixteen or older had some interaction with a public library in the previous year—either through an in-person visit, using a library website, or via a mobile app. About 48 percent of adults specifically visited a library or bookmobile in the previous twelve months, a slight growth from the 44 percent who said that in late 2015. There was a four-point drop, though, in the number who visited library websites in the previous twelve months—falling from 31 percent who said they'd done so in 2015 to 27 percent in 2016.[6]

Figure 9.1. Community demographics graphic. *istock/istrejman*

Community Assessment

Any given library, including public, academic, and school libraries, will have a variety of users that include children, teens, adults, seniors, patrons with special needs, and the homeless. Your demographic, or service population, determines what kinds of materials are offered and in what languages and what kinds of programs are offered and for what ages. To determine this requires an assessment of the community. **Community assessment** is the analysis of the demographics of a community. Statistical data is a good place to start to determine the population, age range, genders, and ethnicities of a particular area, as well as employers, types of households, age, number of schools and libraries, social service providers, languages spoken, and median family incomes.

In conducting a formal community assessment, there are a number of factors to consider. Statistical data is a good place to start to determine the population, age range, genders, and ethnicities of an area. A community assessment can be done in-house by using an analysis survey tool. One example of this is the Community Analysis Scan Form produced by the Colorado State Library.[7] It includes such fields as Census Bureau maps, employers, types of households, age, number of schools and libraries, social service providers, languages spoken, and median family incomes.

It can also be done fairly simply by using census information accessible from the government at American Fact Finder.[8] This brings up a page called Community Facts; by submitting the desired zip code, town, or state, one can choose population, age, business and industry, education, housing, income, languages, and several other categories. It offers a granular search with the availability of detailed breakdowns such as by occupation, by sex, and median earnings by selected year. Since the U.S. Census is only conducted and updated every ten years, the information will necessarily be somewhat out of date, although the site does provide updated information by estimate for succeeding years. Tables 9.1 and 9.2 represent examples created from American Fact Finder: Community Facts. The first one is for a small town with one zip code.

Table 9.1. Sample Community Facts Small Town

Description	Measure	Source
Population		
Census 2010 Total Population	2,270	2010 Demographic Profile
2016 Population Estimate (as of July 1, 2016)	N/A	2016 Population Estimates
2015 ACS Five-Year Population Estimate	2,212	2011–2015 American Community Survey Five-Year Estimates
Median Age	46.4	2011–2015 American Community Survey Five-Year Estimates
Number of Companies	N/A	2012 Survey of Business Owners
Educational Attainment: Percent high school graduate or higher	96.9%	2011–2015 American Community Survey Five-Year Estimates
Count of Governments	N/A	2012 Census of Governments
Total Housing Units	993	2011–2015 American Community Survey Five-Year Estimates
Median Household Income	73,051	2011–2015 American Community Survey Five-Year Estimates
Foreign-Born Population	66	2011–2015 American Community Survey Five-Year Estimates
Individuals Below Poverty Level	10.7%	2011–2015 American Community Survey Five-Year Estimates
Race and Hispanic Origin		
White alone	2,125	2011–2015 American Community Survey Five-Year Estimates
Black or African American alone	14	2011–2015 American Community Survey Five-Year Estimates
American Indian and Alaska Native alone	0	2011–2015 American Community Survey Five-Year Estimates
Asian alone	11	2011–2015 American Community Survey Five-Year Estimates
Native Hawaiian and other Pacific Islander alone	0	2011–2015 American Community Survey Five-Year Estimates
Some other race alone	0	2011–2015 American Community Survey Five-Year Estimates
Two or more races	62	2011–2015 American Community Survey Five-Year Estimates
Hispanic or Latino (of any race)	44	2011–2015 American Community Survey Five-Year Estimates
White alone, not Hispanic or Latino	2,101	2011–2015 American Community Survey Five-Year Estimates
Veterans	184	2011–2015 American Community Survey Five-Year Estimates

The second chart is representative of a very large city of multiple zip codes included in one chart. This city has a multi-branch library system; a further breakdown by zip code might show different results that would influence services and materials for each branch.

Table 9.2. Sample Community Facts Large City

Description	Measure	Source
Population		
Census 2010 Total Population	1,197,816	2010 Demographic Profile
2016 Population Estimate (as of July 1, 2016)	1,317,929	2016 Population Estimates
2015 ACS Five-Year Population Estimate	1,260,688	2011–2015 American Community Survey Five-Year Estimates
Median Age	32.4	2011–2015 American Community Survey Five-Year Estimates
Number of Companies	142,658	2012 Survey of Business Owners
Educational Attainment: Percent high school graduate or higher	74.5%	2011–2015 American Community Survey Five-Year Estimates
Count of Governments	N/A	2012 Census of Governments
Total Housing Units	533,556	2011–2015 American Community Survey Five-Year Estimates
Median Household Income	43,781	2011–2015 American Community Survey Five-Year Estimates
Foreign-Born Population	305,921	2011–2015 American Community Survey Five-Year Estimates
Individuals Below Poverty Level	24.0%	2011–2015 American Community Survey Five-Year Estimates
Race and Hispanic Origin		
White alone	756,302	2011–2015 American Community Survey Five-Year Estimates
Black or African American alone	307,335	2011–2015 American Community Survey Five-Year Estimates
American Indian and Alaska Native alone	3,491	2011–2015 American Community Survey Five-Year Estimates
Asian alone	38,392	2011–2015 American Community Survey Five-Year Estimates
Native Hawaiian and other Pacific Islander alone	512	2011–2015 American Community Survey Five-Year Estimates
Some other race alone	125,668	2011–2015 American Community Survey Five-Year Estimates
Two or more races	28,988	2011–2015 American Community Survey Five-Year Estimates
Hispanic or Latino (of any race)	526,022	2011–2015 American Community Survey Five-Year Estimates
White alone, not Hispanic or Latino	370,257	2011–2015 American Community Survey Five-Year Estimates
Veterans	46,700	2011–2015 American Community Survey Five-Year Estimates

Those are the statistics. Observing who is actually using the library, taking informal surveys, conducting focus groups, or simply talking to and interacting with patrons can also give a pretty good idea of a library's demographic including children, older adults, or languages spoken. In a typical library of any type, there will be a mix of races and ethnicities whose needs must be addressed when choosing materials and services. If yours is an urban library, it is likely to serve a more diverse population. The upshot is that a community assessment, no matter how formally or informally it is conducted, will provide the needed information to inform the needs of that library.

Having such information about the median age, income, and education (among other statistics) of your community helps to determine whom you serve. Building on that allows for library services to be more specifically targeted to those patrons.[9]

Needs Assessment

Closely related to community assessment is **needs assessment**. Once the community assessment is done, the results are used to plan for the needs of the patrons that have been identified. This necessitates a needs assessment of the population. "With patron and community needs always evolving and expanding, how do we know we're providing the right services? When funders ask questions we can't answer, how do we gather evidence of the library's importance?"[10]

A needs assessment begins by determining what you already know about your library's needs, whether it's for additional resources or new technologies (and what library doesn't always need more money and improved technology?). This helps to better understand the gaps (needs) between where you are and where you want to be.

Data Analysis

Data can be collected from library statistics or records or through surveys and the analysis of statistical data that may have been collected during the community assessment. After the data is collected, it is organized and analyzed to create a plan of action for such things as strategic planning, determining changes in the user community, making changes in a library's collection and services, determining the adequacy of facilities and technology, and establishing satisfactory staffing patterns and library hours.

For example, the community assessment may show that the library's target area has a larger immigrant population than it did five years ago. The gap, or need, then, is to figure out how to better serve this community. The data may show that the library does not have up-to-date materials and resources in the languages of this population; therefore the plan of action would be to find the funds to purchase these materials. The library would then advertise this service through marketing, outreach, and community partnerships.

A needs assessment process reveals the influences acting on the library. Information collected shapes the services and programs that best fit the library's strengths and budget. Ultimately it informs a vision for future development.[11]

THE ACADEMIC AND SCHOOL ENVIRONMENT

As we saw in our analysis of community demographics, there are many resources at our disposal to determine the makeup of our communities, into which fall our public libraries. This data also informs the community in which schools and colleges exist in any given town or city by providing a framework. Understanding the needs of students in those school and academic environments, however, requires further analysis. There are four kinds of data that are useful to determine those demographics.

1. About Students: Number of students, class size, race/ethnicity, language proficiency, home backgrounds, special needs, graduation rates, etc.
2. About Staff: Number of teachers, administrators, and paraprofessionals; race/ethnicity; certification; student–teacher ratios; retirement projections; and so on.
3. About the School: Teacher turnover, special qualities and strengths, programs offered, and safety/crime data.
4. About the Community: Location, economic base, population trends, types of employment, projections of growth, and community support.

This information describes the context in which the school operates and is important for understanding the other data. By separating information by demographics (for example, by gender or ethnicity), one can see what impact the education system is having on different groups of students.[12]

Each student's life is composed of different features such as their income level, their family traditions, their parents' education, their community involvement, or race. To be effective, teachers need to understand that these demographic characteristics have influenced every student. The elements that impact education include:

1. Family Income and Socioeconomic Status
   a. The income of a student's family is a predictor of future achievement, such as whether a student is on free or reduced-price lunch.
   b. Adequate nutrition has an impact on focus and learning.
2. Culture
   a. Teachers need to be aware that a student's culture could affect the way the student acts or speaks.
   b. They need to understand the diverse cultures to better understand them.
3. Family
   a. Students come from a variety of families. While the majority of children in the United States live in a two-parent household, 23 percent live with a single mother.[13]
   b. This could mean that these children don't have the resources, such as time and money, that children from dual-parent families might have.
4. Community
   a. Spirituality in a community can have a positive influence on children.
   b. Neighborhoods with high crime or children who come home to an empty house can be negatively influenced and at risk.

c. Teachers must be aware of where their students live and be involved in offering after-school study alternatives.
5. Race and Ethnicity
   a. Diversity in the classroom is relevant to student development; students
      learn from each other.
   b. Teachers must focus less on race and more on the socioeconomic issues in
      the classroom.[14]

What we can conclude then is that the demographics of a community have an
effect not only on its public institutions, such as the library, but also on the schools
and academic institutions that are integral parts of that community.

ELEMENTS OF CUSTOMER SERVICE

You only get one chance to make a first impression, and the one we give the first
time a patron walks through the library door could set the tone for that person's
impression of, and relationship with, the library. It's an accepted concept that customers will remain loyal if they are satisfied with the quality of the service they get.
As libraries are essentially a customer-oriented profession, focusing on customer
needs is a good plan.[15]

What is customer service? **Customer service** is the interaction between the user
and the service provider; good customer service adds value and goodwill. Most people who choose to work in libraries genuinely like what they do, and for them, providing good customer service is second nature. Customer service is two-pronged, as
it can be *transaction* based or *relationship* based. Transaction-based service is *point of
service*, such as checking out an item. Relationship-based service *implies a relationship*
between the LSS and the patron. This can be done, for example, by remembering a
patron's name or knowing their reading preferences.

Determining the library's demographic helps to focus services on patron needs.
As a manager, you need to ensure that your staff understands what the library can
and cannot provide and how to communicate that to the patron. Patrons should be
made to feel that they will be heard, be it a question or a complaint.

Customer Service to a Variety of Patrons

Demographics show that not all the members of a community are alike. The public library, being a microcosm of the community, will reflect that. In addition, the
library serves children and teens, adults and seniors, people with special needs, and
challenging patrons (including the homeless). All are entitled to the same level of
customer service, but their demographic may require a different approach.

1. Service to children
   a. The librarian must be open and friendly, not patronizing.
   b. Since children are smaller; it helps to get down to their level so they can be
      eye to eye.
   c. Do not assume that you know what the child wants. Don't lead them, and
      let them tell you, to the best of their ability, what it is they are looking for.

      d. If possible, encourage the child to ask and answer the questions, not the parent.
2. Service to teens
    a. LSS who serve teens must understand the mind of a teen and how they think at different stages of their development.
    b. Teens are unique, and their needs are legitimate and must be recognized and addressed.
    c. Be approachable, nonjudgmental, tolerant, patient, and respectful.
    d. Talk with them to find out what they are interested in.
    e. Offer activities that appeal to them.
3. Service to older adults
    a. It is important that the LSS not stereotype older patrons. Age alone does not automatically confer infirmity.
    b. Ask them what they want. Let them decide on the services that would make their library use more convenient.
    c. Evaluate shelving to avoid materials placed at very high or very low levels, requiring bending or lifting.
    d. Offer Large Print and books on CD for those whose eyesight may be impaired.
    e. Signage should be clearly printed and well placed.
4. Service to those with special needs
    a. Be familiar with the Americans with Disabilities Act.[16]
    b. Arrange the library to be barrier-free.
    c. Provide adaptive technology as needed.
    d. Not all disabilities are visible.
       i. Patrons may have dyslexia, memory issues, or aphasia. Some may wear prosthetic devices or have temporary disabilities such as broken bones, recent surgery, or injuries that may cause impairment.
5. Service to the challenged patrons: the poor and the homeless
    a. Poverty is an economic condition that limits one's ability to purchase necessary goods and services.
       i. Review fine policies and be creative in implementing alternatives.
       ii. Consult with your town's social services department for available and free services.
    b. People can be on the verge of becoming homeless due to job insecurity, unemployment, underemployment, domestic violence, or other dire situations.
       i. Become familiar with the Homeless Bill of Rights.[17]
       ii. Services for the poor can also be applied to the homeless.
       iii. The homeless population that uses the library will come in all ages, genders, and races. Get specific information about their information needs.

Communication Skills

Communication is the act of exchanging information between two or more people. It can be done verbally, using words, or nonverbally, using gestures. It can be as subtle as raising an eyebrow. We take it for granted, rarely thinking about how we communicate with others. Hopefully we have developed good habits, but that may not always be the case. We may be sending messages to our patrons that we are far from approachable and are not very willing to help with their information needs. Fortunately, there are specific skills that LSS can employ to create effective communication in the library and to show the patron that they are approachable and ready to help with all their information needs. Since we spend more time communicating than we realize, it is an essential skill.

LSS can improve their communication skills by understanding and using the skills in textbox 9.1.

TEXTBOX 9.1: COMMUNICATION SKILLS

- Attending skills show active interest in what patrons say and do and show respect for their needs. This includes:
  o Greeting the patron with a warm smile,
  o Maintaining an open expression,
  o Making eye contact,
  o Maintaining a moderate voice.
- Listening skills are the ability to accurately receive and interpret messages in the communication process. Suggestions are to:
  o Paraphrase—use different words to restate the patron's question.
  o Clarify—be sure the question or statement is made very clear.
  o Provide feedback—be specific about your answer.
- Vocal skills: it's not what you say; it's how you say it:
  o Beware of your inflection, or the highs and lows in your pitch.
  o A monotone suggests you are bored; slow speech might imply that you are depressed; and a very loud tone can be interpreted as anger.
  o Be friendly yet businesslike, and speak distinctly.
  o Smile: it can be heard in your voice.[18]

The final component of communication skills is body language, the constant nonverbal flow of communication. Since we may not always be aware of this, here are some suggestions that can help LSS use it more effectively.

For your face, use a relaxed and pleasant expression. Suggestions:

- Make eye contact: it lets the patron know that you are interested.
- Smile.
- Try for an open, relaxed expression.

Posture shows your energy level and interests. Suggestions:

- Nodding is one of the best ways to show attention.
- Face the patron.
- Lean slightly forward, as leaning back or stepping away gives negative signals.

Your hands are a natural way of expression. Suggestions:

- Use an open-handed gesture, flat hand, palm up or out.
- Avoid a closed hand or pointing fingers.
- Avoid tapping fingers, clicking pens, jingling coins. This conveys annoyance or impatience.

Touch can convey caring and concern. Suggestions:

- The most acceptable form of public touch is handshaking.
- Nonthreatening touch is in the area between the elbow and the wrist.
- Avoid the more intimate gestures such as hugging, putting an arm around someone, or slapping their back.[19]

While almost all communication skills apply to both adults and children, the exception is touch. According to the National Association of State Directors of Teacher Education and Certification, rules of ethics require teachers and school librarians to show respect for all students.[20] The Model Code of Ethics spells out specific behavior that teachers should avoid, including touching students unless there's a clearly defined reason for doing so.[21]

Since communication and customer service skills are essential in our relationships with our patrons, we need to do all we can to know them, understand them, and provide them with our best service.

CHAPTER SUMMARY

In this chapter, we learned how community demographics, data analysis, and needs assessments are used to evaluate library services. We also discussed how communication skills can affect the transmission of information. LSS can use this in a variety of ways to enhance their methods of communication, become more approachable, and become better able to effectively transmit needed information to the user.

DISCUSSION QUESTIONS

1. What are demographics and why do we need them?
2. Would the demographics of a school library differ from that of its community; if so, how?
3. Explain the difference between a community assessment and a needs assessment.
4. Please explain the concept of customer service and how it can vary according to the variety of patrons a library might have.
5. Name several specific skills that LSS can employ to create effective communication in the library.

ACTIVITIES

1. Using information from this chapter, determine the demographics of a community in your state that differs from your own. Based on your findings, describe a library service that would meet the needs of one major community group.
2. Create a bibliography of ten articles that describe programs and services for one of the patron groups for whom libraries provide service (e.g., teens, seniors, the homeless, etc.).

NOTES

1. "What Is Needs Assessment?," video file, Study.com, accessed April 6, 2016, study.com/academy/lesson/what-is-needs-assessment-definition-examples-quiz.html.

2. Don Iannone, "Roots of the Word 'Community,'" Conscious Communities, last modified February 19, 2007, accessed November 13, 2017, consciouscommunities.blogspot.com/2007/02/roots-of-word-community.html.

3. "Demographic," www.merriam-webster.com/dictionary/demographic.

4. Kathryn Zickuhr et al., "How Americans Value Public Libraries in Their Communities," Pew Internet and American Life Project, last modified December 11, 2013, accessed February 10, 2015, libraries.pewinternet.org/2013/12/11/libraries-in-communities/.

5. Rachel Applegate, "Gender Differences in a Public Library," *Public Library Quarterly* 27, no. 1 (October 11, 2008): 19–31, accessed November 14, 2017, doi:10.1080/01616840802122468.

6. John B. Horrigan, "Libraries 2016," Pew Research Center, last modified September 9, 2016, accessed November 14, 2017, www.pewinternet.org/2016/09/09/libraries-2016/.

7. Colorado State Library, "Community Analysis Scan Form," Library Research Service, accessed November 14, 2017, www.lrs.org/public/ca_form.php.

8. U.S. Department of Commerce, "American Fact Finder: Community Facts," U.S. Census Bureau, accessed November 14, 2017, factfinder.census.gov/faces/nav/jsf/pages/index.xhtml.

9. "Explore Topics: Needs Assessment," WebJunction, last modified 2016, accessed April 6, 2016, www.webjunction.org/explore-topics/needs-assessment.html.

10. Idaho Commission for Libraries, "Needs Assessment," accessed November 14, 2017, libraries.idaho.gov/page/needs-assessment.

11. Hali R. Keeler, *Working with Library Collections: An Introduction for Support Staff*, Library Support Staff Handbooks 4 (Lanham, MD: Rowman & Littlefield, 2017), 7–10.

12. Victoria L. Bernhardt, "No Schools Left Behind," *Educational Leadership*, last modified February 2003, accessed November 14, 2017, www.ascd.org/publications/educational-leadership/feb03/vol60/num05/No-Schools-Left-Behind.aspx.

13. Census.gov, "The Majority of Children Live With Two Parents, Census Bureau Reports," United States Census Bureau, last modified November 17, 2016, accessed November 21, 2017, www.census.gov/newsroom/press-releases/2016/cb16-192.html.

14. Allyssa VanderStel, "The Impact of Demographics in Education," Grand Valley State University, last modified April 10, 2014, accessed November 14, 2017, scholarworks.gvsu.edu/cgi/viewcontent.cgi?referer=https://www.google.com/&httpsredir=1&article=1306&context=honorsprojects.

15. Hali R. Keeler, *Foundations of Library Services: An Introduction for Support Staff*, Library Support Staff Handbooks 1 (Lanham, MD: Rowman & Littlefield, 2016), 88–89.

16. U.S. Equal Employment Opportunity Commission, "Facts About the Americans with Disabilities Act," accessed November 21, 2017, www.eeoc.gov/eeoc/publications/fs-ada.cfm.

17. National Coalition for the Homeless, "Building a Movement to End Homelessness," last modified 2014, accessed November 22, 2017, nationalhomeless.org/campaigns/bill-of-right/.

18. Keith Bailey and Karen Leland, *Customer Service for Dummies*, 3rd ed. (Foster City, CA: IDG, 2006), 60–63.

19. Keeler, *Foundations of Library*, 92–93.

20. National Association of State Directors of Teacher Education and Certification, "Model Code of Ethics for Educators (MCEE)," accessed November 27, 2017, www.nasdtec.net/?page=MCEE_Doc#PrinIII.

21. E. A. Gjelten, "What Are Teachers' Responsibilities to Their Students?" Lawyers.com, accessed November 27, 2017, education-law.lawyers.com/school-law/teachers-have-many-responsibilities-to-their-students.html.

REFERENCES, SUGGESTED READINGS, AND WEBSITES

Applegate, Rachel. "Gender Differences in a Public Library." *Public Library Quarterly* 27, no. 1 (October 11, 2008): 19–31. Accessed November 14, 2017. doi:10.1080/01616840802122468.

Bailey, Keith, and Karen Leland. *Customer Service for Dummies*. 3rd ed. Foster City, CA: IDG, 2006.

Bernhardt, Victoria L. "No Schools Left Behind." *Educational Leadership*. Last modified February 2003. Accessed November 14, 2017. www.ascd.org/publications/educational-leader ship/feb03/vol60/num05/No-Schools-Left-Behind.aspx.

Census.gov. "The Majority of Children Live with Two Parents, Census Bureau Reports." United States Census Bureau. Last modified November 17, 2016. Accessed November 21, 2017. www.census.gov/newsroom/press-releases/2016/cb16-192.html.

Collins Dictionary. "Definition of 'Community.'" Accessed November 13, 2017. www.collins dictionary.com/us/dictionary/english/community.

Colorado State Library. "Community Analysis Scan Form." Library Research Service. Accessed November 14, 2017. www.lrs.org/public/ca_form.php.

"Explore Topics: Needs Assessment." WebJunction. Last modified 2016. Accessed April 6, 2016. www.webjunction.org/explore-topics/needs-assessment.html.

Gjelten, E. A. "What Are Teachers' Responsibilities to Their Students?" Lawyers.com. Accessed November 27, 2017. education-law.lawyers.com/school-law/teachers-have-many-responsi bilities-to-their-students.html.

Horrigan, John B. "Libraries 2016." Pew Research Center. Last modified September 9, 2016. Accessed November 14, 2017. www.pewinternet.org/2016/09/09/libraries-2016/.

Iannone, Don. "Roots of the Word 'Community.'" Conscious Communities. Last modified February 19, 2007. Accessed November 13, 2017. consciouscommunities.blogspot .com/2007/02/roots-of-word-community.html.

Idaho Commission for Libraries. "Needs Assessment." Accessed November 14, 2017. librar ies.idaho.gov/page/needs-assessment.

Keeler, Hali R. *Foundations of Library Services: An Introduction for Support Staff*. Library Support Staff Handbooks 1. Lanham, MD: Rowman & Littlefield, 2016.

———. *Working with Library Collections: An Introduction for Support Staff*. Library Support Staff Handbooks 4. Lanham, MD: Rowman & Littlefield, 2017.

Merrian-Webster.com. "Demographic." www.merriam-webster.com/dictionary/demographic.

National Association of State Directors of Teacher Education and Certification. "Model Code of Ethics for Educators (MCEE)." Accessed November 27, 2017. www.nasdtec.net/?page= MCEE_Doc#PrinIII.

National Coalition for the Homeless. "Building a Movement to End Homelessness." Last mod ified 2014. Accessed November 22, 2017. nationalhomeless.org/campaigns/bill-of-right/.

U.S. Department of Commerce. "American Fact Finder: Community Facts." U.S. Census Bu reau. Accessed November 14, 2017. factfinder.census.gov/faces/nav/jsf/pages/index.xhtml.

U.S. Equal Employment Opportunity Commission. "Facts About the Americans with Dis abilities Act." Accessed November 21, 2017. www.eeoc.gov/eeoc/publications/fs-ada.cfm.

VanderStel, Allyssa. "The Impact of Demographics in Education." Grand Valley State Univer sity. Last modified April 10, 2014. Accessed November 14, 2017. scholarworks.gvsu.edu/cgi/ viewcontent.cgi?referer=https://www.google.com/&httpsredir=1&article=1306&context= honorsprojects.

"What Is Needs Assessment?" Video file. Study.com. Accessed November 14, 2017. study.com/ academy/lesson/what-is-needs-assessment-definition-examples-quiz.html.

Zickuhr, Kathryn, et al. "How Americans Value Public Libraries in Their Communities." Pew Internet and American Life Project. Last modified December 11, 2013. Accessed February 10, 2015. libraries.pewinternet.org/2013/12/11/libraries-in-communities/.

CHAPTER 10

The Value of Partnerships

LSS know the principles and the value of forming partnerships with other libraries, agencies, and organizations. (ALA-LSSC Supervision and Management Competency #11)

Topics Covered in This Chapter:

- Principles for Partnerships
  - o Barriers
- Partnerships with Other Libraries
  - o Integrated Library Systems (ILS)
  - o Interlibrary Loan (ILL)
  - o Discount Purchasing
  - o Shared Programming
  - o Technology
  - o Scholarly Research and Communication
  - o Professional Development
- Partnerships with Outside Agencies and Organizations

Key Terms:

Bid list: Items commonly used that are under contract with a purchasing agent at a reduced cost to approved libraries.

Consortium: A partnership of libraries that formally work together to achieve common goals or projects.

Cooperatives: Another name for consortium, this group of libraries typically has a formal agreement that stipulates the goals, expectations, and obligations of its members.

Functions of a shared ILS: Libraries share an integrated library system because of the benefits obtained by sharing circulation, cataloging, reserves, acquisitions, reports, and other applications and databases with other consortium members.

Standards: These are agreed-upon norms, rules, regulations, or other means of measurement of success of an item or project. Standards also identify the quality of the work performed, such as a high standard of cataloging may be used to describe a complete and accurate item record.

Student learning objectives (SLO): These are brief statements that describe what students should know and be able to do at the end of a unit, course, or school year. SLOs may be locally created by educators or relate to state and national learning standards that measure student achievement.

Task force: This typically is an ad hoc or temporary committee composed of working members to delve deeply into an issue and bring a recommendation or resolution to the issue or task to the larger board or committee.

"No man is an island, entire of itself, every man is a piece of the continent, a part of the main."[1] These wise words of poet John Donne, written in 1623, are as applicable to libraries today as they were to Londoners more than four hundred years ago. Likewise, in the United States, there have been periods of isolationism when it was thought prudent for our country to stand aside from world events. History has proven on both individual and institutional levels that the strength of partnerships far outweighs any benefits from disassociation from others.

PRINCIPLES FOR PARTNERSHIPS

Before meaningful partnerships can take place, work must be done to ensure the commitment will be sustained. Library partnerships or **cooperatives** go beyond agreements between staff members. It is most beneficial when the expectations as well as the obligations of each library are clearly stated and agreed to as part of the commitment. While there is no definitive set of guiding principles for successful library partnerships, Stanford University offers a useful set of principles for nonprofit organizations to consider.[2]

TEXTBOX 10.1: PRINCIPLES FOR SUCCESSFUL PARTNERSHIPS

1. Agree-upon values, goals, and measurable outcomes.
2. Develop relationships of mutual trust, respect, genuineness, and commitment.
3. Build upon strengths and assets and also address needs.
4. Have clear, open, and accessible communication.
5. Agree-upon roles, norms, and processes.
6. Ensure feedback to, among, and from all stakeholders.
7. Share the credit for accomplishments.
8. Take time to develop and evolve.

Library partnerships can also be successful when based upon these principles. Below are examples of how LSS engage in these principles to strengthen the cooperation between libraries:

1. Agree-upon values, goals, and measurable outcomes. Libraries that are members of successful partnerships or cooperatives have a common purpose or goal to achieve.
   Example: LSS should know the mission and goals of their library and try to apply them to their everyday work. When working with other libraries, such as in a shared integrated library system (ILS), discuss with the supervisor the values and goals that your library shares with the other member libraries. If a goal of the library is to support teen literacy, discuss with peers in the other libraries ways to build cooperative programs and services. Offer to keep track of data, such as programming, circulation reports, interlibrary loans, or other statistics, that demonstrate the success around this goal.
2. Develop relationships of mutual trust, respect, genuineness, and commitment. As in any other business, relationships among libraries that are built upon trust and commitment have the greatest opportunity to be successful.
   Example: LSS can contribute to the success of the partnership when they follow the rules or regulations established by the cooperative to ensure its **standards** are maintained, such as with inputting data into the shared catalog. LSS perform their work at the highest level because what they do affects the catalogs of all of the partnership libraries. They seek help or training with difficult or unknown procedures or tasks to ensure high record quality.
3. Build upon strengths and assets and also address needs. Each library member will have unique resources, staff, or talents it may offer the partnership.
   Example: LSS share their knowledge and skills with others in the cooperative, such as a willingness to train staff in other libraries on specific **functions of a shared ILS system**. One way to do this is to schedule quarterly meetings of a circulation **task force** where LSS in the member libraries can discuss beneficial ways they customize their use of the ILS with others. The result may be better use of the system as well as needs assessments, such as agreed-upon software updates.
4. Have clear, open, and accessible communication. LSS can support the members' work by using clear language in their oral and written communications.
   Example: Learn and use the preferred way partnership member libraries like to receive communications, including whom to contact for specific functions or questions. Share with the supervisor communications received from **consortium** members if they involve a change of policy, procedures, budget, or other significant issue.
5. Agreed-upon roles, norms, and processes. LSS should seek policy manuals and other procedural documentation from their supervisor about the partnership so that they can be knowledgeable about expected practices.
   Example: Read and follow policy and procedures that affect your work. Ask supervisor for help or support with anything that is unclear or ambiguous. Establish within the library the roles of each LSS whose work involves the

partnership so that there is not a needless duplication of effort or confusion about workflow.

6. Ensure feedback to, among, and from all stakeholders. LSS are important members of any library cooperative, and they have the ability to obtain and provide feedback to their supervisor as well as staff in the participating libraries.

   Example: LSS are most helpful in ensuring feedback is beneficial when they share important information with the other partnership members that is focused on improving the functions or goals of the cooperative. LSS who attend consortium meetings, take notes, and extend themselves in other ways are valuable employees because they fully participate in the ongoing work and decisions of the partnership.

7. Share the credit for accomplishments. Libraries that share the successes of a partnership educate their patrons and community to the benefits of enhanced services because they work with others.

   Example: LSS can help this effort by volunteering to develop publicity about the benefits of the partnership, such as signage about discount savings, enhanced interlibrary loan capacity, and so on. When LSS communicate to other partnership members the positive impact the partnership has for patrons and other advantages for the library, they share the credit for the accomplishments of many.

8. Take time to develop and evolve. The most successful library partnerships occur because they were developed with extensive planning, assessment of alternatives, financial commitment, staff training, and other mutual considerations.

   Example: LSS can participate in many ways during the formation of a partnership. Offer to serve on a subcommittee or task force that looks specifically into how a partnership could improve the work of your department or an area of patron service that you are most interested in. Volunteer to support staff training by offering to attend initial workshops. Help with fundraising or finding cost efficiencies. Look for ways you can support your supervisor and the library in the initial planning and implementation of a partnership or cooperative with other libraries or agencies.

Barriers

Not every collaboration is successful, and it is important to recognize potential barriers to partnerships. Library boards, directors, and staff are cautious when considering the commitment of a partnership with other libraries or outside organizations and should consider the myriad of "what ifs" that could occur both positively and negatively.

There are some common potential barriers from community and nonprofit organizations that libraries should consider when exploring partnerships.[3]

- Minimal organizational capacity: How will the collaborative partnership's organizational capacity be increased? What skills and time do members need to create a more efficient and effective partnership?
- Funding: What strategies are being used to financially sustain the effort and are there more effective ones? How can we avoid having the opportunity for funding, such as a new grant, tear apart working relationships?

- Failure to provide and create leadership within the group: How can new members be encouraged to step up as leaders within the collaborative partnership?
- The perceived costs of working together outweigh the benefits: How can we reduce the costs or increase the benefits of participation in the project by partners and community members? What barriers can be eliminated or overcome?

In addition to these stated barriers, libraries exploring partnerships should also consider:

- Alignment of goals with time schedule: Is the library ready to be a partner, or is the common goal to be achieved, such as joining an ILS consortium, two or three years out? The library may not be ready for the commitment.
- Indirect costs: What is the actual long-range expense? If the partnership is developing with the support of a grant, for example, how does the burden shift to library members in the future? Are there in-kind expectations, such as staff, facilities, utilities, and so on?
- Property rights should be clearly agreed upon: If the library is joining an ILS consortium, are the rights to property, such as data, clearly understood during the agreement and if the consortium dissolves?
- Dissolution of partnership: If the library decides to leave the partnership or the partnership expires or dissolves, what is the process and what guarantees for property and so on are agreed upon?

Before a library board, board of education, or other authorizing agent agrees to the library joining a partnership, these factors or potential barriers should be clearly understood by all parties to ensure a level of trust and agreement among members.

TEXTBOX 10.2: POTENTIAL BARRIERS TO LIBRARY PARTNERSHIPS

1. Organizational Capacity
2. Funding
3. Leadership
4. Costs vs. Benefits
5. Alignment of Goals and Schedule
6. Indirect Costs
7. Property Rights
8. Dissolution Agreement

PARTNERSHIPS WITH OTHER LIBRARIES

It is commonly said in politics, military actions, and many life experiences that there is strength in numbers. Libraries are stronger when they form partnerships with other libraries for specific purposes. These may be economically or services driven. Partnerships may also be formed out of a mutual need, such as shared technology, staffing, or training. Regardless of the reason for the partnership, the result should provide patrons more reasons to use their library.

Another term used for formal library partnerships is a consortium. A consortium is a group of libraries who formally come together to share resources, seek discounts, share expertise, or coordinate programs or activities. Consortia may hire staff to manage the work of the group, such as an ILS coordinator. For example, the Boston Consortium is a group of New England academic libraries that offers services to librarians at member libraries ranging from resource sharing and e-resource licensing to professional development and programming on issues of importance to academic and research libraries.[4] It also promotes digitization of collections and scholarly communication to further the goals of open access and supporting the rights of authors affiliated with its member libraries. Let us examine some of the common endeavors of library consortia and the value they afford patrons.

TEXTBOX 10.3: LIBRARY SERVICES ENHANCED THROUGH COLLABORATIONS

- Integrated Library Systems (ILS)
- Interlibrary Loan (ILL)
- Discount Purchasing
- Shared Programming
- Technology
- Scholarly Research and Communication
- Professional Development

Integrated Library Systems (ILS)

The future of the ILS consortia continues to be strong as libraries seek partnerships to share the expense of the software and technology but also the benefits of offering patrons access to other libraries' collections. Libraries' increasingly complex collections of print, electronic, and digital components demand a unified platform for management and access.[5] Whether libraries use major vendor platforms or open source applications, the majority of libraries do not have on staff the expertise required to run and manage an ILS. Digital magazines, e-books, and other new services have added complexity to ILS designed to manage and circulate print collections.

LSS do much of the functional work of ILS consortia. They work with the circulation patron and item databases every day creating new patron records, managing interlibrary loan, assisting with shelf status, or running reports. By being a circulation task force member who shares expertise with others, LSS learn how to maximize their efficiency and work patterns. Likewise, LSS who work in technical services, cataloging, or reserves find mutual benefit from meeting with and sharing skills and knowledge with colleagues and peers of other ILS consortium member libraries.

If a task force is not in place, LSS may seek to develop one. Discuss with the supervisor the need for a means to exchange ideas and training with others. When LSS can reach out to knowledgeable colleagues in other partnership libraries, there can be cost- and time-saving benefits for all.

Interlibrary Loan (ILL)

Resource sharing or interlibrary loan is a longtime, practical way for libraries to share collections and resources. No one library can develop a collection that meets all of the needs of all of their patrons. When libraries partner with others for resource sharing, significant savings occur. Most importantly, patrons' information and literacy needs are met in a timely way.

ILL may occur between libraries nationally, statewide, regionally, or even in small partnerships. A national consortium membership is OCLC.[6] OCLC is a global library cooperative that provides shared technology services, original research, and community programs for its membership and the library community at large. There are thousands of library members in more than one hundred countries who make information more accessible. Academic and large public or special libraries are members or partners in OCLC to support their patrons' research needs. OCLC also offers full cataloging records to member libraries, which results in savings.

Many states have shared statewide catalogs or support statewide interlibrary loan sharing. For example, the Indiana State Library offers Evergreen Indiana, whereby every resident in Indiana is eligible to check out circulating items from the state library.[7] The Office of Library and Information Services in Rhode Island offers LORI, a directory system of all public libraries and eighteen academic libraries that work together to support interlibrary loan.[8] Many other states also financially support public and academic libraries lending of items to nonpatrons. This kind of library partnership at the state level in Wisconsin provided all residents of the state improved library service, as well as the ability to use whichever library or libraries best serve their needs. Municipal libraries participated in library systems because residents benefit from this arrangement.[9]

The majority of K–12 schools share library materials within regions or districts. Montgomery County Public Schools in Maryland is an example of a large county system that uses Destiny Library Manager for its shared catalog.[10] By having one centralized county-wide online catalog system, there is a timely sharing of materials among students and staff, while simultaneously library media center staff members can work more efficiently to create collaborative learning environments that promote and support student achievement.

Discount Purchasing

Every consumer knows that savings accrue from discount purchasing. When vendors can guarantee large orders, they can pass on savings to the consumer. Likewise, libraries that form partnerships with others around purchasing library supplies, books, furniture, and computer hardware and software can reap similar benefits.

The way library discounts typically work is through the initiative of a district, consortium, county, or state that brokers with vendors for savings from guaranteed large purchases. The Connecticut Library Consortium (CLC) is a legislated, nonprofit organization created to save money and accomplish projects too large or costly for a single library.[11] With more than eight hundred library and school members, CLC "saves Connecticut libraries millions of dollars each year by leveraging the collective buying power of our members. CLC negotiates discounted prices on a wide variety of library resources and services essential to excellent library service for Connecticut citizens. CLC's statewide contracts for books, non-print media, and supplies enable members to waive their own bidding requirements and realize savings of up to 80% on mission-critical library materials." It seeks discounts on everything libraries need: e-resources, books, nonprint media, supplies, technology, continuing education, and more.[12]

LSS can follow state, district, and consortium discounts their library may be eligible for. Many school districts have a **bid list** that school library media centers are encouraged to use for purchasing of school supplies or furnishings.

Shared Programming

Often a presenter who offers a program for adults, teens, or children will discount his or her fee if two or more libraries contract the program. This may be done between two library directors who seek to have the presenter at each of his libraries, or it may be accomplished on a regional or district scale, such as the One Book, One Community: Our Region Reads program in Pennsylvania.[13] For twelve years, this program has invited collaboration among ninety-three school, public, and academic libraries in six counties and the Pennsylvania State Library. More than two million people read the selected book, participate in programming related to the story, and engage in conversations about the book via social media supported by the libraries.

Programming is a major service and, in these days of online access, is one of the main reasons for the need of community libraries. It takes an enormous amount of staff resources to plan, implement, and evaluate each program. Many public libraries offer multiple programs each day from children's story times in the morning to teen after-school events to adult programs in the evening. Many patrons do not have the mobility to drive distances to out-of-town libraries. Libraries who partner in programming find efficiencies in speaker fees, transportation costs, staff planning, administration such as contracts, and so on. It behooves LSS who are involved with programming to seek regional task forces or committees whereby they can plan out shared programs months ahead with other libraries.

Technology

Acquiring technology is an important yet expensive part of any library budget. Patrons want and need up-to-date technology to support their information and personal needs. Libraries that partner with others find cost savings in the purchase of hardware and software. Typically the larger the number of libraries, the better the discount.

Libraries also seek discounts through state and national programs. Since the mid-1990s, Internet service for libraries has been available at significant savings through the federal government's e-rate program. Many states also provide networks for schools, libraries, and universities.

LSS can support technology acquisitions by becoming knowledgeable of the discount programs their library qualifies for. For example, a town public library may be able to partner with other town departments when purchasing technology. Speak with IT support staff to explore all options.

Scholarly Research and Communication

Many consortia or partnerships exist for academic libraries who have common goals and needs. These goals may be around such topics as sharing of scholarly materials, professional learning, research, publishing, curriculum, or library administration. Consortia tend to be developed by type of university, geographic region, academic league, or large statewide university system with multiple sites. LSS who work in academic libraries should seek information about their consortium and introduce themselves to colleagues in member libraries for shared work interests.

One example, the Boston Library Consortium (BLC) supports its members in many ways.[14] It began in 1970 for resource sharing, but today includes eighteen research libraries in Massachusetts, New Hampshire, Rhode Island, and Connecticut. Not only do BLC members share print, digital, and electronic content, the consortium also acts as an incubator for projects and initiatives important to academic and research libraries, including digitization programs, new research methods, and publication of scholarly works. BLC also offers a wide range of professional development opportunities for staff focused on skill building, from project management for libraries to events more focused on expanding services such as marketing of expensive e-resources.

Professional Development

Library budgets are always stretched, and often professional learning or development for LSS is underfunded. In today's world, there will always be the need for LSS to acquire expertise in new technology, standards, or methods for improved library service. LSS who seek new learning may not be offered workshops or conferences routinely to hone their skills. However, LSS who perceive themselves as leaders can work collaboratively with their managers in ways to acquire professional development. Using key ideas from an article on professional development, LSS can work in these ways with their managers or supervisors to enhance their leadership skills.[15]

- Be identified as a leader: LSS who take on informal leadership roles may have their managers help them grow their skill sets for the good of the library organization.
- Go outside the library: If the manager cannot send staff to state and national conferences, do not overlook the benefit of joining local community service organizations that offer opportunities to develop leadership skills.
- Take initiative: Do not wait until you are assigned a leadership role. Step up and offer your expertise to the library organization.
- Make time: Try new ideas or accomplish projects outside of the daily work expectations.
- Welcome innovation: Rather than a manager saying "no," convince her to say "not yet" if an idea is not going to work at the current time. It may be needed in the future.
- Think holistically: Think on the larger-scale impact of a program or service you are involved with. How does it fit into the goals of the library?

- Share what we do and why: It is important to share what we do with the outside world to inform others and to gain continued support for the important work LSS do.

PARTNERSHIPS WITH OUTSIDE AGENCIES AND ORGANIZATIONS

Alliances or partnerships with community agencies and nonprofit and business organizations most often benefit the users of libraries. Public, academic, and school libraries, while their purposes may differ, all have in common the mission to provide a high level of services for their patrons that involve lifelong learning, technology, civic duty, social inclusion, and literacy. None of these can be solely delivered by the library staff; rather it takes a community partnership to support these goals.

School libraries partner with other school libraries, but they are also a member of the school and local communities. School media specialists know that when they collaborate with faculty to support **student learning objectives (SLO)**, students' learning is enhanced through the resources and instructional supports of the library. The ongoing collaboration between school media center staff and teachers informs the purpose of the school library. In addition to faculty, another group within the school community that provides important support to the library is the parents' organization, who often raise funds and encourage library volunteers.

Another important organization the school media center partners with is the local public library. Public libraries and schools share school-age patrons. Collaboration between school and public libraries enhances children's success with summer reading, homework, and projects. Collaboration also supports and sustains students' literacy and civil and social responsibilities.

School libraries extend their partnerships to nonprofit institutions, government agencies, and businesses for specific mutual collaborations or projects. An example of partnership cooperation that made national headlines occurred among a middle school library media center, Mystic Aquarium, and a 3-D systems business. A penguin at Mystic Aquarium had an injury to the flexor tendon in her ankle, making it difficult for her to walk or swim normally.[16] Mystic Aquarium reached out to its long-standing middle school partner who had recently acquired a 3-D printer for their own studies. Working with ACT Group, a 3-D systems partner, students, with the support of the school media specialist, were able to design, create, and print a new boot for the penguin. The final boot design was printed on a 3-D printer that was able to use multiple materials, allowing the boot to be flexible for comfortable movement and rigid to support the injured tendon.

Public libraries continually work with and cooperate with their governing agencies or municipal governments of the town or city. They also collaborate with other town agencies such as police, health and human services, public works, and so forth. Many libraries have agreements for resource sharing and patron visitations with local museums and historical societies. Libraries today may create and share local history collections through shared digitization efforts.

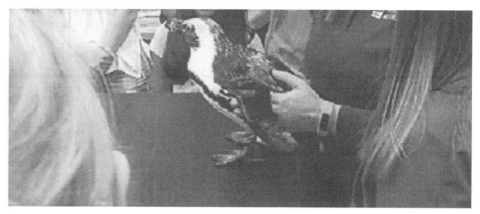

Figure 10.1.   Penguin boot—Partnership of Mystic Middle School Library Media Center, Mystic Aquarium, and ACT. *Mystic Middle School*

TechSoup for Libraries provides ten examples of successful library cooperative projects around the country.[17] From these examples are the following:

- **Salt Lake City Public Library** has established itself as the community gathering place. The city block it occupies, called Library Square, includes retail outlets such as the Community Writing Center of Salt Lake Community College, a nonprofit artist's cooperative, public radio station KCPW, a delicatessen, a coffee shop, and Night Flight Comics, a graphic novel and comics shop. The library's contract with the retailers stipulates that they must be community-focused. They share programming, training, broadcasting, and implementation of large events. More than one thousand other groups and organizations meet at SLCPL, including the League of Women Voters, Wasatch Coalition for Peace and Justice, Utah Quilters, Utah Storytelling Guild, the Authors Club, Women in Recovery, and Leukemia and Lymphoma Society. Most of these groups partner in programming with SLCPL, making the library not only the place to meet in Salt Lake City but the place to develop events as well.[18]
- **Laramie County Library System, Wyoming**, has formed alliances that include the Wyoming State Museum, Old West Museum, Laramie County Head Start, Stride Learning Center, Cheyenne Animal Shelter, YMCA, Cheyenne Boys and Girls Club, Cheyenne Lions Club, Cheyenne Rotary Club, Cheyenne Eye Clinic, Starbucks, Cheyenne Women's Civic League, and Susan G. Komen Breast Cancer Foundation. The collaborations are evidence of a strong and valued community library.[19]
- **Nashville Public Library** and their community partners provide programs in literacy, culture, public affairs, education, design, and local history. Partners include the Vanderbilt Symphony, the Hispanic Chamber of Commerce, the National Association for the Education of Young Children, the Nashville Kurdish Association, the Women's Bar Association, and the Intermuseum

Figure 10.2. Rotunda exhibit. *Courtesy of Cheyenne Frontier Days, Old West Museum*

Figure 10.3. Civil rights. *istock/emarto*

Council. To educate the community about the significant role that Nashville citizens played in the civil rights movement, the library built a Civil Rights Room and presents programs with the National League of Cities, Fisk University, the First Baptist Church, the First Amendment Center, and the Winter Institute for Racial Reconciliation. According to the Tennessee state librarian, the Nashville Public Library is "a diverse and welcoming activity hub and a center for public discourse."[20]

Every public library should have many collaborative success stories. When the community believes in the mission of their library, common interests and goals can be achieved through the power of outside partnerships.

The primary collaborations of academic libraries are within the university or college that they serve. The staff of the academic library support faculty in their delivery of curriculum and instruction as well as their research endeavors. Students are likewise supported with resources and instruction in the tools of research. The academic library may also be the archive of the university, digitizing and preserving original artifacts and materials from important donations.

Academic libraries also support each other in formal collaborations, often around materials found via OCLC or consortium catalogs. They participate in interlibrary loan and may assist with the research of other universities' patrons. At conferences and meetings, academic library staff share professional learning, training, and expertise.

Academic libraries also partner with national and state government agencies around topics of history, health, medicine, law, science, and other professions. Distinguished academic libraries are members of the Digital Library Federation, a group of leading libraries and institutions who, along with the Library of Congress and the Smithsonian, set standards for creating and sharing exemplar and important digital collections.

Special libraries can be nonprofit, such as medical libraries, government or military libraries, or libraries of humanities councils or museums. These libraries form partnerships with their colleagues in similar professions in the United States and around the world. The National Institute of Health National Library of Medicine has formal partnerships with the following medical libraries in order to share important and most current research, materials, and resources:[21]

- American Library Association (ALA)
- American Society for Information Science and Technology (ASIS&T)
- Association for Information and Image Management (AIIM, U.S.)
- Association for Library and Information Science Education (ALISE)
- Association of Moving Image Archivists (AMIA)
- Association of Research Libraries (ARL)
- Coalition for Networked Information (CNI)
- Communication Institute for Online Scholarship (CIOS)
- Council on Library and Information Resources (CLIR)
- European Association for Health Information and Libraries (EAHIL)
- International Council of Scientific and Technical Information (ICSTI)
- International Federation of Library Associations (IFLA)

- National Federation of Advanced Information Services (NFAIS, U.S.)
- Special Libraries Association (SLA)

In a second example, the Scherer Library of Musical Theater is the premier library for archiving and preserving artifacts of American musical theater.[22] It is also a research center for musicians, actors, writers, and others who produce theatrical works. The library staff collaborate with other artists and theaters around the world as they share historical information, scripts, screenplays, musical scores, and other important artifacts of original plays. Using the tools of metadata and cataloging, the Scherer is developing a digital collection to one day be accessed and shared electronically with other libraries and patrons. The work of this special library is preserving a unique part of American culture and history.

Other special libraries are found in for-profit business. These libraries support the research and economic growth of the corporation. Special libraries archive, manage, and disseminate collections of comprehensive information and research databases on topics related to the parent business. A special library also develops its own collections of files and documents of its work in a subject of its business. While special libraries safeguard and protect classified information of the organization, they also collaborate and share best practices by being members of the Special Libraries Association (SLA).

CHAPTER SUMMARY

LSS support the goals of the library when they are actively involved in the consortia or partnerships formed with other libraries and outside organizations. While barriers may exist to the success of a partnership, LSS who understand the successful principles of partnerships can serve as valued members of task forces or committees that solve problems or set standards for the group. LSS who appreciate and contribute to the success of their library's partnerships with other libraries, agencies, and organizations are valued employees who help the library meet its goals of programming, cost sharing, professional development, or other benefits to the community.

DISCUSSION QUESTIONS

1. Review the principles of successful partnerships. What other ways can LSS support these principles?
2. What other barriers have you personally encountered in forming partnerships? Explain how one of these barriers could also apply to a library partnership.
3. Of the library services described in this chapter that may be enhanced through partnerships with other libraries, which one do you think would have the greatest benefit for your library and why?
4. What partnerships (other than those described in this chapter) would benefit your public library? Who would be the other partnership members, and why would the collaboration between the library and these agencies be beneficial to all?

ACTIVITY

Write a proposal for a new library partnership.

- Identify a potential partnership for your library that would improve programming, purchasing, or technology.
- To whom is the proposal being addressed? Who will take action on it?
- Write a brief abstract of the issue to be enhanced or resolved through consortium membership.
- Who would be the potential consortium members and why would they be interested in joining?
- What would be the estimated expense for your library?
- Who would provide leadership for the consortium and oversee its work?
- What obligation would there be for library staff? What benefits would they obtain?
- How would the consortium know that it is successful?
- What is the time frame of consortium membership for your library?
- What other considerations do you have for the proposal?

NOTES

1. John Donne, "No Man Is an Island," accessed September 9, 2017, www.oatridge.co.uk/poems/j/john-donne-no-man-is-an-island.php.

2. Stanford University, "Principles of Partnerships," Haas Center for Public Service, accessed September 9, 2017, haas.stanford.edu/sites/default/files/principlesofpartnerships.pdf.

3. Community Tool Box, "Creating and Maintaining Partnerships," Toolkit, last modified 2017, accessed September 19, 2017, ctb.ku.edu/en/creating-and-maintaining-partnerships.

4. Boston Library Consortium, "Boston Library Consortium—for Librarians," last modified 2017, accessed September 10, 2017, blc.org/.

5. Marshall Breeding, "The Rush to Innovate," *Library Journal* 138, no. 6 (April 20, 2013), search.ebscohost.com/login.aspx?direct=true&db=aph&AN=86373836&authtype=cookie,cpid&custid=csl&site=ehost-live&scope=site.

6. OCLC, "About OCLC," last modified 2017, accessed September 18, 2017, www.oclc.org/en/about.html.

7. Indiana State Library, "Evergreen Indiana," State Library Evergreen Indiana Catalog, last modified 2017, accessed September 18, 2017, www.in.gov/library/catalog.htm.

8. Office of Library and Information Services, "Directory of LORI Libraries," State of Rhode Island Office of Library and Information Services, last modified 2017, accessed September 18, 2017, www.olis.ri.gov/libraries/directory.php.

9. Wisconsin Department of Public Instruction, "AE 17: Membership in the Library System," Public Library Development, last modified 2017, accessed September 18, 2017, dpi.wi.gov/pld/boards-directors/administrative-essentials/system-membership.

10. Montgomery County Public Schools, "Destiny Library Manager," School Library Media Programs, last modified 2017, accessed September 18, 2017, www.montgomeryschoolsmd.org/departments/media/destiny/.

11. Connecticut Library Consortium, "Our Mission," About CLC—What We Do, last modified 2017, accessed September 18, 2017, www.ctlibrarians.org/?page=WhatWeDo.

12. Ibid.

13. One Book, One Community, "What is 'One Book'?" One Book, One Community: Our Region Reads, last modified 2017, accessed September 18, 2017, www.oboc.org/what-is-one-book.html.

14. Boston Library Consortium, "Boston Library."

15. Abby Johnson, "Leadership in Librarianship: Professional Development Isn't Just for Managers," *American Libraries* 48, no. 9/10 (September/October 2017), search.ebscohost.com/login.aspx?direct=true&db=lxh&AN=124915493&authtype=cookie,cpid&custid=csl&site=ehost-live&scope=site.

16. Sea Research Foundation, Inc., "Mystic Aquarium Partners with Local Middle School Students and Technology Group to Help Enhance Mobility of Injured African Penguin," Mystic Aquarium Research, last modified July 18, 2016, accessed September 18, 2017, www.mysticaquarium.org/2016/07/20/mystic-aquarium-partners-with-local-school-tech-group-to-help-injured-penguin/.

17. TechSoup, "Ten Examples of Successful Library Collaborative Project," TechSoup for Libraries, last modified 2017, accessed September 18, 2017, www.techsoupforlibraries.org/planning-for-success/communication-and-partnerships/tools/ten-examples-of-successful-library-collabo.

18. Ibid.

19. Ibid.

20. Ibid.

21. U.S. National Library of Medicine, "Partners of NLM," last modified 2017, accessed September 19, 2017, www.nlm.nih.gov/about/partners.html.

22. Goodspeed Musicals, "Library," last modified 2017, accessed September 18, 2017, www.goodspeed.org/education-library/library?gclid=CLuXoob4r9YCFZiEswodLagM1w.

REFERENCES, SUGGESTED READINGS, AND WEBSITES

Boston Library Consortium. "Boston Library Consortium—for Librarians." Last modified 2017. Accessed September 10, 2017. blc.org/.

Breeding, Marshall. "The Rush to Innovate." *Library Journal* 138, no. 6 (April 20, 2013): 32. search.ebscohost.com/login.aspx?direct=true&db=aph&AN=86373836&authtype=cookie,cpid&custid=csl&site=ehost-live&scope=site.

Community Tool Box. "Creating and Maintaining Partnerships." Toolkit. Last modified 2017. Accessed September 19, 2017. ctb.ku.edu/en/creating-and-maintaining-partnerships.

Connecticut Library Consortium. "Our Mission." About CLC—What We Do. Last modified 2017. Accessed September 18, 2017. www.ctlibrarians.org/?page=WhatWeDo.

Donne, John. "No Man Is an Island." Accessed September 9, 2017. www.oatridge.co.uk/poems/j/john-donne-no-man-is-an-island.php.

Goodspeed Musicals. "Library." Last modified 2017. Accessed September 18, 2017. www.goodspeed.org/education-library/library?gclid=CLuXoob4r9YCFZiEswodLagM1w.

Indiana State Library. "Evergreen Indiana." State Library Evergreen Indiana Catalog. Last modified 2017. Accessed September 18, 2017. www.in.gov/library/catalog.htm.

Johnson, Abby. "Leadership in Librarianship: Professional Development Isn't Just for Managers." *American Libraries* 48, no. 9/10 (September/October 2017): 56. search.ebscohost.com/login.aspx?direct=true&db=lxh&AN=124915493&authtype=cookie,cpid&custid=csl&site=ehost-live&scope=site.

Montgomery County Public Schools. "Destiny Library Manager." School Library Media Programs. Last modified 2017. Accessed September 18, 2017. www.montgomeryschoolsmd.org/departments/media/destiny/.

Mystic Aquarium. "Mystic Aquarium Partners with Local School & Tech Group to Help Injured Penguin." Mystic Aquarium Press Releases. Last modified 2016. Accessed September 18, 2017. www.mysticaquarium.org/2016/07/20/mystic-aquarium-partners-with-local -school-tech-group-to-help-injured-penguin/.

OCLC. "About OCLC." Last modified 2017. Accessed September 18, 2017. www.oclc.org/en/ about.html.

Office of Library and Information Services. "Directory of LORI Libraries." State of Rhode Island Office of Library and Information Services. Last modified 2017. Accessed September 18, 2017. www.olis.ri.gov/libraries/directory.php.

One Book, One Community. "What is 'One Book'?" One Book, One Community: Our Region Reads. Last modified 2017. Accessed September 18, 2017. www.oboc.org/what-is -one-book.html.

Sea Research Foundation, Inc. "Mystic Aquarium Partners with Local Middle School Students and Technology Group to Help Enhance Mobility of Injured African Penguin." Mystic Aquarium Research. Last modified July 18, 2016. Accessed September 18, 2017. www .mysticaquarium.org/2016/07/20/mystic-aquarium-partners-with-local-school-tech-group -to-help-injured-penguin/.

Stanford University. "Principles of Partnerships." Haas Center for Public Service. Accessed September 9, 2017. haas.stanford.edu/sites/default/files/principlesofpartnerships.pdf.

TechSoup. "Ten Examples of Successful Library Collaborative Project." TechSoup for Libraries. Last modified 2017. Accessed September 18, 2017. www.techsoupforlibraries.org/plan ning-for-success/communication-and-partnerships/tools/ten-examples-of-successful-li brary-collabo.

U.S. National Library of Medicine. "Partners of NLM." Last modified 2017. Accessed September 19, 2017. www.nlm.nih.gov/about/partners.html.

Wisconsin Department of Public Instruction. "AE 17: Membership in the Library System." Public Library Development. Last modified 2017. Accessed September 18, 2017. dpi.wi .gov/pld/boards-directors/administrative-essentials/system-membership.

CHAPTER 11

Library Marketing

LSS know the principles of marketing the library and its services and can develop and implement a marketing plan. (ALA-LSSC Supervision and Management Competency #12)

Topics Covered in This Chapter:

- Library Marketing
  - o Marketing Plans
  - o Marketing Tools
- Promotion
  - o Displays and Signage
  - o Public Relations
- Branding
- Library Programs and Activities

Key Terms:

Branding: Branding is the process involved in creating a unique name and image in the consumer's mind for a product (or library) through advertising campaigns with a consistent theme.

Marketing: Marketing is the advancement of an idea through publicity or promotion. It is based on thinking about the library in terms of customer needs and satisfaction. It relies on designing the library's offerings in terms of those needs and on using effective communication to inform and motivate patrons.

Marketing plan: A marketing plan is a document that outlines the library's advertising efforts. It describes activities involved in achieving specific goals and objectives for the library in a set time, such as one year.

Promotion: Promotion is a variety of activities designed to educate patrons about the materials and services that the library offers. It refers to the overall process, rather than a specific activity.

Public relations: Public relations are activities that help the public or user group to understand, accept, and support the programs or initiatives of a library.

Marketing is part of any library's public service. Besides wanting to bring attention to programs or services, libraries are in competition with so many other options including bookstores and the Internet. There are those, of course, who predict the end of libraries, but we are finding that they are still relevant both as a place to find materials and services and as the "third place"—the social area separate from home and work. People are living increasingly more isolated lives, as evidenced by the upswing in social networking. Libraries are often the social center of a community. LSS who work in supervisory positions must recognize this and work with other library staff to effectively communicate it.

LIBRARY MARKETING

Marketing, for libraries, is based on thinking about customer needs and their satisfaction. It consists of an effort to discover, create, and satisfy customer needs. In other words, marketing has less to do with getting customers to "buy" a product than it does developing a demand for that product, and thus fulfilling the customer's needs.[1] This is done all the time on television and in magazines—products and services are designed to meet a need; marketing lets the potential market know these products are available and, in turn, influences our behavior. In effect, they suggest we have needs we didn't know we had. QVC, the Home Shopping Network, and product infomercials even let you call in *right now* before you can change your mind. Marketing relies heavily on designing the library's offering in terms of the target market's needs and desires and on using effective communication to inform and motivate. We want the public to know what we offer and to come in right now to get it before it's gone! It is "necessary to help nonprofits promote their values, accomplish their mission, and develop increased resources to address a wide range of compelling concerns."[2] Libraries have been slow to come to the marketing table. After all, we're libraries and everyone knows what we do. Or do they? Libraries have changed so much that it is no longer good enough to rest on our former reputation. If we don't let the public know what we are about these days, who will? Libraries have a product, and we need to make the public aware of that product and that the library is the best place to get it. We need to get our patrons to think of the library not just as a place for books or meeting space, but as a place of cultural preservation of information in its various formats.

Marketing Plans

A **marketing plan** is a document that outlines the library's marketing efforts. It describes activities involved in achieving specific goals and objectives for the library in a set time, such as one year. It will provide a strategic framework for the ways you communicate with the audiences that are important to your efforts. The plan should support the overall mission and goals of your library and should be reviewed and updated annually. The marketing plan typically has several components:

1. Introduction: What is the environment?
2. Goals: What do you want to happen?
3. Objectives: What will be accomplished?
4. Positioning statement: How do you want the library to be perceived?
5. Target audience: Who needs to hear your message?
6. Key messages: What is the most important message you want to deliver?
7. Strategies: How will you deliver the message?
8. Evaluation: How will you know what worked and didn't work?
9. Summary of findings.[3]

Let's look at these elements. The introduction should address the challenges and opportunities to be considered. An example of this could be *"Because our library is in an old building, people think our materials and services are out of date."* How can this be addressed? This leads to setting goals, such as *"The public will recognize that we are a vibrant and modern facility."* The objective then could be *"We will see an increase in attendance and use of materials within one year."* How then you want the library to be perceived becomes *"Our library offers free access to information for people of all ages and backgrounds; they can get assistance from our trained staff."* Who are we targeting with these services, and why are our resources and services important to them? *"Our internal audience might include the staff, trustees, and friends, while our external audience could include parents, students, school principals, and the mayor."*

Next, what is your key message? It could be something like *"The library—it connects—people to people, people to place, people to learning,"* or, *"Your link to the past & gateway to the future."*[4] Now what is your strategy going to be? Identify publicity and outreach aimed at your target audience and ways to deliver it. We will examine specific strategies later in the chapter when we talk about library promotion. Finally, you can evaluate your success by measurable factors such as circulation statistics, program attendance, website visits, surveys, word of mouth feedback, and so on. Once you have gathered all this information and put it together, you will have your marketing plan.[5]

Marketing Tools

One strategy that libraries have adopted is to mimic the services of a bookstore.[6] Many libraries are borrowing the best of bookstores by offering more comfortable seating, coffee bars, face-out shelving, and more staff on the floor. Some are even choosing to do away with traditional library cataloging in favor of subject cataloging, or grouping like topics together. According to the Maricopa County Library District in Arizona, "The library was designed to be customer-centric. That emphasis included placing low shelving at the entrance to draw people into the collection, tripling the number of lounge chairs, creating reading nooks, and adding signage to help patrons navigate."[7] Variations of this theme are being used in libraries all over the country.

Figure 11.1.   Library with coffee and book sign. *istock/cgj0212*

Besides changing the layout of the library, other marketing methods are being used to highlight library services in an ever-competitive market. "The advertising arena has changed. Today there are so many more choices and so much clutter. . . . The average person is exposed to 3,000 advertising messages a day."[8] That is a lot of information, and with those odds, we have to make sure that our message doesn't get lost in the barrage. However, although we may be hit with a lot of advertising, we usually remember what a friend tells us—especially if it's positive. This is a concept called word-of-mouth marketing (WOMM). It's personal, immediate, honest, and free. The LSS at the front desk are the first people encountered when someone walks through the door. It starts with them—they should be greeting patrons and telling them what's new today. Staff, trustees, town officials, and other patrons should be talking about the library. Word of mouth is a powerful marketing tool that all libraries should be using. "There is no more powerful communication technique than one person talking with and listening to another, whether it's on social media (good) or live and in person (best). WOMM tops the chart."[9]

Social media is pervasive and as such is an invaluable marketing tool as well. Facebook, blogs, Twitter, Instagram, Tumblr, e-mail, and texts are great tools to get the word out, particularly these days when most people are constantly connected to their mobile devices. Be sure you know who your target audience is, find out what their needs are, and market to them. Libraries have a diverse clientele. It's up to the library to recognize this, target their needs, and then get the word out in the most appropriate way for each group.[10]

Figure 11.2. Social media graphic. *istock/3D_generator*

PROMOTION

Libraries constantly look for new ways to engage their patrons and to draw in new ones. They can use a combination of traditional and digital methods to **promote** the library successfully.

Displays and Signage

Part of the marketing strategy includes displays. Think of the grocery or drug store: magazines and candy displayed at the checkout and aisle end cap displays of sales and specials. By highlighting inventory and making it available, the store draws attention to something it wants you to buy. These items are displayed for precisely that reason. The same can be true in the library—we want to get your attention, and it begins at the entrance.

Imagine someone new to the community walking into the library for the first time. One of the first things they might see is the circulation desk with people behind it—do they look approachable? They might see some basic informational signs. They'll see patrons, who all seem to know what they are doing. Perhaps there is a guard on duty. This could intimidate the patron and cause him to wonder if he needs permission to enter or if he needs to show his ID or library card. Some of these things may confuse or disturb a patron. No one likes to walk into an unfamiliar place, and each library differs in its arrangement. This patron may feel uneasy because he hasn't been in a library since childhood or he doesn't know what he wants or how to ask for help. He has no idea of how the library is arranged, and he may wander into the wrong room or feel confused that everyone else seems to know where they are going and what they are doing. There may be all kinds of information he needs, but it may be hard to ask.

Now imagine this same scenario with displays and signage that clearly identify the information desk; the children's, teen, and reference rooms; the computers; newspapers; magazines; and restrooms. Maybe there is an interesting display that, at the very least, gives him an excuse to loiter while he tries to get his bearings. There are different kinds of signage and displays with different purposes.

- Directional signage can provide a floor plan and a guide to the rooms within the library, such as the reference room, children's room, or restrooms.
- Location indicators on shelving can direct the patron to the content of the collection and can also be used to cross-reference parts of the collection.
- Library informational policies should be prominently displayed, such as the circulation policy, the code of conduct, and rules for Internet use, for example.
- There may be displays on topics of interest or new materials.

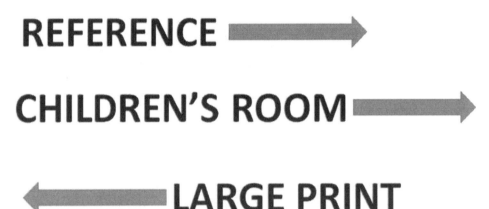

Figure 11.3.   Library signage. *Courtesy of the author*

The opportunity exists for any number of special displays—thematically linked to a holiday, season, or subject. Examples of such displays include putting flowerpots, trowels, gloves, and gardening books in a small wheelbarrow during spring; pumpkins and hay in a small wagon with fall books; highlighting cookbooks by creating a display with pots, pans, and wooden spoons or place settings. The school library displays can "sell" books. Using—or reusing—items found in the classroom or library can create excitement. Be sure that all displays use bright, clean paper and items.

There are also non-library-related displays: most libraries will have a community bulletin board or shelving with a variety of local events, information, and resources. Libraries are the go-to place for tax forms and voter registration cards. If they have the space, many libraries will also host art exhibits of local artists or schoolchildren. Other proven marketing ideas include providing passes to your patrons for local museums and other attractions (although this can get costly as the library must purchase them).

These are nonrelated in the sense that they are not directly related to library service, but they tie the library to the community. This connection can "sell" services and functions so the taxpayer and library funders can see where their dollars are going.

Public Relations

Once you have determined that you are having a program, it's the job of the LSS to get the word out. It can be the best program you ever offered, but if no one knows about it, no one will come. Most libraries can't afford billboards or signs on buses, but we can do a media campaign. This means sharing your information with as many media outlets as you can identify:

- social media
- newspapers
- radio stations
- local television
- the library website
- other libraries
- the senior center and other local organizations, clubs, and community centers
- schools and colleges

Press releases are crucial to the media campaign, and they are free. Gather all the facts, or what is referred to as the five Ws and sometimes H:

- *Who* will be speaking or presenting?
- *What* is the primary topic?
- *Where* will it take place?
- *When* will it take place?
- *Why* are you having this program?
- *How* did it happen?

The LSS will use these elements when writing a press release. The time-tested "inverted pyramid style" structure is a good model. Following this structure, the "base" of the pyramid—the most fundamental facts—appears at the top of the story, in the lead paragraph. Nonessential information appears in the following paragraphs in order of importance. Editors cut from the bottom up, and while all the information in your press release is important, the most critical news needs to be first.[11]

Identify and develop a contact within each media outlet that is used, and keep this list updated as personnel can change or get reassigned. Find out how they want the press release delivered—most will want an e-mail or an electronic form. Know when the deadlines are for each one; a minimum of two weeks is what most media outlets require, but don't assume they are alike. Send releases in advance, and make ancillary materials—photos, audio, and video—readily available. For headlines, go with clear over cute if you can't manage both. The same goes for the copy. Don't bury the lead, and don't get bogged down in jargon. In both instances, readers will turn off before they get to the message. In any case, prepare to have your words edited or rewritten; make your release precise and concise.[12]

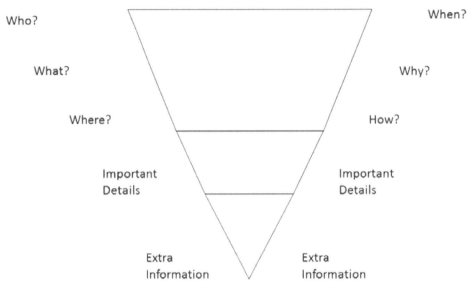

Who?   When?

What?   Why?

Where?   How?

Important   Important
Details   Details

Extra   Extra
Information   Information

Figure 11.4.   Press release inverted pyramid diagram. *Courtesy of the author*

Good illustrations (photos, charts, etc.) are a vital way to communicate to your audience why they should care about your offering. Provide ample but not overwhelming background, including your own—don't make it difficult to contact you for further details. Don't bombard contacts with irrelevant releases, or harass someone who chooses not to give you coverage. Take no for an answer, or you may lose the contact altogether.

Follow up with a phone call, if possible, to make sure they got your information. Think of it from their point of view: there are a lot of organizations with events

---

TEXTBOX 11.1: SAMPLE PRESS RELEASE

Contact: Susan Smith
Phone (123) 456-7890; Fax (123) 456-7891
E-mail: s.smith@anytownpl.org

FOR IMMEDIATE RELEASE

Outdoor Art Show at Anytown Public Library

Enjoy the soft summer breezes as you experience inspiring works of art at the first annual Anytown Public Library Outdoor Art Fair on Saturday, July 18, from 11 to 4. Families and art lovers are invited to come and make a day of it by exploring the grounds, picnicking in a lovely setting, watching an artist at work, or purchasing a beautiful original piece of art. There will be something fun for everyone in the family.

This event is free and open to the public. The Anytown Public Library is located at in the heart of the historic district at 46 Main Street, Anytown, USA. Parking is free and refreshments will be available for sale. For more information, please call the library at (123) 456-7890 or check us out on the web at anytownlibrary.org.

and they may be inundated at any given time with hundreds of press releases from schools, libraries, local businesses, and organizations. Make sure that yours has been received and acknowledged. If possible, include a photo with your press release to a newspaper or on your web page or newsletter. Try to establish a relationship with the photography department at the local paper; they will be more likely to send a photographer to cover your event if they know who you are.

If it is a very special event and the budget permits, you can place a paid ad in your local newspaper. Most newspapers include all press releases and paid ads in their digital version as well so it increases the visibility. However, it can be quite expensive, as newspapers charge by the column inch—the larger the ad, the higher the price. The rate for a nonprofit in a local newspaper may cost about $33 per column inch for a weekday ad. The price increases to $38 for the Sunday paper. For a small town with a circulation of only about 29,000 subscribers, you can imagine this can be a costly venture, but one worth considering depending on your event and your budget.

Public relations is an ongoing job. We've been talking about it in terms of a specific program, but ultimately *all* libraries want to maintain a high profile in the community. Good PR supports the library's resources and collections. Libraries must prove their value to their funders. The greater the number of people who are aware of the library, the more who will use it, promote it, and support it. This is particularly important at budget time when the library may be competing with other town departments for limited dollars.

We know that competition for money is not the only threat to the viability of libraries: the Internet has made it easier for people to think that everything they need can be found on the web. It is incumbent upon us to reinforce that we are the proponents of information literacy and that the LSS can direct patrons to quality information from reliable resources. We need to do everything we can to increase our visibility and remain relevant.[13]

BRANDING

Another way to increase your visibility is by **branding**. Branding is different from marketing; rather, it is an important first step and part of the "marketing mix." Branding is part of the marketing *strategy*, while promotion and publicity are part of the marketing *tools*.[14] Branding is the process involved in creating a unique name and image for a product in the consumer's mind, through advertising campaigns with a consistent theme. Branding aims to establish a presence in the market that attracts and retains loyal customers. It's making your library known for something.

Think about commercial brands. You see an image or logo and instantly think of what it represents. In business the brand is for a product, but in libraries it is for a service. "Within a service profession the staff's relationships and interactions with customers play a pivotal role in influencing brand quality and brand values."[15] That is the purpose behind branding a library. It can be an image, a logo, a tagline, or anything that makes the library instantly recognizable. Using the library's brand in all marketing and public relations reinforces its value to the community. Examples of library branding can include an eye-catching logo as well as a tagline, such as Wa-

Figure 11.5. Display of brands. *istock/OfirPeretz*

terford Pubic Library in Connecticut: *Discovery Begins Here*; Curtis Memorial Library in Maine: *A World of Possibility*; and the Cuyahoga County Public Library in Ohio: *browsing is just the beginning*.

Possibilities for branding are limitless, but it can be a challenging process that takes a lot of time and energy. Having an objective facilitator for a series of brainstorming sessions is helpful, as she can keep the group on task and mediate, if necessary. It can be an emotional process, but the result can go a long way toward making your marketing strategy more effective.

LIBRARY PROGRAMS AND ACTIVITIES

Libraries can also market themselves through programs and activities. In doing so, they bring people into the library for a variety of reasons: to expose patrons to art, music, and the humanities; for the sake of community spirit and connections; and for all manner of learning opportunities.

There are a variety of things that libraries can offer to make themselves both visible and essential to the community. For example, educational programs can include offering lifelong learning with classes on foreign languages, finance, health and fitness, nutrition, aging, and more. Many libraries offer lectures on a variety of topics relevant to the community, such as local history, medical issues, and health insurance. Using library resources and services in collaboration with facilitators in the community can provide a wealth of opportunity, for the public and for the library.

For those who have limited reading or language skills, the library can offer classes in literacy by collaborating with literacy volunteers or English as a Second

Language (ESL) tutors. For the poor, homeless, or otherwise underserved, classes on résumé writing and interviewing are invaluable as are classes on life skills, how to manage a budget, or how to apply for local, state, or federal aid. This may be a group that is unaware that the library has these vital services. LSS must find these populations and get this information to them, perhaps through social service agencies and community centers.

For children, teens, the newly literate, or GED candidates, the library can offer homework help by collaborating with schools or student mentors. LSS can offer this opportunity for teens needing community service hours, and it can be promoted by teachers and counselors at school. For the college bound, informational programs are popular to help with the universal application or writing the college essay or assisting parents with issues of financing and student support. The library, collaborating with the school system or board of education, can market these resources directly to those who need them.

Recreational programs are another important part of library service. Less structured perhaps than educational programming, it is no less instructive. As an example, book discussions, a staple of library programming, offer an opportunity for stimulating thought and can be on any topic, such as science fiction and fantasy, history, political novels, or any number of themes. Held in the library and marketed to the community through both traditional and social media, book clubs can be a great marketing tool.

TEXTBOX 11.2: SOCIAL MEDIA POST OF LIBRARY EVENT

Join Seattle author Bharti Kirchner in a warmhearted conversation with American librarian Nancy Pearl about her debut novel *George and Lizzie*. Q & A follows.
   Get tips on reading and writing from authors.
      www.spl.org/calendar-of-events?trumbaEmbed=view%3Devent%26eventid%3D126132073

Also included as recreational programming are summer reading programs for children that reinforce skills while out of school and promote reading-related activities. Widely marketed by libraries and local schools, they are a popular summer library activity. Many states participate in the Collaborative Summer Library Program, which provides themes and supporting materials to libraries, as well as online programs with components for children, teens, and adults.[16] For example, CSLP's theme for the summer of 2018 was music, and the slogan, "Libraries Rock." For summer of 2019, the theme is space and the slogan is "A Universe of Stories"; for 2020, fairy tales/mythology/fantasy. Reading programs solve the problem of how to keep kids involved in literacy—and using the library—all year round. Another children's activity that has proven popular is the international "Take your Child to the Library Day" to market the library to families. Held the first Saturday in February, this program for families and literacy has a dual purpose in that the library can use this and similar programs and services to inform elected officials and taxpayers, who get to see a positive example of how their dollars are being used.

Gaming is a recreational offering for all ages, ranging from board games and scavenger hunts to mentally and physically challenging interactive computer games for all ages. Teens especially like gaming, and they are likely to utilize word-of-mouth marketing to get their friends involved.

Films are always popular (but as an aside, it is important to know that if movies are shown, the library must obtain a Public Performance License, available from a variety of vendors. This is an umbrella license that covers many film studios and allows for the free showing of anything in their catalog).[17] Ideally all programs reinforce the value of the library and the services it provides. When planning a movie night, rather than just set up the equipment and leave the room, plan to discuss the movie when it is done. Perhaps set up a display of books and other materials that relate to the theme of the film. Choose movies that have name recognition and model your event after Sundance, Cannes, and the Oscars. Be aware of whom your target audience is: that of a public library will differ from that of a K–12 school and requires different licensing.[18] Regardless, films can attract a wide audience for an inexpensive night out, something libraries want to encourage.

Figure 11.6. People attending a library program. *istock/Rawpixel*

Outreach programming is yet another way LSS can connect with patrons. It can include library service to the homebound, nursing homes, or day-care centers—sending books or volunteer readers to these locations. Outreach also refers to book mobiles, a boon to rural communities and those without regular access to a library. A 2007 book by Masha Hamilton, *The Camel Bookmobile*, is a novel based on the true events of book delivery by camel to far-flung villages in Africa.[19] While this is an extreme example of outreach, it does serve to illustrate the need to get library materials to those who cannot physically come to a library. Outreach does not necessarily mean off the premises, though. Providing multicultural collections and materials in other languages is also a means of reaching underserved populations. By contacting social service agencies, LSS can obtain and display brochures and flyers about community services and food and shelter resources, and vice versa for library programs.

Network with your colleagues to see what they have done lately and if it was successful. LSS cannot ignore the value that marketing through these services can bring to the library.

CHAPTER SUMMARY

Libraries are many things to many people in a community; they therefore offer a multitude of materials, activities, and services to their constituents. Library staff must have a plan to promote and market these services. A marketing plan and the relevant tools will help to get the message out. Using public relations and targeted promotion will ensure the message gets to the people who will most want to know about and use these services.[20]

DISCUSSION QUESTIONS

1. What is a marketing plan?
2. It is almost impossible to escape the barrage of advertising in the media. What makes you pay attention to an ad? How would you adapt that for library marketing?
3. Using your local print or online newspaper and social media sites, find five examples of library press releases. Do they tell you all you need to know? Is there any pattern that *makes them similar?*
4. How do displays and signage fit into library promotion and marketing?
5. Do you think that library branding is necessary? Why or why not?

ACTIVITIES

1. Using your local library, or one that you use frequently, create a marketing plan. Take into consideration your perception of what their strengths and weaknesses might be.
2. Look at some programs that your library has given in the past. Using the information that you have, write a press release for one of them. To whom would you send this information and through what means?

NOTES

1. WebFinance, Inc., "Marketing," Business Dictionary, last modified 2017, accessed December 4, 2017, www.businessdictionary.com/definition/marketing.html.

2. Amy Shaw and Peter Deekle, *Outstanding Public Relations: 60 Years of the John Cotton Dana Award* (Chicago, IL: American Library Association, 2007), 4.

3. American Library Association, "Marketing @ Your Library," last modified 2007, accessed December 4, 2017, www.ala.org/ala/pio/campaign/prtools/marketing_wkbk.pdf.

4. Brandon Gaille, "List of 37 Catchy Library Slogans and Taglines," BrandonGaille.com, last modified September 8, 2013, accessed December 4, 2017, brandongaille.com/list-37 -catchy-library-slogans-and-taglines/.

5. ALA, "Marketing @ Your Library."

6. Steve Coffman, "What If You Ran Your Library Like a Bookstore?" *American Libraries*, last modified March 1998, accessed December 4, 2017, search.ebscohost.com/login .aspx?direct=true&db=aph&AN=306538&authtype=cookie,cpid&custid=s1024272&site= ehost-live&scope=site.

7. Barbara Fister, "The Dewey Dilemma," *Library Journal*, last modified October 1, 2009, accessed December 4, 2017, search.ebscohost.com/login.aspx?direct=true&db=aph& AN=44468055&authtype=cookie,cpid&custid=s1024272&site=ehost-live&scope=site.

8. Peggy Barber and Linda Wallace, "The Power of Word-of-Mouth Marketing," *American Libraries*, last modified November 2009, accessed December 4, 2017, search.ebscohost .com/login.aspx?direct=true&db=aph&AN=45315135&authtype=cookie,cpid&custid= s1024272&site=ehost-live&scope=site.

9. Ibid.

10. Hali R. Keeler, *Working with Library Collections: An Introduction for Support Staff*, Library Support Staff Handbooks 4 (Lanham, MD: Rowman & Littlefield, 2017), 158.

11. Ibid., 154–55.

12. Laurie Russo, "Mastering Marketing | Library Promotion," *Library Journal*, last modified March 9, 2017, accessed December 4, 2017, lj.libraryjournal.com/2017/03/lj-in-print/master ing-marketing-library-promotion/.

13. Anita Rothwell Lindsay, *Marketing and Public Relations Practices in College Libraries*, CLIP Notes 34 (Chicago, IL: American Library Association, 2004).

14. Elisabeth Doucett, "Branding for Public Libraries," Lyrasis, last modified December 8, 2009, accessed February 5, 2015, www.slideshare.net/conniemassey/branding-for-public-li braries.

15. Keeler, *Working with Library Collections*, 158.

16. Collaborative Summer Library Program, "Future Programs," last modified 2017, accessed December 4, 2017, www.cslpreads.org/programs/future-programs/.

17. Motion Picture Licensing Corporation, "Welcome to The Motion Picture Licensing Corporation," accessed December 4, 2017, www.mplc.org/.

18. Swank Motion Pictures, Inc., "K–12 Schools Movie Licensing USA," accessed December 4, 2017, www.swank.com/k-12-schools/.

19. Masha Hamilton, *The Camel Bookmobile* (New York: Harper Collins, 2007).

20. Keeler, *Working with Library Collections*, 150–52.

REFERENCES, SUGGESTED READINGS, AND WEBSITES

American Library Association. "Marketing @ Your Library." Last modified 2007. Accessed December 4, 2017. www.ala.org/ala/pio/campaign/prtools/marketing_wkbk.pdf.

Barber, Peggy, and Linda Wallace. "The Power of Word-of-Mouth Marketing." *American Libraries*. Last modified November 2009. Accessed December 4, 2017. search.ebsco host.com/login.aspx?direct=true&db=aph&AN=45315135&authtype=cookie,cpid& custid=s1024272&site=ehost-live&scope=site.

"Branding for Libraries: New Opportunities, New Behaviors, New Consumers." Video file, 1:13. Vimeo. Posted 2015. Accessed December 4, 2017. vimeo.com/125032399.

Coffman, Steve. "What If You Ran Your Library Like a Bookstore?" *American Libraries*. Last modified March 1998. Accessed December 4, 2017. search.ebscohost.com/login .aspx?direct=true&db=aph&AN=306538&authtype=cookie,cpid&custid=s1024272&site= ehost-live&scope=site.

Collaborative Summer Library Program. "Future Programs." Last modified 2017. Accessed December 4, 2017. www.cslpreads.org/programs/future-programs/.

Doucett, Elisabeth. "Branding for Public Libraries." Lyrasis. Last modified December 4, 2009. Accessed December 5, 2017. www.slideshare.net/conniemassey/branding-for-public-libraries.

Fister, Barbara. "The Dewey Dilemma." *Library Journal*. Last modified October 1, 2009. Accessed December 4, 2017. search.ebscohost.com/login.aspx?direct=true&db=aph&AN=44468055& authtype=cookie,cpid&custid=s1024272&site=ehost-live&scope=site.

Gaille, Brandon. "List of 37 Catchy Library Slogans and Taglines." BrandonGaille.com. Last modified September 8, 2013. Accessed December 4, 2017. brandongaille.com/list-37 -catchy-library-slogans-and-taglines/.

Hamilton, Masha. *The Camel Bookmobile*. New York: Harper Collins, 2007.

Keeler, Hali R. *Working with Library Collections: An Introduction for Support Staff*. Library Support Staff Handbooks 4. Lanham, MD: Rowman & Littlefield, 2017.

Lindsay, Anita Rothwell. *Marketing and Public Relations Practices in College Libraries*. CLIP Notes 34. Chicago, IL: American Library Association, 2004.

Motion Picture Licensing Corporation. "Welcome to the Motion Picture Licensing Corporation." Accessed December 4, 2017. www.mplc.org/.

Russo, Laurie. "Mastering Marketing | Library Promotion." *Library Journal*. Last modified March 9, 2017. Accessed December 4, 2017. lj.libraryjournal.com/2017/03/lj-in-print/mas tering-marketing-library-promotion/.

Shaw, Amy, and Peter Deekle. *Outstanding Public Relations: 60 Years of the John Cotton Dana Award*. Chicago, IL: American Library Association, 2007.

Swank Motion Pictures, Inc. "K–12 Schools Movie Licensing USA." Accessed December 4, 2017. www.swank.com/k-12-schools/.

———. "Public Libraries: Movie Licensing USA." Accessed December 4, 2017. www.swank .com/public-libraries/.

WebFinance, Inc. "Marketing." Business Dictionary. Last modified 2017. Accessed December 4, 2017. www.businessdictionary.com/definition/marketing.html.

CHAPTER 12

Planning, Goal Management, Objectives, and Assessment

LSS develop realistic goals and measurable objectives after careful consideration of benefits, risks, and impact on library current and future needs. (ALA-LSSC Supervision and Management Competency #13)

Topics Covered in This Chapter:

- Needs Assessment
- Planning Elements
  - o Vision
  - o Mission
  - o Core Values
  - o Goals
  - o Objectives
  - o Outcomes
  - o Action Plans
  - o Activities and Daily Work
- Assessment

Key Terms:

Improvement plan: This is a formal process where a team is established to recommend significant change in one or more aspects of the library program that is in need of new services, modification, or retraction.

PIE: This is an acronym for the three actions of planning, implementation, and evaluation of programs and services that LSS can identify in the improvement process.

SMART: This is an acronym that identifies five steps in the goal-writing process. A successful goal for library improvement will be specific, measurable, achievable, relevant, and time-bound.

Stakeholders: These are the community of supporters such as patrons, staff, students, faculty, taxpayers, donors, board members, and any others who use or have a connection to the library.

Strategic plan: This type of plan is a review of the full library for the purpose of significant change for the near future. Often referred to as a long-range plan, it is usually developed for three to five years and may take a year or more to implement. This time-consuming process involves all library staff and many of its stakeholders.

Student learning outcomes: Also known by the acronym of SLO, these are statements of what students will know and be able to do based on instruction.

Successful administrators and leaders plan their work around the current and future goals and needs of the library that have been identified by representatives of the library community. There are many models for planning in business, education, libraries, and other nonprofits. Each model develops steps and actions to best achieve target goals. This chapter explains how the need for a new plan is determined, the elements of planning, and how LSS can align their work to help meet the library mission.

NEEDS ASSESSMENT

Planning is spurred by some type of major need the library board and director have identified. A needs assessment process reveals the influences acting on the library. Information collected shapes the services and programs that best fit the library's strengths and budget. Ultimately, it informs a vision for future development.[1] Based on the assessment, the library may create a team who may determine there is an inadequacy of facilities, technology, staffing, or resources and begin a planning process to address the need.

The needs assessment may also reveal an urgency for an overall review of the purpose of the library and how it does its work. A long-range or **strategic planning** process that involves staff, resources, and the community would be required to resolve the significant issues discovered in the needs assessment. Often libraries do not have the expertise to lead a strategic planning process on staff and will hire a consultant to guide them in this work. A consultant is also neutral to the personalities, culture, and issues of the library and can move people to think "out of the box" or away from how services are traditionally offered.

A major needs assessment typically takes place prior to the planning process, but smaller assessments may crop up as needed. For example, during the planning process, an idea of improving interlibrary loan may be discussed. A task force may be convened to investigate and assess and evaluate the current and future needs of this service and provide their input to the larger planning team.

Needs assessments are critical to the success of the planning process. The assessment or data provides the information that influences the direction of the work of the team. Without knowing the "state of the ship," a team could devise a plan that does not address the real needs of the library. LSS are very important members of a needs assessment team because they work daily with the programs, services, and resources of the library and see the strengths and deficits. Their opinions are invaluable to others who do not have this firsthand, primary experience.

How do you conduct a needs assessment? The most important idea is to obtain reliable data from the library's users. This can be done through surveys, mail, telephone, and e-mail. Data can also be obtained from interviews with a sampling of key users and staff who use or work with the service or program. Libraries can conduct public focus group meetings or forums where a leader guides the discussion to obtain ideas and opinions. A task force or an advisory group could be formed—an ideal opportunity for LSS—who are given the time and resources to delve into the issues that surround the need. Finally, if the library is part of a larger institution such as a school, university, or corporation, employees in that community can be good sources of data. Public libraries will want to gain ideas from other town or municipal employees as well. The data from these assessments should be organized into a readable report with statistics to be shared with the improvement or strategic planning team so that they have this information as they go forward with the planning process.

LSS have many roles in the needs assessment process. First and foremost, LSS have the most direct contact with patrons and practice a high degree of customer service. Working with the library director and supervisor, LSS can support the data collection process in many ways.

- Volunteer to serve on the needs assessment task force or committee to both share your input and help with data collection from the community.
- If there is an anonymous patron survey, invite patrons to participate. Explain why it is important to gather data and how this is an opportunity for library users to express their opinions.
- Be informed about the purpose of the needs assessment in order to be able to answer questions patrons may have.
- Volunteer to be interviewed by the task force if your work is related to the service being assessed.
- If telephone or mail surveys are being used, offer to help with making calls or with distributing materials.
- Volunteer to help compile data once it is collected. If you have the skills to make charts, tables, or graphs, help in this effort to tell the results of the data.

With the data reported and the needs analyzed, the library management team has sufficient information to support the implementation of a planning process.

PLANNING ELEMENTS

Well-ordered goals and objectives develop from a plan. As individuals, we can plan some of our daily and long-range activities. Other activities happen spontaneously or are planned by others. This occurs in libraries as well. Library staff and community can maximize the potential excellence of the library when there is a plan in place that has been developed and approved by many of its **stakeholders**. The

Figure 12.1. Library stakeholders. *istock/Rawpixel*

need for a library plan can come about in many ways. The most common way is the library director and his board or supervisors determine there is a need for improvement or a renewed purpose. Sometimes this occurs on a regular basis of every three to five years. Other times, a plan may be needed because of a financial change or other immediate need.

There are several types of library plans, all of which affect LSS and the essential work that they do. Four of the most common plans are performance plans, business plans, **improvement plans**, and strategic plans.

Performance plans are mutually agreed upon between the supervisor and the LSS and describe specific goals the LSS should work toward or achieve in order to be a successful employee. Performance expectations are discussed in chapter 4.

Business plans are created when the library board or other management group decides the library needs to find a new and steady income stream. Business plans may be created by the larger institution, such as a private school or college. They may also be important mechanisms for both private and public libraries that need another source of revenue. Funding for libraries is discussed in chapter 8.

Library improvement plans are the result of a process established to create significant change in one or more aspects of library services or programs. A library improvement team is formed as needed. The improvement efforts require problem solving and figuring out effective solutions that involve complex issues. In libraries where staff and funding are scarce, improvements should involve the most efficient use of resources. The result of this work is connected to the mission of the library and is written into a plan with specific goals, objectives, and assessments.

The last type of plan, the strategic plan, is a review of the full library for the purpose of significant change for the near future. Often referred to as a long-range plan, the plan is usually developed for three to five years and may take a year or more to implement. Strategic planning is a time-consuming process that involves all library staff and many of its stakeholders. Long-range or strategic plans have the greatest chance of being successful when they are developed in an inclusive, transparent, and purposeful way. Strategic planning for the Boston University Libraries resulted in an intentional redefinition of all its libraries to develop programs, services, and information sources to support learning and scholarship in the twenty-first century.[2] The actions of the plan affect every patron, faculty, and library staff member. Ultimately a strategic plan is a statement of how the library will use its finite resources to accomplish and sustain its mission.

Both improvement plans and strategic plans involve LSS who have a key position on the work teams. LSS are stakeholders who have experience with handling library resources and direct contact in delivering patron services. They often have firsthand experience with the issues or systems that need to be improved. They can provide feedback about what works due to their unique view of processes, programs, and services. The perspectives of LSS team members from different departments add to their potential to positively serve on committees and task forces to affect the results of the strategic or improvement plan. This chapter will address the process of improvement and/or strategic planning and how the LSS are integral to both.

Regardless of the type of library, there are specific elements or parts of improvement and strategic planning that should take place in either process. Textbox 12.1 lists important element of improvement or strategic plans.[3]

Each of these elements is an important part of planning. Likewise, each element does not stand alone but is related to the other elements. For example, an activity that does not relate to a goal may be fun but lacks meaning. There is also a hierarchy or order among all of the elements of planning, beginning with the vision that is the broadest statement of why the library exists. We will examine each element of strategic planning and discuss how each influences the work of LSS.

TEXTBOX 12.1: ELEMENTS OF AN IMPROVEMENT OR STRATEGIC PLAN

- Vison
- Mission
- Goals
- Objectives and Outcomes
- Action Plans
- Activities
- Assessment

Vision

The vision is the broadest statement of why the library exists. It is typically a brief statement that everyone who works in the library can understand and support. Another way to describe the library vision is to ask: What is the purpose of this library? The vision is the big picture of what the library wishes to achieve. What does good library service look like to the community of users? Using an analogy of a road map, the vision provides a destination for the organization.[4] Without vision or purpose, the library community is at a loss for direction for its programs and services. Vision statements are static or fixed, meaning that they do not change from year to year or from library board to board or even from library director to director. In the strategic planning process, if there is already a working vision statement, the statement may be slightly updated because of a newly added service.

Vision statements are only successful if they are in tune with and have input from the community.[5] In developing the vision statement, library boards and staff may visit similar-type libraries and talk to peers to understand how they developed their visions. Many academic, public, and school libraries create their vision around equity of access to information and lifelong learning. Vision statements may focus on the expansion of existing services or the offering of new services. Holding public meetings can help identify a vision as well.[6] The committee charged with drafting the vision statement will, upon consensus, bring it to the larger library community for approval. The vision must be in place before the other elements of strategic planning can move forward.

The Montana State Library provides these example vision statements:[7]

- The library will promote lifelong reading habits.
- Adults will have access to information that will help them in their home and business enterprises.
- Through the library district, our community members will access information from around the world.
- The district library may contain materials in a variety of formats, for example, print, video, and computer accessible information.
- The library may serve as a gateway to electronic networks.

The University of Toledo describes its vision statement as what they are aiming for.[8] It reads, "*University Libraries will become the intellectual center of The University of Toledo by fully integrating its services, state-of-the-art technologies, and unique collections into all aspects of our institution.*" From this simple statement, the community knows this academic library aims to be the intellectual center for the university by integrating its services, technologies, and collections into all aspects of university life. In other words, the library aims to have its services and collections infused into everything the university does.

Mission

If the vision statement is *what a library aims for*, the mission statement is *what it actually does*. The mission of the libraries at the University of Toledo states, "*The mission of the University Libraries is to drive excellence in life-long learning, discovery and engagement. Within a collaborative and interdisciplinary environment, we enrich the student learning experience, facilitate research at all levels and engage the community through innovative educational services, resources and technologies.*" If one was to ask the question of what these libraries do, they could list from the mission that they:

1. promote lifelong learning,
2. promote discovery,
3. promote engagement,
4. create a collaborative and interdisciplinary environment,
5. enrich student learning,
6. facilitate research at all levels, and
7. engage the community through innovative services, resources, and technology.

Note that each of these parts of the mission begins with an action verb. An action verb describes the process, motion, act, deed, or performance being done. The mission is a general statement of how the library will achieve its vision. In our example above, *how* the university libraries will become the intellectual center is by the above seven actions.

These seven actions are simple in words but complex in how they can be accomplished. For example, what may it take to engage the college community (students, faculty, and staff) through innovative services, resources, and technology? Who are the library staff and how would they accomplish this? How would success be measured? What kind of funding would be needed?

Because the mission affects all aspects of how the library conducts its work, it is a very important statement that is researched and drafted in committee and, upon consensus, is brought to the larger library community for approval. Sometimes it takes months for a mission statement to be developed and approved, as it is critical to how the library will do its work.

The American Association of School Librarians, a division of the American Library Association, suggests this mission statement for K–12 schools to consider: *"The mission of the school library program is to ensure that students and staff are effective users of ideas and information; students are empowered to be critical thinkers, enthusiastic readers, skillful researchers, and ethical users of information."*[9] What do school libraries want students to be?

In this example, the mission of the school library program is directly linked to what students will be able to do. The success of the library program can be measured through student performance and achievement.

TEXTBOX 12.2: KEY ELEMENTS OF A K–12 LIBRARY MISSION

1. users of ideas and information
2. critical thinkers
3. enthusiastic readers
4. skilled researchers
5. ethical users of information

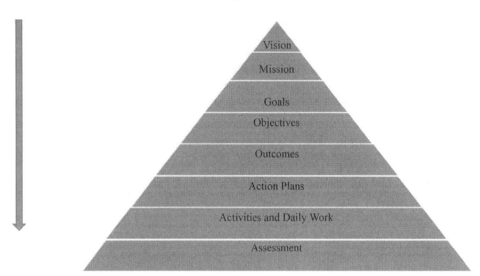

Figure 12.2.   Planning hierarchy. *Courtesy of the author*

Both the vision statement and mission statements affect how LSS work, but they do not provide specificity. The next levels or descending order of the hierarchy—goals, objectives, action plans, and activities—provide guidance and direction on how the work of LSS can contribute to the overall vision and mission of the library and effect positive change.

Core Values

While implicit in the vision or mission statements, organizations need to have a set of core values before they can develop meaningful goals. These values define the library in terms of principles, beliefs, and expected ethical behavior of its leaders in carrying out their work. What is valued by the library should extend into its program goals. Examples of library core values most often sought are around freedom of speech, the right to read, lifelong learning, access to resources, privacy, nondiscrimination, respect, flexibility to meet changing needs, and a focus on innovation. Core values are part of library policy and are integrated with program goals.

Goals

Library goals are general statements of what the library aims to accomplish as a result of its program. Goals flow from the library mission and describe overarching expectations such as "the library will support the development of literacy" or "the library will be a leader in technology." Library goals should be aligned with the mission and the core values of the library. Goals are broad, long-term expectations of what the library aims to achieve as a result of its services, management, and programs.

Before LSS can develop realistic goals and measurable objectives related to their work, they need to know the current and future needs of the library. This is why it is so important for LSS to be involved in an improvement or strategic planning process. Do the personal performance goals of the LSS benefit the library mission?

But as noted earlier in this chapter, mission statements are very broad and do not give staff enough specificity on how to do their work. Ideally, LSS goals should be in harmony with the library mission. The next hierarchical levels, goals and objectives, break down the mission into more clearly defined statements that LSS can relate to their daily work.

Embedded within goals are strategies on how to achieve something to make it work. A strategy is a unique approach of how you will use your mission to achieve your vision. Strategies are critical to the success of an organization because this is where you begin outlining a plan for doing something.[10] For example, a school library improvement team may have a broad goal to support and increase children's literacy. As they develop the goal, strategizing may take place on ways this could happen such as more parent involvement, summer reading programs, tangible incentives for children, and so on. These strategies provide a direction in which the goals, and later objectives and action plans, will be formulated. Goals are progressive steps in the strategy. Goals will differ depending upon the type and needs of the library. School library goals tend to be around student achievement such as literacy while academic libraries' goals may have a focus on research and career development. Public libraries' goals often seek community involvement. Examples of goals for school, academic, and public libraries that could also relate to LSS work are found in the following table:

Table 12.1.   Examples of Library Goals by Library Type

School	Academic	Public	Special
Teach advanced bibliographic citation to all ninth-grade students so that they can successfully cite sources by the end of the fall term.	Explore new databases to improve student and faculty access to current scientific discoveries to support research by the end of the spring term.	Increase access to library resources to underserved community members within eighteen months.	Develop a service within three months that will alert managers to new information as it arrives in the library so they can share current research and reports with others.

There are several steps to writing effective goals.[11] Each goal should begin with an action verb, followed by an activity and a purpose. If possible, a goal statement should end with a date by when the goal could be accomplished. In figure 12.3, the program goal in the example for a public library to *increase access to library resources to underserved community members within eighteen months* is broken into the component parts of goal writing.

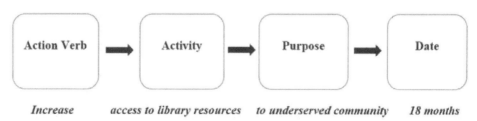

Increase   *access to library resources*   *to underserved community*   *18 months*

Figure 12.3.   Program goal. *Courtesy of the author*

Program goals should always begin with an action verb. The activity or what will be done by taking this action comes next. Goals without purpose lack meaning, and while the purpose may be understood by the goal-writing committee, it is important to include the purpose as part of the goal so that everyone who reads the goal will know why it is important to accomplish. Finally, a reasonable time frame is important because it adds urgency and importance to the activity and its purpose. Goals without time frames are more difficult to measure and may languish for lack of a sense of urgency.

Objectives

If goals are broad long-term expectations of what is expected as a result of the library program, then objectives are the statements of what and how the goal is to be achieved. There typically are several objectives to address a single goal. Another way of thinking about objectives is these are the steps that should be taken to successfully achieve a goal.

A successful method for writing objectives is called **SMART**, which stands for Specific, Measurable, Achievable, Relevant, and Time-bound. Objectives are intended results or consequences of activities. Objectives can be process or outcome orientated. Textbox 12.3 provides an example of how LSS can develop SMART program objectives.

TEXTBOX 12.3: LSS DEVELOP SMART OBJECTIVES

Specific: As with goal writing, begin the objective with one action verb that best describes what response needs to be done. Include the "who," "what," or "where."

Measurable: Decide how much change needs to be made. Is it a partial change or is it a totally new direction or replacement of an existing program or service?

Achievable: The writer should pause and take a reality check. Can this really be done with the library resources available?

Relevant: Go back and read the program goal that this objective will support. Does it directly relate to it and will it help achieve the goal?

Time-bound: This is where the "when" appears. Is there a time limitation within which the objective should be accomplished? Be sure to provide an allowance for contingencies. Objectives may be short, medium, or long term.

To become proficient at developing goals and objectives, one has to practice. A first level of practice is to write a personal goal with objectives. We all have personal goals. For example, the goal may be to "lose five pounds before the end of the year in order to fit into new clothes." As you read this, identify the action verb (lose), the activity (reduce weight by five pounds), the purpose (to fit into new clothes), and time frame (end of the year).

Next let's write three SMART objectives that support this goal.

1. Eat three hundred less calories per day.
2. Purchase three snack foods per week instead of four.
3. Monitor weight on the scale each day.

Simply written, these personal objectives are achievable, relevant, and time-bound. They each begin with an action verb and each one is measurable.

Using this exercise as a model, the next example provides LSS practice writing realistic and measurable objectives with consideration of benefits, risks, and impact on a library's current need. The goal for special libraries is found in table 12.1. With each objective, LSS may have a key role in being the person who does the action within a specific time frame and reports results to the supervisor on its potential impact for a new library service.

Goal: *Develop a service within three months that will alert managers to new information as it arrives in the library so they can share current research and reports with others.*

Objective 1: Contact by listserv or e-mail other special librarians to learn how they inform company employees about new information sources within the next two weeks.

Objective 2: Discuss with information vendors ways their information sources may be added to an RSS feed or other means for alerting employees to new information sources.

Objective 3: Meet with company IT to explore ways to use technology to create communication channels for alerting and forwarding new information to employees within six weeks.

Objective 4: Pilot new options with two managers to evaluate the options and obtain feedback from them during the third month.

For each objective, LSS may be the person who assumes the actions of communicating with other special libraries' staff, vendors, and the company IT support. They may work with their supervisors once a new service is developed to pilot the process with a department manager to evaluate its effectiveness. LSS who are involved in strategic or improvement planning are aware of new goals and can volunteer to help develop objectives that will meet the goals.

Objectives may be about a process or an outcome.[12] Process objectives describe the activities, services, or strategies that will be delivered as part of the goal. The actions above for developing a new information delivery service are process objectives because they enhance the library program.

Outcomes

The second kind of objectives are outcome objectives. Outcome objectives specify an intended effect on a target population, such as library patrons, students, or other users. An outcome objective describes what a person will know and be able to do as a result of the program or activity. As an example of outcome objectives, we will look at the goal in table 12.1 for school libraries. The school library media specialist will *teach advanced bibliographic citation to all ninth-grade students so that they can successfully cite sources by the end of the fall term.* A question LSS can ask is: Who is the recipient of the teaching? The recipients or target population of the goal are ninth-grade students. Here are four outcome objectives LSS can help develop and support around the teaching of students advanced bibliographic citation.

Outcome 1: Students will know the elements of a bibliography for MLA and APA formats.

Outcome 2: Students will know when to use citations in doing research.

Outcome 3: Students will be able to use citation tools, such as online bibliography-generating applications.

Outcome 4: Students will successfully cite sources using advanced formats 85 percent of the time in their research papers.

When the LSS is involved in the development of the outcome objectives, he can support the teaching of the school media specialist by obtaining his own training in this goal and then by working individually with students who will need support when they are in the library. In libraries, outcome objectives often focus on what the patrons will be able to do. School and academic libraries most often have outcomes related to student learning while public and special libraries may have more outcomes related to how patrons will be able to better use services.

Goals, objectives, and outcomes always use action verbs. Some of the more common action verbs LSS may consider are in textbox 12.4.

TEXTBOX 12.4: ACTION VERBS

acquire	create	identify	perform	review
analyze	delegate	improve	plan	select
assist	deliver	inform	prepare	support
collaborate	develop	maintain	promote	survey
collect	establish	modify	provide	teach
communicate	explore	motivate	recommend	train
conduct	facilitate	organize	report	update
construct	foster	participate	research	verify

Action Plans

Action plans are statements of specific actions or activities that will be used to achieve a goal within the constraints of the objective.[13] Action plans tell how an objective will be conducted or achieved. Very practical statements, action plans may be chronological or sequential. Just as we do in our daily lives, we give order to our actions. LSS who may work with *Outcome 3: Students will be able to use citation tools, such as online bibliography-generating applications* may develop an action plan of updating their own knowledge and skills in writing citations so that they can correctly support students at times when the school media specialist is not available. Action plans may involve one or many people, depending upon the desired objective or outcome. The more people involved, the more formalized process the action plan should be with assignments, responsibilities, and deadlines clearly understood. Without a well-thought-out action plan, objectives will not be met. Current and future needs of the library can only be met when LSS are involved and committed to the work of action plans. Action plans are most effective when they are made collaboratively and are committed to paper. Successful action plans have these key elements:

Table 12.2.   Action Plan Template

Actions and Activities	*What will be done?*
Responsibilities	*Who will do it?*
Timeline	*By when? (Day/Month)*
Resources	*Resources available*
	Resources needed (financial, human, political, and other)
Potential Barriers	*What individuals or organizations might resist? How?*
Communications Plan	*Who is involved? What methods? How often?*

In all aspects of an action plan, LSS can be essential support. Action plans require staff and resources, and LSS who work most closely with patrons and resources are able to effectively contribute to important library goals and objectives at this level of information gathering, communications, and other responsibilities. Accomplishing the work of an action plan feels good in a tangible way because we feel good about the positive contribution and impact we can have on the future of the programs and services of the library.

Figure 12.4.   Elements of action plans. *istock/tumsasedgars*

Activities and Daily Work

In the daily work and activities of the LSS, we support current and future goals and objectives of the library. LSS are often on the front line of implementation of new programs and services. In order for LSS to be able to convey the benefits of new services, they should be involved in the implementation process.

A simple way to think about how a service or program is realized is the acronym **PIE**, which stands for planning, implementation, and evaluation. Planning begins with the vision through the development of objectives and outcomes. Implementation of the plan occurs with action plans and activities. The final letter "E" is the evaluation of both formal and informal assessments of the improvement to programs and services.

In order for LSS to competently offer and support the new goals and objectives, they may need training and mentoring from others. In the strategic or improvement plan, there should always be objectives and action plans for LSS professional development and training. LSS provide the most direct customer service to patrons, and they need to be knowledgeable and competent with any new methods, technology, or services. LSS are also in the position to provide feedback to supervisors about the implementation of a new program and service and where it may fall short from the intended goal. For example, when a public library implemented self-checkout, there was an intermittent problem in the children's department. Instead of a pleasant experience, parents with tired and unruly children found it frustrating to deal with an unreliable self-checkout system when leaving the library. LSS were observant and always offered their support and help to patrons to minimize the frustration. Because of their knowledge of how the system was supposed to work and their continued feedback to the library administration of their observations with this unit, an inherent problem was found. Due to the monitoring and support of LSS, self-checkout is now successful at this library.

ASSESSMENT

We began this chapter with an introduction to needs assessments. Needs assessments are important at the beginning of the planning process because they identify areas of library programs and services that can be added or improved.

Assessment also takes place throughout the planning process and then again at the end of implementation of the action plans. In the larger picture of the overall strategic or improvement plan, stakeholders need to know if it was successful. Likewise, throughout the implementation, each action plan also needs to be evaluated so that the change is incorporated, modified, or rejected.

There are many types of assessment methods, and they all require the collection of data. Data is information that will help provide feedback to decision makers and can be in the form of statistics, customer surveys, interviews, observations, visuals, and so forth. Each goal and objective may require its own assessment. An example of an assessment used by an academic library that had an objective to implement self-checkout included a method of assessment, results of the assessment, and an action plan in case the results were not what were hoped for.[14]

- Objective: Increase student and faculty use of self-checkout station to check out library materials.
- Methods of Assessment and Performance Target: Analyze and compare statistics from both mediated and self-checkout processes. Analysis of data will report the use of self-checkout stations will increase 10 percent from fall semester to the end of spring semester.

- Assessment Results: Use of self-checkout in fall semester peaked at 16 but then fell to 13 percent of circulation the following spring. Data indicates there was not an increase in use from fall to spring but actually a decrease in the use of the self-checkout unit.
- Action Plan for Use of the Results of Improvement: Results indicate a need to increase awareness of students of the self-checkout unit through staff training and marketing and to reevaluate its location.

By the college library collecting statistics and other data during the first year of implementation, it found there was a need for staff training and marketing, and perhaps a new location, in order for the objective to be successful. Monitoring use and collecting data were essential to the success of this new service.

LSS are important members of assessment teams for both long-range plans and for short-term objectives. Stakeholders at the beginning of a strategic or improvement planning process ask the team to assess which aspects of the library mission are effective and which are not. In a full assessment, each service and program may be examined. Essential questions may be asked such as:

- Are patrons satisfied with library services, programs, and resources? Which ones are most important to them and are used the most? The least?
- Are patrons' research needs being meet effectively and efficiently?
- Are faculty and student teaching and learning needs being adequately met? Are information technologies and resources being appropriately applied?

In order to obtain feedback to these questions, specific team or library staff may be recruited to draft surveys, interview samplings of patrons and staff, collect circulation and program statistics, and so forth. In school libraries, anonymous comparative student data from standardized tests may also be used to help determine how library instruction and resources are affecting **student learning outcomes** (SLO) and achievement.

The purpose assessment is to identify actions and to make recommendations for improvement of resources, staffing, programs, and services that will support the vision and mission of the library. Summarized are the important elements of the planning process:

- Vision: what the library aims to do;
- Mission: what the library does;
- Goals: general statements of what the library aims to accomplish as a result of its program;
- Strategies: an approach on how to achieve something to make it work;
- Objectives: the statements of what and how the goal is to be achieved;
- Outcomes: specify an intended effect on a target population, such as library patrons, students, or other users;
- Action plans: how an objective will be conducted or achieved;
- Activities and daily work: how goals and objectives are implemented in services, programs, and resources;

- Assessment: the collection of data where each action in the plan is evaluated so that the change is incorporated, modified, or rejected.

LSS who work directly with patrons have an important role in helping decide which programs and services are beneficial and where certain ones may fall short. LSS who are strategic or improvement team members can have a significant impact on the current and future direction of the library.

CHAPTER SUMMARY

Library services, resources, and programs support the vision and mission of the library. Through a strategic or improvement planning process, the mission, or what the library actually does, can be refined to best meet patrons needs. LSS who primarily deliver services and resources to patrons are in an important positon to serve as members of a planning team to influence new services and change. By understanding the relationship among goals, objectives, outcomes, and actions, LSS see that their work is critical to the success of the library mission. In the assessment phases, LSS collect data and help analyze the story it tells about how the plan is implemented and may recommend refinements to ensure success.

DISCUSSION QUESTIONS

1. Why is the needs assessment an important first step of the strategic or improvement planning process?
2. What is the relationship among a library's vision, mission, and goals?
3. What are the parts of a well-written goal statement?
4. Why does each library goal require objectives? What is the difference between a process objective and an outcome objective?
5. Why is assessment both a final and an ongoing part of the implementation process? What can LSS do if the implementation is not successful?

ACTIVITY

Using the template shown in figure 12.3, develop a goal, objectives, and an action plan for a service in the library you work in or frequent that is important to you.

1. Write a goal that begins with an action verb and identifies the activity, purpose, and time frame.

   Goal: _____

2. Write three objectives that support this goal. Write at least one objective as an outcome for patrons.
   a.
   b.
   c.

3. Complete an action plan for one of the objectives.
    Actions and Activities: *What will be done?*
    Responsibilities: *Who will do it?*
    Timeline: *By when? (Day/Month)*
    Resources: *Resources available/Resources needed (financial, human, political, and other)*
    Potential Barriers: *What individuals or organizations might resist? How?*
    Communications Plan: *Who is involved? What methods? How often?*
4. Write a short assessment plan for the objective that includes the type of data that will be collected, a measure for success, and an alternative action if the results are not satisfactory.

NOTES

1. Idaho Commission for Libraries, "Needs Assessment," Programs and Services, last modified 2017, accessed October 20, 2017, libraries.idaho.gov/page/needs-assessment.

2. Boston University Libraries, "Strategic Plan: 2010–2017," last modified 2017, accessed October 20, 2017, www.bu.edu/library/about/strategic-plan/.

3. Idaho Commission for Libraries, "Planning Process Elements," last modified 2017, accessed October 14, 2017, libraries.idaho.gov/page/planning-process-elements.

4. Iowa State University Extension, "Vision and Mission Statements—a Roadmap of Where You Want to Go and How to Get There," Business Development Process, accessed October 14, 2017, www.extension.iastate.edu/agdm/wholefarm/html/c5-09.html.

5. Montana State Library, "Task a Three: Creating a Vision," Public Library District Handbook, last modified 2017, accessed October 14, 2017, libraries.msl.mt.gov/consulting/online_publications/publiclibrarydistricthandbook/assessment/vision.

6. Ibid.

7. Ibid.

8. University of Toledo, "University Libraries Mission, Vision, and Policies," last modified August 21, 2017, accessed October 19, 2017, www.utoledo.edu/library/info/college.html.

9. American Library Association, "Outline of Guidelines," American Association of School Librarians, last modified 2017, accessed October 20, 2017, www.ala.org/aasl/standards/guidelines/outline.

10. Iowa State University Extension, "Vision and Mission Statements."

11. Bowling Green State University, "How to Write Program Goals," Human Resources, accessed October 25, 2017, www.bgsu.edu/content/dam/BGSU/human-resources/.../i9.../action-verbs.pdf.

12. Ibid.

13. Iowa State University Extension, "Vision and Mission Statements."

14. University of South Florida, "USF Libraries Assessment Report," Sample Assessment Plan Template, accessed October 26, 2017, www.usf.edu/provost/offices/assessmentsupport.aspx.

REFERENCES, SUGGESTED READINGS, AND WEBSITES

American Library Association. "Outline of Guidelines." American Association of School Librarians. Last modified 2017. Accessed October 20, 2017. www.ala.org/aasl/standards/guidelines/outline.

Boston University Libraries. "Strategic Plan: 2010–2017." Last modified 2017. Accessed October 20, 2017. www.bu.edu/library/about/strategic-plan/.

Bowling Green State University. "How to Write Program Goals." Human Resources. Accessed October 25, 2017. www.bgsu.edu/content/dam/BGSU/human-resources/.../i9.../action-verbs.pdf.

Center for Disease Control. "Developing Program Goals and Measurable Objectives." Accessed October 25, 2017. www.cdc.gov/std/program/pupestd/developing%20program%20goals%20and%20objectives.pdf.

Idaho Commission for Libraries. "Needs Assessment." Programs and Services. Last modified 2017. Accessed October 20, 2017. libraries.idaho.gov/page/needs-assessment.

———. "Planning Process Elements." Last modified 2017. Accessed October 14, 2017. libraries.idaho.gov/page/planning-process-elements.

Iowa State University Extension. "Vision and Mission Statements—a Roadmap of Where You Want to Go and How to Get There." Business Development Process. Accessed October 14, 2017. www.extension.iastate.edu/agdm/wholefarm/html/c5-09.html.

Montana State Library. "Task A Three: Creating a Vision." Public Library District Handbook. Last modified 2017. Accessed October 14, 2017. libraries.msl.mt.gov/consulting/online_publications/publiclibrarydistricthandbook/assessment/vision.

University of Connecticut. "Assessment Primer: Goals, Objectives and Outcomes." Accessed October 20, 2017. web2.uconn.edu/assessment/primer/goals1.html.

University of South Florida. "USF Libraries Assessment Report." Sample Assessment Plan Template. Accessed October 26, 2017. www.usf.edu/provost/offices/assessmentsupport.aspx.

University of Toledo. "University Libraries Mission, Vision, and Policies." Last modified August 21, 2017. Accessed October 19, 2017. www.utoledo.edu/library/info/college.htm.

CHAPTER 13

Conducting Meetings and Effective Decision Making

LSS know the basic principles and conduct meetings effectively and efficiently. (ALA-LSSC Supervision and Management Competency #15)

LSS know the concepts of effective decision-making and are able to make decisions as appropriate. (ALA-LSSC Supervision and Management #16)

Topics Covered in This Chapter:

- Meeting Basics
  - o Private vs. Public Meetings
  - o Internal vs. External Meetings
- Parliamentary Procedure
  - o Roles
  - o Planning an Efficient Meeting
  - o Agenda
  - o Decision-Making vs. Information-Sharing Meetings
  - o Motions
  - o Executive Session
  - o Voting
  - o Remote Attendance
- Making Decisions
  - o Individual Decision Making
  - o Group Decision Making

Key Terms:

Abstain: The decision members make when they choose not to vote for or against an issue.

Agenda: Developed by the chair, this is an outline for how the upcoming library meeting will be conducted and the order in which each item will be presented for either discussion or action.

Amend: Any member of a library meeting may request to change a motion under consideration as long as the person who made the original motion and the person who seconded it agree.

Bylaws: These are the written rules that control the internal affairs of a library, defining such things like the library's official name, purpose, requirements for board membership, officers' titles and responsibilities, how meetings should be conducted, and how often meetings will be held. They also serve as the legal guidelines of the library, and the library could be challenged in court for its actions if it violates them.[1]

Consensus: When a group of key people gather together to discuss ideas or solutions under consideration for the library, instead of taking a formal vote, they are asked to informally show their level of support and agreement in various ways such as nodding their heads, saying "Aye," or raising hands.

Minutes: Minutes are the record of the discussions and actions that take place at a library meeting. The secretary takes minutes during the meeting and is responsible for preparing a draft version to be considered for acceptance at the next meeting.

Motion: This proposal for action is made by one member for all participants of the meeting to discuss and vote upon. The proposal is made in the form of a statement that begins with the phrase "I make a motion to . . ." or "I move to . . ." The proposal must be seconded by another member to be voted upon by the membership.

Parliamentary procedure: Synonymous with Robert's Rules of Order, these are the rules that define how particular situations should be handled or outcomes achieved in meetings.

Simple majority: In the process of voting on an action or issue, this is half of the voting membership plus one more that sways the final outcome or decision.

All libraries are governed by boards who represent the community they serve. School libraries are governed by boards of education; public libraries are managed or advised by boards of trustees. Most academic libraries, as a department of the college institution, are governed by a board of regents or trustees. Special libraries such as a museum library or corporate library could be governed by a board of directors or a management board. Common to all of these governing boards are the regular meetings that take place where important group decision making and actions take place about mission, goals, facilities, policies, personnel, and fiscal oversight. Library directors represent the library's interest at the governing board meetings. In many situations, the library director is managed by and reports to the board.

There are many other types of meetings that involve library staff and the community to discuss ideas and take action. These could be meetings for staff or departments, project management teams, special events, new programming, or friends groups. In schools and universities, there may also be meetings around curriculum and instruction, student learning objectives (SLO), delegation of tasks, and other academic activities. LSS make important contributions when they are participants of meetings.

This chapter will discuss how LSS can better understand the basics of meetings and how to participate in and conduct meetings effectively and efficiently. It will also introduce strategies LSS can use to help make appropriate decisions both as individuals and with others in meetings.

MEETING BASICS

The purpose of a library meeting is to get work done through discussion and actions. Meetings are the means by which a person or group can exercise choice and affect outcomes.[2]

Private vs. Public Meetings

According to current statistics, there are 119,487 libraries in the United States.[3] How a library receives its funding classifies it as public or private. Publicly funded libraries rely on taxpayers for their operating and capital budgets, while privately funded libraries must obtain their finances through a variety of means such as fund-raising, gifts, endowments bequests, and sound financial planning. Publicly funded libraries are typically municipal libraries, public K–12 school libraries, public academic libraries, government libraries, and some special libraries. Private libraries are those found in independent schools and universities, business corporations, and medical, legal, and other professions. In addition, many libraries serve the public but have not been incorporated as municipal departments and are privately funded. Depending upon the type of funding the library receives, its governing board meetings are either open or closed to public taxpayers.

Why is this important to library meetings? Simply stated, if the library is publicly funded, then anyone can speak their opinion or bring up an issue of concern during the public comment time at governing meetings. **Minutes** of public meetings are also recorded and available for the public to access, such as from the library or town website. If the library is private, unless invited, the public is excluded from attending the governing meetings. While minutes of the meeting are most likely taken, the library board is not required to make them available to all. Fundamental to how library governing boards conduct their meetings is whether the library is privately or publicly funded.

Internal vs. External Meetings

Internal library meetings are those that take place within the library building to support its work. LSS attend many internal organization meetings such as:

- regularly scheduled meetings with individual staff members and department meetings;
- meetings with selected staff on special topics, such as planning a winter craft festival or the upcoming summer reading program;
- open-ended meetings with some or all staff to brainstorm ideas about future directions of library initiatives, services, facilities, or projects.

TEXTBOX 13.1: TYPES OF INTERNAL LIBRARY MEETINGS AND ATTENDEES

Type of Meeting	Attendees
Personnel	Library director, librarians, LSS
Department	Department supervisor, librarians, LSS
Team Meetings	Library director, librarians, LSS, consultants, community members
Planning or Events	Library director, librarians, LSS, volunteers, patrons, board members
Library Friends	Library director, librarians, LSS, patrons, board members

Internal library meetings are not open to the public. While the public may be invited to such meetings as friends groups, team meetings, or planning special events, personnel and department meetings are closed to the public. Textbox 13.1 is a sampling of the internal types of library meetings and key people most likely to attend them.

There is always the need for regular meetings within any library organization, small or large. LSS are key participants of these meetings. Small to medium-size libraries may hold weekly or biweekly full-staff meetings before the library opens where the library director, librarians, and LSS can share information, seek advice on new ideas, or solve problems. The frequency of meetings is important because with overlapping staff to cover extended hours, meetings are the means to ensure all library staff are in communication with each other. Large libraries may have unit or department meetings. For example, the library director may meet regularly with supervisors who then, in turn, schedule department meetings with LSS. The frequency of meetings may be crucial depending upon the nature of the work and the initiatives that are ongoing. Finding a regular common meeting time for all staff members can be challenging in libraries that have extended hours. An alternative is for the supervisor to hold two meetings to accommodate the shifts and schedules of LSS.

External meetings, on the other hand, take place outside of the library and with people other than building staff. LSS represent the library at many different types of external meetings. Examples of external meetings LSS may attend are:

- regional meetings with staff from neighboring libraries that share technology or common projects;
- consortium meetings such as for the Integrated Library System (ILS) where LSS serve on circulation or bibliographic task forces;
- statewide or regional meetings held by professional organizations, associations, the state library, or other institutions;
- teleconferenced meetings where participants are in multiple locations around the state or country for common professional learning or initiatives, such as LSS who participate in state interlibrary loan meetings.

When LSS represent the library at an external meeting, it is important that they take detailed notes about the discussion and actions taken at the meeting so that they can accurately report the work of the meeting. It is the nature of libraries needing to be open extended hours that they do not close for all staff to attend an external meeting. Usually one or two people are designated to represent the library at an external meeting. It is important for the returning LSS to share handouts and any other materials that were distributed with others to inform them of the new information learned.

PARLIAMENTARY PROCEDURE

A meeting is called for the purpose of accomplishing work. A key way to keep members on track and to get the work done in an efficient and thorough manner is to apply a set of rules or standards to how the meeting will be conducted. These standards of rules for conducting meetings were developed by an engineer named Henry Martyn Robert.[4] Born in 1837 and a West Point graduate, Robert designed many large locks, dams, and seawall infrastructures still in use today across the United States. As he moved around the country for his work, he was also active in community and church groups, where he discovered each had their own interpretation of **parliamentary procedure**. He often was asked to take on a leadership position in these groups and found himself ill equipped to conduct meetings in an orderly fashion. Assemblies wasted enormous amounts of time deciding how meetings should be run.[5]

It wasn't until 1874, while assigned to supervise lighthouse construction on Lake Michigan, that Henry Robert began writing his 176-page *Pocket Manual of Rules of Order for Deliberative Assemblies*. His publisher thought the book's title was too long and arbitrarily changed it to *Robert's Rules of Order*. Both Robert and the publisher expected the book's initial press run would last for two years; however, it sold out in four months. Today in its eleventh edition, *Robert's Rules of Order* is used by more than 80 percent of professional societies worldwide as the standard on how to conduct business meetings.[6]

Internal meetings conducted by library governing boards, teams, and departments use Robert's Rules of Order as a fair and efficient way to get work done. External library organizations, consortia, and associations also rely on Robert's Rules. Government agencies from local municipalities to the U.S. Congress conduct their meetings using the complex standards of parliamentary procedures that are clearly referenced and available in Robert's Rules for all to understand and apply.

It is important for LSS to know and understand Robert's Rules of Order because our work is determined and supported through the many decisions made in library meetings. LSS who can apply Robert's Rules are respected for how they appropriately participate in meetings. Those who can use and apply Robert's Rules are often sought for leadership roles because they know how to efficiently run a meeting.

Roles

The number of meeting participants and the purpose of the meeting influence the formality of how the meeting is conducted. Meetings that are regularly scheduled, have eight or more members, and are called for the purpose of making decisions about actions should be conducted using parliamentary procedure with elected or appointed officers. These officers serve for a specific term, such as one or two years, and they may be reelected according to the library bylaws. Following is a list of the specific roles officers perform to enhance the effectiveness of meetings:

1. President or Chair: leads and conducts the meeting; is responsible for setting the meeting agenda; may vote on any issue.
2. Vice President: steps in for the president or chair in his or her absence; often heads an important subcommittee, such as budget or personnel.
3. Treasurer: oversees the fiscal transactions of the organization; may sign the checks for the organization; reports the monthly fiscal health and activities to the board and may recommend sound financial policies.
4. Secretary: records the minutes of the meetings; assists in official correspondence of the organization; oversees a filing system of meeting minutes and other important documents.

The success of a meeting is the key responsibility of its leader or chair. The chair's priority is to conduct the meeting. She should make all members feel welcome and accommodate any who have special needs, such as considering seating arrangements, microphones, and so on. It is always appreciated when the chair starts and ends the meeting on time. In order to do this, she must pay careful attention to the agenda and not be reluctant when necessary to summarize a speaker's main points to move the discussion along. The chair should have a solid knowledge of parliamentary procedure and use it to conduct meetings that are deemed fair, orderly, legal, and efficient. During the meeting, the chair may summarize key points, repeat action items, and clarify responsibilities. Not only does this help the participants follow the work of the meeting; it also serves as a check for the secretary who is

Figure 13.1.   Library board meeting. *istock/monkeybusinessimages*

recording minutes. At the end of the meeting, the chair confirms or sets the date, time, and location for the next meeting.

Minutes are the official written recording of the actions that take place during the meeting. Public libraries and those funded by taxpayers are subject to the Freedom of Information Act and must post meeting minutes in an accessible location for the public to view. The minutes are the official record of the actions and decisions made by the members for each item.

Planning an Effective Meeting

It is the responsibility of the chair to plan the meeting. The tool used to share the plan with others is called the **agenda**. Before the agenda can be created, the chair should follow these suggested steps:[7]

1. Define results first. What is the purpose of the meeting and what results does the group aim to achieve? If there is not a defined purpose, then perhaps there is no need to hold the meeting.
2. List the meeting's topics. Identify the topics that need to be covered to accomplish the results. Think through what has to be done and consider a logical order for discussing the topics or making decisions. Consider the information that the group needs in order to discuss a topic or make a decision knowledgably. An effective agenda considers the following:
   a. What topics do we have to cover to accomplish our goal?
   b. What outcome/s do we want for each topic?
   c. What information do we need?
   d. Who will make the decisions?
3. How much meeting time is needed? Visualize the amount of time it will take for the meeting from its beginning to the end. To do this, determine how much time should be allotted for each agenda item. For example, it may only take five minutes to approve the last meeting's minutes, where a half hour may be needed to conduct a discussion on budget planning. Consider the total time available, and assign realistic time slots for each item. During the meeting, if the group hasn't reached a decision within the time provided, suggest next steps or refer the item to a next meeting or committee.
4. Plan strategies to address each topic. Different methods of discussion can be used to make the best use of the group for each topic. It may be helpful to plan for breakout sessions into smaller groups if the membership is large. Be clear about expectations for involving participants to assure that involvement builds trust and gets authentic action.
   a. Seek feedback either in the form of a survey before the meeting or during the meeting by asking each participant to share an idea or opinion. As members speak, record and summarize their contributions on a whiteboard or flip chart for everyone to see.
   b. Prioritize the feedback either through consensus (nodding of heads, a show of hands), a rank ordering by a show of hands, or other means to identify the ideas the group would prefer to work with.

Sending an agenda before a meeting lets participants know what will be discussed and gives them time to think about what you will discuss.

Agenda

Meetings are most efficient and effective when the chair distributes an agenda a few days before the meeting. The agenda is the road map of how the meeting will be conducted and what topics will be discussed. Members of boards, teams, or departments may be asked to contribute to the agenda, and if not, any member may ask to have an item placed on it. Following is a sample public library board agenda:[8]

Sample Public Library Board Agenda

1. Call to order by chair
2. Roll call and introduction of guests
3. Public comment
4. Communications
5. Approval of minutes of previous meeting
6. Financial reports
7. Audit and approval of monthly expenditures
8. Director's report and statistical report
9. Committee reports or other reports
10. Discussion items
11. Action items
12. Old business
13. New business
14. Adjournment

Agendas vary by library and type of meeting. Typically boards of public libraries seek public comment prior to their beginning the work of the meeting. Once the comment period is concluded, the public may not speak again during the meeting without recognition by the chair. Public are invited to observe the meeting but may not participate without invitation. Communications are any correspondence received by the chair, library director, or other members of the board that are deemed important to share and file as part of the official record of the meeting.

Regular reports come next. These are the review and approval of the minutes of the previous meeting and the financial reports and approval of expenditures by the treasurer and library director. The library director next provides his or her monthly report of the key activities, successes, and concerns since the last meeting. He also provides a comparison of performance measures such as circulation and other usage statistics of the same month the previous year or other measures for analysis.

Next are committee reports. The committees have been appointed by the chair, and they are composed of board members who have agreed to work in smaller groups to accomplish specific tasks related to policies, fundraising, personnel, and so forth.

In setting the agenda, the chair and library director may determine items that need to be discussed and items that need action or voting upon. For example, the library board must vote approval of the library director's application for a state library grant to digitize the library collection of local historic newspapers. The chair would have on the agenda as an action item "approval of application for state library grant." She would ask the library director to explain the grant and entertain any questions by board members. Once discussion is complete, the chair would ask for a motion to approve the application of the grant.

Old business is when any member may bring up or continue the discussion of an item that was presented at a previous meeting. These items do not need to be identified prior to the meeting. New business is the opportunity for any member to introduce a topic that was not on the agenda. Typically new business items are not fully discussed or voted upon but may spark enough interest that members agree to add the item to the agenda for discussion or action at the next meeting. Once the meeting is adjourned, the work of the meeting is complete and no additional work can be done.

While these rules apply strictly to governing boards, library teams, internal department meetings, and external meetings that LSS participate in often follow agendas. Chairpersons of many library meetings that warrant formality adapt the practices of parliamentary procedure or Robert's Rules of Order.

Decision-Making vs. Information-Sharing Meetings

There are two different reasons for calling library meetings. The first reason to call a meeting is to make a decision or create or amend a library policy. At these meetings, members are invited to vote their opinion for the action to be taken or decision to be made. Action items are clearly listed on the agenda and should always follow discussion. The discussion may have occurred at the previous meeting or, most likely, before the vote.

The second reason for calling a library meeting is to solicit and share information. Items may be on an agenda for discussion purpose only. Discussion can only be established by the chair. At these meetings, it is clear to members that it is too early to take a vote. If an item is for discussion only, no action or vote may be taken. These meetings are specifically called to get public comments, to have discussion among members, or as brainstorming work sessions. Recommendations may be made, but they are not acted upon. The purpose of information-sharing meetings is to hear from all concerned parties and ensure that all opinions are considered in the decision-making process.[9] After this type of meeting, the chair states when the vote may occur, most likely at the following meeting.

To vote is the responsibility of all meeting members. In order to fulfill this responsibility to the best of one's ability, LSS who are voting members should study the issue, participate in discussions, seek opinions of others who are knowledgeable and have experience with the subject, and thoughtfully form an opinion on either side of the issue. When discussion has been thoroughly conducted and no new information is presented, the chairperson of the meeting may call for a vote to decide the question.

Motions

The question or item to be voted upon is called a **motion**. A motion is a clearly spoken sentence or two, made by a board member. Motions are made when a member wants action to be taken. Only a member of the committee or board may call for a motion to vote on an item. In order for a motion to be considered, another member of the board must second the motion. By seconding the motion, this other member agrees with the motion and wants discussion and a vote to take place around it. Once the motion is seconded, discussion and action may follow.

An effective chairperson will not let too much discussion occur without asking for a motion. This technique serves as a control for those members who have much to say but with little support from others. Discussion can occur once the motion has been made and seconded.

A motion may be amended or slightly changed by another committee member *only* with the approval of the person who made the original motion. Motions can be withdrawn prior to the vote by the person who made the motion. After discussion, the chair calls for a vote on the motion. Motions can be approved, defeated, or withdrawn. For example, a motion to accept a change in library fines could be phrased, *"I make a motion to raise library fines for books to ten cents per day and media to twenty cents per day."* The chair would ask for another member to second the motion. By seconding the motion, this means that this person agrees to this change in fines. The motion must be seconded by another member to be eligible to be voted upon. Textbox 13.2 has the format of a straightforward motion.

TEXTBOX 13.2: STRAIGHTFORWARD MOTION

Member 1: *I would like to make a motion to . . .*

Member 2: *I second the motion.*

Discussion takes place. Chair calls for a vote.

Motions, however, are not always straightforward. In the discussion, another person may like to **amend** or change the original motion. It is up to the person whose motion is on the floor (a phrase that means the motion is actively under consideration and has not been voted upon yet) to allow an amendment to his motion. If he does not, then his motion has to be voted upon. If he agrees to have his motion amended, textbox 13.3 provides the protocol:

TEXTBOX 13.3: AMENDING A MOTION

Member 1: *I would like to make a motion to . . .*

Member 2: *I second the motion.*

During the discussion (before the vote), any member may move to amend the motion with the agreement of the person who made the motion.

Member 1: *I agree to Member 3 amending my motion.*

Member 2: *I second.*

Member 3: *I amend the motion to read . . .*

Member 2: *I second the amended motion.*

Another way to amend the motion is to have Member 1 withdraw his motion. Member 2 will have to second the withdrawal. Once done, Member 3 (or any other member) can create a new motion to be considered.

Executive Session

At times at public library meetings, it is important that the discussion does not get recorded in the minutes. Most often this need is around discussions about personnel. No library should ever publish minutes with individual personal performances as part of their public meeting record. Yet a managing board must have these discussions.

Robert's Rules provide for a way to do this called executive session. During executive session, there is no recording of minutes. It is a time simply for discussion. Executive session is not separate from an open meeting but rather is a portion of an open meeting during which the public may be excluded. In order to close the meeting and go into executive session, a motion must be made and seconded during an open meeting to enter into executive session. Next, the motion must also identify the general area or areas of the subject or subjects to be considered; and third, the motion must be carried by a majority vote of the total membership of a public body.[10]

During executive session, members may "try out" or frame motions, but no actions or vote may be taken. In other words, the public meeting has been suspended temporarily and closed for private discussion. In order for the meeting to go into executive session, the process outlined in figure 13.2 must be followed. Likewise, for the meeting to come out of executive session and now be open to the public where motions can be made and voted upon, there is protocol to follow.

To go into executive session:

I make a motion to move the meeting into executive session.	*I second the motion.* It passes with a majority vote of the total membership.

Figure 13.2. Executive session. *Courtesy of the author*

Executive session should be used sparingly and reserved only for times when there is the most need for confidential discussion. Chairs of library meetings should know when and how to use executive session for the purpose of getting important work done.

Voting

Immediately after a motion is seconded, the chair allows purposeful and focused discussion on the motion. Once discussion has been had, the chair calls for a vote. If any member deems that the discussion is repetitive and not productive, she may call for the vote. This indicates to the chair the member(s) do not think any more discussion is necessary, and they are ready for the vote to take place.

Robert's Rules provide for one vote per member. The chair has the right to vote the same as all members. Many library organizations determine the vote by **simple**

majority, meaning one vote more than half the membership will determine the outcome. Other organizations may require in their bylaws that motions must have two-thirds majority to pass.

Voting members have the option to **abstain** from the vote. An abstaining member has chosen not to cast her ballot either for or against the action or decision. She has simply chosen not to exercise her right to vote and will not be counted on either side of the issue.[11]

Voting Process

Who?   Each member who casts his or her opinion is counted as one vote.

What?   A motion is made by a member for a decision or a specific course of action.

When?   A vote takes place when the presiding officer or chair calls for it.

Where?   A vote takes place during an authorized meeting with a quorum of members.

How?   Each member's vote is recorded and tallied. Depending upon the organization, actions can be approved or defeated by a simple majority (one more than half of members present) or by a super majority (two-thirds, three-fourths, etc., of members present).

Remote Attendance

It has become more common for people today to ask if they may attend meetings remotely using phone, Internet, or video conferencing rather than miss a meeting.[12] While in-person attendance is always encouraged, the library may, in accordance with its own and/or municipal **bylaws**, allow occasional remote attendance and remote voting by members. The library board chairperson may require advance notification so as to prepare for the remote participation.

Voting electronically may occur at the discretion of the library bylaws or as determined by the chair. If a member is attending the meeting remotely, they may voice their vote as those who are in the room. Occasionally the chair may ask for a vote on an issue outside of a board meeting. Seeking group consensus on a timely issue, rather than an official vote, is most appropriate by e-mail. However, the chair may have the authority, depending upon the library bylaws, to ask for an official vote via e-mail under certain circumstances. If this cannot be done, then the chair and officers can decide if a special meeting needs to be called where members will assemble and vote for the purpose of this business.

In this section, basic or fundamental concepts of parliamentary procedure, codified by Robert's Rules of Order, were explained. There are numerous other situations that are not addressed here. In addition to reading full versions of *Robert's Rules of Order*, LSS would benefit by obtaining an abridged or summary "cheat sheet" of Robert's Rules. LSS may also attend or view streamed library board meetings to observe how Robert's Rules are applied. Volunteer to serve in leadership positions on both internal and external library meetings and exercise your knowledge of Robert's Rules. The more LSS practice and apply Robert's Rules in meetings, the more confident they will grow in their understanding and skills of parliamentary procedure.

Table 13.1. Example of a Robert's Rules "Cheat Sheet"

To:	You Say:	Second Needed	Debatable	Amendable	Vote
Make a motion	I move that . . .	Yes	Yes	Yes	Majority
Amend a motion	I move this motion be amended by . . .	Yes	Yes	Yes	Majority
Suspend further consideration	I move that we table it.	Yes	No	No	Majority
Postpone	I move we postpone the matter until . . .	Yes	Yes	Yes	Majority
End debate	I move the question.	Yes	No	No	Majority
Recess	I move we recess until . . .	Yes	No	Yes	Majority
Adjourn	I move we adjourn.	Yes	No	No	Majority

MAKING DECISIONS

Related to participating in meetings, LSS who learn the concepts of effective decision making are able to make decisions as appropriate. Every day we are confronted with making decisions. Some decisions are inconsequential, such as what we choose to eat for breakfast. Other decisions have much greater impact on others. At work LSS constantly make decisions. Many of our decisions are rote or routine, from determining how to file resources to deciding when to contact patrons about their overdue materials. Other decisions have far greater impact on coworkers, patrons, and library services.

There is much in the psychology, education, health, and business literature about how to make good decisions. Underpinning all of the advice is that people make the best decisions when they adopt a decision-making process or strategies. Having a decision-making process is effective whether the decision is a personal one or one that contributes to a group process.

Making a decision is using a thought process of selecting a logical choice from the available options. When trying to make a good decision, an LSS must weigh the positives and negatives of each option and consider all the alternatives. For effective decision making about library issues, LSS must be able to forecast the outcome of each option as well and, based on all these items, determine which option is the best for that particular situation.[13]

To make an effective decision, LSS need information. Given the information available, LSS make choices that produce the best results for the library. Decision makers need to be efficient in that it does no good to delay making a decision for a timely question or matter. If the LSS does not make the decision, someone else will do so. For all decisions LSS make that affect coworkers, it is best to discuss options with them and listen to what they have to say. Without agreement with others in the library, any decision we make is less likely to be implemented by the people we work with. If getting complete information could take a long time, it is almost always better for LSS to accept some degree of risk in the outcome in order to make a timely decision. Unanimity is also essential: without consensus many decisions will never get implemented, in which case all of the effort in making the decision was wasted. Unfortunately, getting unanimity reduces efficiency because it requires additional effort during the decision-making process to involve the people who will implement the decision.[14]

Individual Decision Making

There are many things that influence individual decision making. LSS who make the most effective decisions for themselves consider these concepts that influence individual decision making:[15]

1. Dominant Incentive: LSS have something to gain by the decisions they make at work. Dominant incentives are often not obvious to others but can be identified based on how people talk about things. Similarly, many people are not really aware of their own dominant incentives.
   Example: LSS believes she could offer better programs and services if she had a promotion.
2. Goal Setting: A person has to have some idea of what the possible ends are in order to set goals that inform their decisions.
   Example: LSS aims to advance his career by making work decisions that support his performance goals established with his supervisor at his annual review.
3. Framing: The way something is described influences how LSS think about their work.
   Example: LSS decides to participate on a building program committee because she is proud of the statewide recognition the library received for its community outreach.
4. Heuristics and Biases: Heuristics are rules of thumb that people use to make decisions. Heuristics are derived from past experience and are often just short-cuts to decision making based on a person's past experiences. Heuristics are also informed by our individual biases that can cut both ways.
   Example: LSS decides to create a display around the benefits of locally grown food and organic gardening.
5. Uncertainty and Risk: Uncertainty refers to things that are unknown and harder or impossible to judge while risk refers to things that are known and therefore can be predicted and acted upon.
   Example: LSS opts to require preregistration with a cap of twenty for a new program for teens because he is uncertain how to conduct the program if the number is larger.

All of these concepts affect how LSS make individual decisions about how they plan and perform their work. Knowing oneself and having clear personal goals informs how we think about things. When the LSS adopts and believes in the mission, goals, and priorities of the library director and supervisors, he can better align his decisions on the job to the broader expectations of the library community.

Group Decision Making

Because library work is collaborative, LSS often make decisions with others. They informally make decisions with coworkers and supervisors. When attending meetings, they are part of a group decision-making process. We have already presented

Figure 13.3.   Gathering input is important in the decision-making process. *istock/AndreyPopov*

how LSS who are members of formal teams, boards, or committees make decisions using the parliamentary process of voting. More likely in their day-to-day work, LSS participate in informal group decisions.

There are several steps for a group decision-making process to be successful. While everyone will not always be happy with the end result, the more active role LSS can have in participating in the process, the more likely they will accept and adopt the change. The following lists the four steps for group decision making.[16]

1. Gather a wide range of input before making a decision.
2. Facilitate a **consensus**-building process that is inclusive.
3. Once the decision has been made, announce it early so everyone knows about it.
4. Don't reconsider the decision unless there is significant new information.

The first step in the group decision-making process is to collect input from a wide variety of sources. The quality of the decision is likely to be enhanced with the good ideas from many people rather than just a few. Asking for input also improves agreement: people who have been consulted about a decision feel better about it, even if the decision goes against their input. LSS who gather input early in the decision-making process can adopt many good ideas into the early design of their program or new service rather than asking people what they think about it once the decisions are practically made. Early input also allows for time for feedback that can help refine an idea.

Example: LSS would like to change some of the procedures currently required by the university consortium for interlibrary loan (ILL) to make it more efficient. He hosts a meeting with his coworkers for staff of other libraries in the ILL consortium to gather input and ideas to better improve ILL services.

The second step in a group decision-making process is to gain consensus by gathering key people together to discuss all options and then take a poll to see what the majority of the group would like. A decision made in consensus is more likely to be the right one than one without consensus because the majority believes in it. To achieve consensus, LSS should get key people together at the same time where everyone can respond to ideas presented. In a consensus-building meeting, the problem should be framed clearly with a process in place on how to evaluate the options. Visually on a board or flip chart display the choices and arguments for and against the proposed solutions. Run an open meeting by allowing people to disagree with each other without fear of reprisal. Keep control of the discussion by continually seeking new ideas, being inclusive, and avoiding redundancy.

Example: LSS leads contract negotiations for the municipal library staff. She calls a meeting to discuss benefits, conditions, and compensations staff would like to see in the new contract with the city. She runs an open meeting where all ideas are written on the board. No suggestion is discounted. After discussion has been fully vetted, she leads a polling process where any suggestion to be included in negotiations needs to have a 75 percent show of hands.

After the group decision has been made, it is important to make a timely announcement so that everyone knows what it is so that it can be quickly implemented without confusion. If the decision affects all library staff, an all-staff meeting should be called or a clearly written e-mail by the leader or chair should announce it via all staff e-mail.

Example: To all staff: This morning all LSS met to discuss ways they can contribute to supporting patrons' reading. A consensus decision was made that all LSS will each week select one of their favorite books to recommend to patrons and place it on a designated display shelf with his or her name near the front of the library. By being a part of the reading initiative, LSS want patrons to know they also are readers.

Finally, LSS should not reconsider a group decision unless there is significant new information. Be prepared to make corrections to new ideas or start-ups, as they are in a pilot stage. Only reconsider if there is substantial new information that convinces the group that they made the wrong choice and catastrophic results could occur if they continue. People will become untrusting and frustrated if LSS reconsider decisions lightly because this dishonors the work and investment they personally made to the process and its result. If LSS widely gathered information and data in the input step, the first step of group decision-making, and used consensus-building strategies to formulate the decision, it would be highly unlikely there would be a need to rescind it.

CHAPTER SUMMARY

LSS who know the basic principles and are able to conduct meetings effectively and efficiently are using their knowledge and experience to become leaders in their libraries. Parliamentary procedure is an orderly and effective way to conduct meetings so that work can be accomplished. LSS who learn how meetings work within the nuances of Robert's Rules of Order may acquire respect and support among their peers and supervisors for leadership roles.

LSS make decisions each day on the job as individuals and in groups. Decisions are made more effectively and appropriately when LSS know the concepts and adapt the skills to make appropriate decisions that affect their work and that of their colleagues.

DISCUSSION QUESTIONS

1. What are the key differences between the funding of public and private libraries and how do these differences affect how their governing board meetings are conducted?
2. What are five of the key basics of meetings and why should LSS know about them?
3. Why should LSS know parliamentary procedure and when would they use it?
4. What is executive session and how can it be effectively used in library meetings?
5. Why should LSS know and understand how to apply key concepts behind individual and group decision making?

ACTIVITY

Attend or view (cable TV, streaming website) one *live* public meeting this week where you will identify the main actions and work of the meeting. This meeting should be for a library or school board.

As a member of the public, you have a right to attend any open public meeting. The only time government meetings are not public is when the meeting is called into executive session for personnel or other confidential reasons. These occasions are rare.

1. Obtain a copy of a meeting agenda to follow along with the work of the meeting. Do this before the meeting if possible—it may be posted online.
2. Obtain a copy of previous meeting minutes of the agency beforehand. Often minutes are posted on the agency's website.
3. Make notes of what you observe during each part of the meeting. Follow the agenda. You will use your notes for writing your assignment.
4. Observe participants behaviors. Make notes of what you see. Are members listening to each other? Do they work as a team? Are there subgroups within the board or council? Is behavior overall cordial and polite or sometimes disruptive?
5. Identify the purpose or purposes of the meeting. Does the content of the meeting align with the agenda?
6. Does the chair use parliamentary procedure (Robert's Rules)?
7. What action items (where a vote was taken) were discussed and voted upon? How did the discussions prevail?
8. What overall impressions do you have as an observer?

Write a two- to three-page report about your observation of the meeting. Use your notes (above) from the meeting you attended as research data.

1. Describe the library and purpose of the meeting. How many members are on the board and how many attended? How often does this group meet? Date, time, and location should also be included.
2. Using your notes, describe the behaviors of the participants and the actions discussed or voted upon during the meeting. Quote from your notes. Describe what you think went very well at the meeting based on information in this chapter. Explain any problems you observed. You are encouraged to judge, predict, and evaluate the success of this board.
3. What recommendations would you have for the presiding officer about the meeting? How could he or she improve upon either his or her own performance or the performance of the members?

NOTES

1. University of Kansas, "Writing Bylaws," Community Tool Box, last modified 2017, accessed December 15, 2017, ctb.ku.edu/en/table-of-contents/structure/organizational-structure/write-bylaws/main.

2. State of Alaska, "Conducting Effective Public Meetings," Department of Commerce, Community, and Economic Development, last modified December 24, 2014, accessed December 7, 2017, www.commerce.alaska.gov/web/dcra/LocalGovernmentOnline/LocalGovernmentElectedOfficials/ConductingEffectivePublicMeetings.aspx.

3. American Library Association, "ALA Library Fact Sheet 1," Number of Libraries in the United States, last modified 2017, accessed December 7, 2017, www.ala.org/tools/libfactsheets/alalibraryfactsheet01.

4. Edward P. Becker, "Robert's Rules of Order," *Tribology & Lubrication Technology* 64, no. 3 (March 2008), search.ebscohost.com/login.aspx?direct=true&db=brb&AN=501227219&authtype=cookie,cpid&custid=csl&site=ehost-live&scope=site.

5. Robert's Rules Association, "Short History of Robert's Rules," The Official Robert's Rules of Order Website, accessed December 9, 2017, www.robertsrules.com/history.html.

6. Becker, "Robert's Rules of Order."

7. Regents of the University of Minnesota, "How Do We Plan for an Effective Meeting?" Civic Engagement, last modified 2017, accessed December 9, 2017, www.extension.umn.edu/community/civic-engagement/tip-sheets/plan-for-effective-meeting/.

8. Wisconsin Department of Public Instruction, "Effective Library Board Meetings," Public Library Development, last modified 2017, accessed December 9, 2017, dpi.wi.gov/pld/boards-directors/administrative-essentials/board-meetings.

9. State of Alaska, "Conducting Effective Public Meetings."

10. New York State, "FAQ—Open Meetings Law (OML)," Department of State Committee on Open Government, accessed December 9, 2017, www.dos.ny.gov/coog/openmeetinglawfaq.html.

11. Robert's Rules Association, "Short History of Robert's Rules."

12. Union County, Illinois, "Addendum 'A' Governmental Unit Remote Attendance Policy," Code of Ordinances of Union County Illinois, accessed December 10, 2017, code.unioncountyil.gov/administration/meeting-procedures/remote-meeting-participation/governmental-unit-remote-attendance-policy/.

13. Web Finance Inc., "Decision-making," Business Dictionary, accessed December 9, 2017, www.businessdictionary.com/definition/decision-making.html.

14. John Ousterhout, "Open Decision-Making," Stanford University, last modified April 16, 2014, accessed December 9, 2017, https://web.stanford.edu/~ouster/cgi-bin/decisions.php.

15. Pennsylvania State University, "Individual Decision Making Concepts," The Arthur W. Page Center, last modified 2017, accessed December 9, 2017, pagecentertraining.psu.edu/index.php/public-relations-ethics/ethical-decision-making/lesson-2-ethics-and-decision-making/individual-decision-making-concepts/.

16. Ibid.

REFERENCES, SUGGESTED READINGS, AND WEBSITES

American Library Association. "ALA Library Fact Sheet 1." Number of Libraries in the United States. Last modified 2017. Accessed December 7, 2017. www.ala.org/tools/libfactsheets/alalibraryfactsheet01.

Becker, Edward P. "Robert's Rules of Order." *Tribology & Lubrication Technology* 64, no. 3 (March 2008): 4. search.ebscohost.com/login.aspx?direct=true&db=brb&AN=501227219&authtype=cookie,cpid&custid=csl&site=ehost-live&scope=site.

New York State. "FAQ—Open Meetings Law (OML)." Department of State Committee on Open Government. Accessed December 9, 2017. www.dos.ny.gov/coog/openmeetinglawfaq.html.

Ousterhout, John. "Open Decision-Making." Stanford University. Last modified April 16, 2014. Accessed December 9, 2017. web.stanford.edu/~ouster/cgi-bin/decisions.php.

Pennsylvania State University. "Individual Decision Making Concepts." The Arthur W. Page Center. Last modified 2017. Accessed December 9, 2017. pagecentertraining.psu.edu/index.php/public-relations-ethics/ethical-decision-making/lesson-2-ethics-and-decision-making/individual-decision-making-concepts/.

Regents of the University of Minnesota. "How Do We Plan for an Effective Meeting?" Civic Engagement. Last modified 2017. Accessed December 9, 2017. www.extension.umn.edu/community/civic-engagement/tip-sheets/plan-for-effective-meeting/.

Robert's Rules Association. "Short History of Robert's Rules." The Official Robert's Rules of Order Website. Accessed December 9, 2017. www.robertsrules.com/history.html.

State of Alaska. "Conducting Effective Public Meetings." Department of Commerce, Community, and Economic Development. Last modified December 24, 2014. Accessed December 7, 2017. www.commerce.alaska.gov/web/dcra/LocalGovernmentOnline/LocalGovernmentElectedOfficials/ConductingEffectivePublicMeetings.aspx.

Union County, Illinois. "Addendum 'A' Governmental Unit Remote Attendance Policy." Code of Ordinances of Union County Illinois. Accessed December 10, 2017. code.unioncountyil.gov/administration/meeting-procedures/remote-meeting-participation/governmental-unit-remote-attendance-policy/.

University of Kansas. "Writing Bylaws." Community Tool Box. Last modified 2017. Accessed December 15, 2017. ctb.ku.edu/en/table-of-contents/structure/organizational-structure/write-bylaws/main.

Web Finance Inc. "Decision-making." Business Dictionary. Accessed December 9, 2017. www.businessdictionary.com/definition/decision-making.html.

Wisconsin Department of Public Instruction. "Effective Library Board Meetings." Public Library Development. Last modified 2017. Accessed December 9, 2017. dpi.wi.gov/pld/boards-directors/administrative-essentials/board-meetings.

Glossary

501(c)(3): Section 501(c)(3) is the portion of the U.S. Internal Revenue Code that allows for federal tax exemption of nonprofit organizations, specifically those that are considered public charities, private foundations, or private operating foundations. It is a public benefit category under which libraries fall.

Abstain: The decision members make when they choose not to vote for or against an issue.

Active listening: This is a communication technique that requires the listener to fully concentrate, understand, and respond to the speaker. In a library, active listening is the process by which staff repeats what is said so that the speaker knows he has been heard. Managers who perfect this skill enhance their ability to discuss and communicate issues with their staff.

Advocacy: This is the process of demonstrating support, usually to government officials, library administration, or the public, for a policy, a decision, or the people with whom you work.

Agenda: Developed by the chair, this is an outline for how the upcoming library meeting will be conducted and the order in which each item will be presented for either discussion or action.

Amend: Any member of a library meeting may request to change a motion under consideration as long as the person who made the original motion and the person who seconded it agree.

The Americans with Disabilities Act (ADA): The Americans with Disabilities Act, or the ADA, was passed in 1991 as an act of Congress and bans discrimination against the approximately fifty-seven million Americans—19 percent of the population—who are hearing impaired, legally blind, epileptic, paralyzed, developmentally disabled, speech impaired, mentally impaired, and HIV positive. It applies to anyone with a condition that substantially limits one's life actions. It is of interest to libraries in regard to patrons and staff alike.

Anniversary date: An employee's anniversary date corresponds to the date on which they were hired. It is significant in the library in that this date may be the beginning

237

of the employee's fiscal year, used for annual evaluations, salary increases, vacations, or promotions.

Annual appeal: An annual appeal is a solicitation of individuals that asks for support for the library and its programs. It is carried out through a combination of direct mail (usually solicitation letters and, if available, brochures) and one-on-one individual solicitations between a volunteer for the library and the individual being solicited.

Annual performance plan: The annual plan provides the link between long-term strategic goals outlined in the library's strategic plans and what managers and LSS are expected to accomplish in a single fiscal year.

Assets: These items are the investment funds, real estate, and financial resources the library may use to meet future operating costs, expenditures, building projects, or other commitments.

At will employment: At will employment means that library employees can be fired anytime and for any reason other than those that are illegal (discrimination for age, disability, gender, genetic information, national origin, race, religion, or sex).

Audit: In this formal process, a certified accountant who does not work for the library or parent institution is contracted annually to review the library's income and expenditures to ensure all financials are in order.

Balanced budget: In any library budget, the income is expected to equal the amount of expenditures. In other words, the amount of funds taken in each year by a library must be expended on personnel, operating expenses, or investments.

Benefits: In the library and other workplaces, benefits refer to compensation other than wages, such as holidays, sick time, medical insurance, and pensions.

Bid list: Items commonly used that are under contract with a purchasing agent at a reduced cost to approved libraries.

Branding: Branding is the process involved in creating a unique name and image in the consumer's mind for a product (or library) through advertising campaigns with a consistent theme.

Budget: A budget is an estimate of income and expenses over a defined period of time, usually the library's fiscal year. It is critical for libraries to keep a budget in order to determine where funds are needed for allocation and the source from which they will come. This is an annual process of planning the income and expenditures required to operate the library for the coming year.

Budget narrative: This is an amount of detail, description, or justification written by the library director to explain what the numbers in the budget spreadsheet represent, how the costs were arrived, and how the library objective will be achieved if the budget is approved.

Bylaws: These are the written rules that control the internal affairs of a library, defining such things as the library's official name, purpose, requirements for board membership, officers' titles and responsibilities, how meetings should be conducted, and how often meetings will be held. They also serve as the legal guidelines of the library, and the library could be challenged in court for its actions if it violates them.

Calendar year: This is a twelve-month period that begins January 1 and ends December 31.

Code of conduct: These are the written expectations of behavior that govern how employees act on the job or in the community.

Cohort: This is a group of people, for example, LSS students, who are together in a similar situation or academic course and that help and support each other through the process.

Collapsed budget: This type of budget document or presentation is a summary of the main income, personnel, and operating expenses for the library.

Communication skills: Communication is the act of exchanging information between two or more people. It can be done verbally, using words, or nonverbally, using gestures. There are specific skills that staff can use to show patrons that they are approachable and ready to help with all of their information needs.

Community: A community is usually considered to be all the people who live in a particular area or place.

Community assessment: Community assessment is the analysis of the demographics of a community. This information informs library services.

Consensus: When a group of key people gather together to discuss ideas or solutions under consideration for the library, instead of taking a formal vote, they are asked to informally show their level of support and agreement in various ways such as nodding their heads, saying "aye," or raising hands.

Consortium: A partnership of libraries that formally work together to achieve common goals or projects.

Convergent thinking: In this type of learning, such as an LSS course, the instructor expects students to deduce the "right" or correct answer.

Cooperative: Another name for consortium, this group of libraries typically has a formal agreement that stipulates the goals, expectations, and obligations of its members.

Cost center: This is a library department, service, or other unit to which annual expenses are estimated in the annual budget or charged for accounting purposes.

Crowdsourcing: Crowdsourcing is soliciting goods and services from the online community instead of from traditional outlets. It is often used to raise funds for a cause or an event.

Curriculum: This is the specific content or material taught in a course, such as an LSS course in foundations, that can be measured through types of testing or assessments.

Customer service: Customer service means assisting patrons (users, customers) with their needs in person, by phone, or electronically by providing high-quality service. Library support staff and management do this to achieve a goal or complete a transaction while showing respect, courtesy, and interest in the patron.

Demographics: Demographics are the statistics of a given population by age, sex, race, and income. This is important for libraries so they can know whom they are serving and for whom they can provide the appropriate resources.

Displays and exhibits policy: Libraries must determine what displays and exhibits they can host. Depending on wall, floor, and bulletin board space, libraries can offer a wide range of material to their constituents.

Divergent thinking: In this type of learning, there is no one correct or "right" answer. LSS students, for example, may interpret the problem differently and seek multiple creative solutions.

Diversification: This is a strategy used to avoid extreme financial risks whereby the library endowment is invested in multiple ways, such as mutual funds, bonds, income property, and so on.

Diversity: Diversity refers to hiring and maintaining a staff that represents a variety of backgrounds and abilities. Having diversity in the staff is important for serving a multicultural and multiethnic demographic.

Documentation: Documentation is information that serves as a record of what took place, the record of an employee's performance.

Employment laws: Employment laws and regulations seek to protect employees from discrimination and harassment. Employment legislation is important because it provides protection and job security for employees against malpractices in all workplaces, including libraries.

Endowment: A library endowment is an income or property given to the library to help sustain its operation. An endowment fund can be made up of past and current donations or bequests by individuals or estates for sustained support of the library. An endowment is invested in equities (stocks) and fixed income (bonds and CDs, etc.) in order to increase its size annually.

The Equal Employment Opportunity Commission (EEOC): The U.S. Equal Employment Opportunity Commission (EEOC) is responsible for enforcing federal laws that make it illegal to discriminate against a job applicant or an employee because of a person's race, color, religion, sex (including pregnancy, gender identity, and sexual orientation), national origin, age (forty or older), disability, or genetic information. These rules must be part of library employment practices.

Evaluation: An evaluation is an assessment of the work that a library staff member is doing. Also referred to as a performance review, it is a measurement of an employee's success in meeting goals and objectives for his or her position. Usually performed annually, it is based on a predetermined set of standards.

Fairness: Fairness includes the concept of equal employment opportunity for all regardless of race, religion, origin, gender, or sexual orientation. Fairness is a key component of the hiring process in libraries.

The Family and Medical Leave Act (FMLA): The Family and Medical Leave Act (FMLA) is a federal labor law that allows an eligible employee to take an extended leave of absence from work due to illness or to care for a sick family member and is guaranteed for libraries, and all employers, with fifty or more employees.

Feedback: Feedback is the process whereby the results of something you do are "fed back" or returned to you; between manager and LSS, it is an important part of the performance review process.

Fiscal year: This is a twelve-month period used for accounting purposes and preparing financial statements, such as the library budget. A common fiscal year many libraries use begins July 1 and ends June 30.

Formative: The term means beginning form or shape and idea or development of a skill or process. In a staff supervision context, the term refers to informal steps or the initial processes of evaluation.

Functions of a shared ILS: Libraries share an integrated library system because of the benefits obtained by sharing circulation, cataloging, reserves, acquisitions, reports, and other applications and databases with other consortium members.

Fundraising: Fundraising is the process of getting voluntary donations from individuals and businesses to benefit a specific purpose. Fundraising is also known as development.

Grants: A grant is a sum of money given by an organization to a library (or other nonprofit) for funding a project or initiative that will improve services or otherwise benefit the organization. The library must apply for a grant and meet certain qualifications to be considered.

Hierarchy: Used in the context of the library, it is the system of management organization in which people or groups are ranked one above the other according to authority.

Hiring: Hiring, for most organizations including libraries, is a complex process involving several steps: applications from interested candidates, selecting those who qualify for an interview, checking their references, and so on to determine who is offered the job.

Improvement plan: This is a formal process where a team is established to recommend significant change in one or more aspects of the library program that is in need of new services, modification, or retraction.

Internet use policy: Because the Internet is an unmonitored global network, libraries cannot control or monitor content; they must establish guidelines for proper use so patrons are not in violation of federal, state, and local laws.

Interview: An interview is a meeting between a prospective employee and employer to determine the subject's qualifications and suitability for a position in a library or other workplace.

Job description: A job description is a statement or document that describes the duties and responsibilities of an employee in the workplace.

Labor laws: The Department of Labor (DOL) administers and enforces more than 180 federal laws. These mandates and the regulations that implement them cover many workplace activities, including all types of libraries, for about 10 million employers and 125 million workers.

Laissez-faire: A policy or attitude of letting things take their own course, without interfering. A library manager who has this style of leadership will not intervene even if warranted.

Level services: This type of budget is a funding plan that allows for providing current services "as is" in the next budget cycle. Libraries that are funded for level services typically only receive an increase for personnel contracts and anticipated inflationary costs for materials, supplies, or equipment. New library initiatives or services are not budgeted.

Liabilities: The opposite of assets, liabilities are financial obligations that are reported on the library balance sheet. Liabilities must equal or total the same amount as the assets in a budget. They account for how the assets are being used for library expenditures, operating costs, or investments.

Library board of trustees: Typically a volunteer group of people who represent the community and serve the library and its director in an advisory capacity. Some boards also have management oversight of the library director and/or fiscal responsibility for the library budget.

Library leadership: These are the supervisors and administrators who manage the library to assure staffing, policies, services, and all operational details are taking place appropriately.

Library use and borrower policy: A library use and borrower policy refers to borrowing privileges that are restricted to residents of a town or students of a school or college. This relates to the library and its funding structure and is solved by issuing library cards. Library cards identify eligible users and their level of access to services.

Line item: This is a line that appears on a separate entry in a fiscal budget, balance sheet, or accounting ledger.

Listserv: This is an application or program that distributes messages to subscribers interested in specific topics, such as on the topic of library children's programming, on an electronic mailing list.

Marketing: Marketing is the advancement of an idea through publicity or promotion. It is based on thinking about the library in terms of customer needs and satisfaction. It relies on designing the library's offering in terms of those needs and on using effective communication to inform and motivate patrons.

Marketing plan: A marketing plan is a document that outlines the library's advertising efforts. It describes activities involved in achieving specific goals and objectives for the library in a set time, such as one year.

Material selection policy: A collection policy, also known as a material selection policy, is a document that provides guidance for the librarians or LSS who do collection development. It follows a set of guidelines to consider when choosing materials and includes such criteria as positive reviews, reputation of the author, local interest, demand, and budget limitations.

Meeting room policy: Libraries that have meeting rooms must have a policy that clearly outlines who may use the room and for what purpose.

Minutes: Minutes are the record of the discussions and actions that take place at a library meeting. The secretary takes minutes during the meeting and is responsible for preparing a draft version to be considered for acceptance at the next meeting.

Mission: This is a guiding statement of the purpose of the library and its work. All employees should know the library mission and align their work with it.

Motion: This proposal for action is made by one member for all participants of the meeting to discuss and vote upon. The proposal is made in the form of a statement that begins with the phrase "I make a motion to . . ." or "I move to . . ." The proposal must be seconded by another member to be voted upon by the membership.

Needs assessment: A needs assessment is a systematic process for determining and addressing needs, or "gaps" between current conditions and desired "wants." The discrepancy between the current condition and wanted condition must be measured to appropriately identify the need.

Nonprofit: Libraries and other institutions that either are publicly funded or have endowments and other means of raising revenue that cover the annual operating expenses. They are not "in business" to have a profit. Nonprofits typically do not pay state or federal taxes.

Occupational Safety and Health Administration (OSHA): OSHA's mission is to ensure that every working man and woman in the nation is employed under safe and healthful working conditions. Nearly every employee in the United States comes under OSHA's authority. The only exceptions are those who are self-employed, workers in mining and transportation industries (who are covered by other agencies), and most public employees.

Operating expenses: In addition to staff, these are the items such as postage, utilities, fuel, maintenance, materials and supplies, vehicle replacement, and so forth required to open the library and provide its services each year.

Parliamentary procedure: Synonymous with Robert's Rules of Order, these are the rules that define how particular situations should be handled or outcomes achieved in meetings.

Pedagogy: These are the traditional classroom methods of teaching academic or theoretical subjects that most students, including those who are in library degree programs, are exposed to in school.

Performance appraisal: A performance appraisal, also known as a performance evaluation, is a process by which a manager examines an employee's work by comparing it to a set of previously determined standards.

Personnel policies: Personnel policies define the rights, obligations, treatment, and relations of people in a workplace. Personnel policies can vary from library to library but generally cover the hours worked, schedules, vacation and sick time, and rules for dealing with issues and obstacles.

PIE: This is an acronym for the three actions of planning, implementation, and evaluation of programs and services that LSS can identify in the improvement process.

Pilot: Before adapting a new policy or procedure in final form, this is a trial run to evaluate and make improvements, such as to a new library policy, before full implementation.

Planned giving: Planned giving is a program designed for donors to gift financial support to the library during their lifetimes and after their deaths. It is a form of charitable giving that is arranged through wills and estate plans.

Policies: Policies are clear, simple statements of how your organization intends to conduct its services or business and guidelines that help employees know what is expected of them with respect to standards of behavior and performance. In libraries, policies determine who can use the library, patron behavior, and material selection.

Policy and procedural manuals: A policy and procedural manual is a book or a binder of all of the library's policies and procedures that can be easily accessed and is helpful for all LSS.

Probationary period: The probationary period, often the first sixty or ninety days of a new job in a library, determines if the new employee is suited for the job and serves as a time for training and evaluation. Benefits may begin to accrue at the end of the probationary period.

Procedures: Procedures are the step-by-step tasks that support the policy—the action plan. Procedures describe how each policy will be put into action in your organization.

Promotion: Promotion is a variety of activities designed to educate patrons about the materials and services that the library offers. It refers to the overall process, rather than a specific activity.

Public relations: Public relations are activities that help the public or user group to understand, accept, and support the programs or initiatives of a library.

Qualitative data: The opposite of statistics, these are ways to confirm a hypothesis or theory, such as do self-checkout units improve library service, using interviews, observations, and other social or humanistic methods.

Reconcile: This is an accounting process whereby the library director and other staff review line items during the year to ensure transactions are complete and review spending and income accounts to be certain they are consistent with the approved budget.

Recruitment: Recruitment, in a library, is the process of finding appropriate candidates for an open position. Usually carried out by Human Resources, it may also be done by others in library management.

Rules: Rules are accepted principles or instructions that state the way things are or should be done and tells you what you are allowed or are not allowed to do.

Rules of conduct policy: Rules of conduct, patron responsibility, code of conduct, and other terms describe a policy that explains what is expected of the patron. They begin with a statement of inclusion—that everyone has the right to use the library.

Self-regulation: This type of self-management occurs when a person takes charge of his or her own learning or makes other decisions that guide his or her actions, such as when an LSS decides to return to college for an advanced degree.

Shadowing: Shadowing is a strategy where a new staff member follows another staff member during their daily routine. They can observe how a task is done by watching someone doing it. This is useful for new LSS to learn hands-on how to do their job.

Simple majority: In the process of voting on an action or issue, this is half of the voting membership plus one more that sways the final outcome or decision.

Situational leadership: This adaptive and flexible leadership style may be temporarily needed when there is a contingency or event, such as an emergency in the library after hours, that requires someone with confidence and experience to step in to make decisions.

SMART: This is an acronym that identifies five steps in the goal-writing process. A successful goal for library improvement will be specific, measurable, achievable, relevant, and time-bound.

Staff development: Also called professional learning, library staff continue to learn new skills, issues, and theories to improve their work performance by taking courses, attending workshops, reading journals, and learning from others in various other formats.

Stakeholders: These are the community of supporters such as patrons, staff, students, faculty, taxpayers, donors, board members, and any others who use or have a connection to the library.

Standards: These are agreed-upon norms, rules, regulations, or other means of measurement of success of an item or project. Standards also identify the quality of the work performed, for example, a high standard of cataloging may be used to describe a complete and accurate item record.

Stewardship: Stewardship is the cultivation and maintenance of relationships and is an important aspect of fundraising. Showing appreciation for past contributions and staying in contact with donors for future donations greatly increases the chances of continued giving.

Strategic plan: A strategic plan is the clearly worded description of the library's mission, what it wants to achieve over the next few years, and the strategic priorities to guide the organization toward achievement of the vision. Often referred to as a long-range plan, this time-consuming process involves all library staff and many of its stakeholders.

Student learning objectives (SLO): These are brief statements that describe what students should know and be able to do at the end of a unit, course, or school year. SLOs may be locally created by educators or relate to state and national learning standards that measure student achievement.

Student learning outcomes: Also known by the acronym of SLO, these are statements of what students will know and be able to do based on instruction.

Summative: This term as it relates to evaluation means a cumulative or summary assessment of what a person can do or perform. For library staff, the summary evaluation could be an annual performance appraisal or review.

Supervision: The act or process of monitoring work performance of others that includes administering and delegating library activities and responsibilities.

Task force: This typically is an ad hoc or temporary committee composed of working members to delve deeply into an issue and bring a recommendation or resolution to the issue or task to the larger board or committee.

Termination: Simply stated, this is when an employee is severed from their employment and let go due to just cause.

Transformational leadership: A style of leadership whereby library supervisors place a high value on forming a personal relationship with their LSS employees, firmly believing that they have a role to empower others to develop their potential for the long-term good of the institution and its goals.

The USA PATRIOT Act: This is the acronym made by the Uniting and Strengthening America by Providing Appropriate Tools Required to Intercept and Obstruct Terrorism act. Created by Congress in the wake of 9/11, it substantially expanded the authority of U.S. law enforcement for the stated purpose of fighting terrorism in the United States and abroad. It expanded the authority of the FBI to gain access to library records, including stored electronic data and communications.

Index

About the Authors

Hali R. Keeler, MLS, MA, is the author of the books *Working with Collections: An Introduction for Support Staff* (Rowman & Littlefield, 2017); *Foundations of Library Public Services: An Introduction for Support Staff* (Rowman & Littlefield, 2015); and *Ghosts of Groton Bank* (2016), as well as the article "Library Technician Training Programs," *Library Mosaics* magazine (January/February 2005). She is the former coordinator for the Library Technology Certificate Program at Three Rivers Community College (2003–2011) and has been an adjunct professor since 1998. She teaches courses in public services, technical services, and management strategies. In addition to library instruction, Ms. Keeler worked as a children's librarian and is the retired executive director of a public library. She has been a speaker and presenter at library conferences and workshops and has served in leadership roles on library boards and committees at the state and local levels.

Marie Keen Shaw is the program coordinator for the library technical assistant certificate program at Three Rivers Community College in Norwich, Connecticut, where she has also been an adjunct professor since 1999. She teaches courses in cataloging and classification, digital resources, reference services, and management strategies. She serves on the boards of the Connecticut Library Consortium and the Groton Public Library. Marie received her doctorate of education from the University of Connecticut in educational leadership and adult learning, a sixth-year degree from Southern Connecticut State University in educational leadership, and her MS from Purdue University in library and information science and educational media. A retired certified high school library media specialist and curriculum instructional leader, she has been a speaker at state library and educational media conferences in Rhode Island, Illinois, and Connecticut. Marie is the author of the books *Cataloging Library Resources: An Introduction* (Rowman & Littlefield, 2017), *Library Technology and Digital Resources: An Introduction for Support Staff* (Rowman & Littlefield, 2015), and *Block Scheduling and Its Impact on the School Library Media Center* (1999). Her doctoral dissertation, *Teacher's Learning of Technology: Key Factors and Process*, was accepted by the University of Connecticut in 2010.